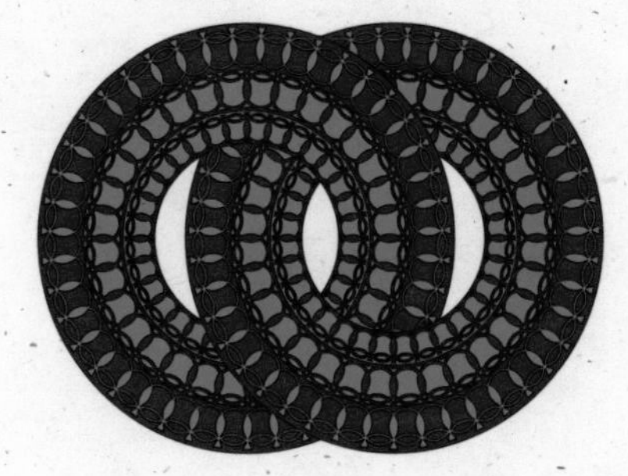

W9-BID-939

Judith Hannan

MOTHERHOOD EXAGGERATED

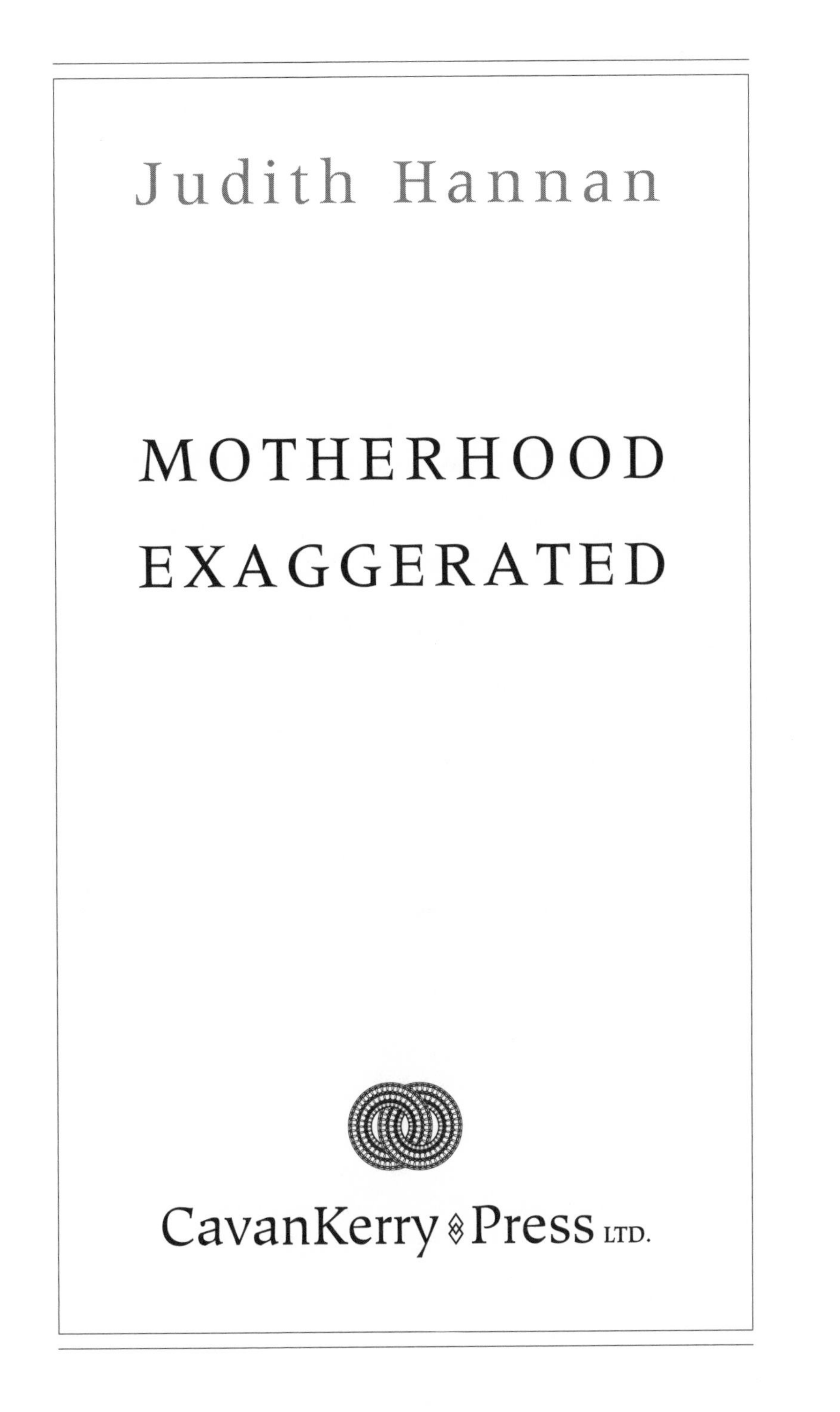

Judith Hannan

MOTHERHOOD EXAGGERATED

CavanKerry Press LTD.

CavanKerry Press Ltd.
Fort Lee, New Jersey
www.cavankerrypress.org

Library of Congress Cataloging-in-Publication Data

Hannan, Judith, 1953-
Motherhood, exaggerated / Judith Hannan. -- 1st ed.
p. cm.
ISBN-13: 978-1-933880-27-3 (alk. paper)
ISBN-10: 1-933880-27-9 (alk. paper)
1. Mothers and daughters. I. Title.

PS3608.A71557M66 2012
813'.6--dc23

2011034438

Cover and interior text design by Gregory Smith

First Edition 2012, Printed in the United States of America

Motherhood Exaggerated is the ninth title of CavanKerry's Literature of Illness imprint. LaurelBooks are fine collections of poetry and prose that explore the many poignant issues associated with confronting serious physical and/or psychological illness.

CavanKerry is grateful to the Arnold P.Gold Foundation for the Advancement of Humanism in Medicine for joining us in sponsoring this imprint. Offering LaurelBooks as teaching tools to medical schools is the result of shared concerns--humanism, community, and meeting the needs of the underserved. Together with the Gold Foundation, CavanKerry's two outreach efforts, GiftBooks and Presenting Poetry & Prose, bring complimentary books and readings to the medical community at major hospitals across the United States.

CavanKerry Press is grateful for the support it receives from the New Jersey State Council on the Arts.

For Nadia

For the patients whom Nadia and I befriended in the hospital and their families: their names have been changed to respect their privacy, but the connection of our hearts to theirs remains undiminished.

Contents

I Discovery

II Rebirth

III Recovery

Introduction

There is before. And there is forever after.

And

There

Is

The

Frozen

Moment . . .

that marks the rent in a family's life, their Stygian introduction to the new, upside down world that they are about to enter when they first hear the words, "Your child has cancer." For those parents who remember anything, who can recall anything more than the white noise of the doctor's voice as he droned on about scans and biopsies and catheters and chemotherapy and side effects and prognosis, it is the moment that their dreams of a perfect life for their beloved child were shattered. When thoughts of a first day at kindergarten, or a Bat Mitzvah, or a prom, or a college graduation, were replaced by the primal instinct to sacrifice, to protect, to save. Please, just let my child live—I will take anything else that comes . . . until it comes.

Today, 60 families will hear those dread words and have their lives changed forever. Today, 60 innocent children, adolescents, and young adults will enter my world and the world of my pediatric oncology colleagues around the country. "Fortunately" (except for the 10 who don't . . .), 50 of them will survive their illness but with scars on not only their bodies and souls, but those of their parents, their siblings, and their extended families. This year, more than 20,000 children, adolescents, and young adults will make their way to pediatric oncology practices for treatment of leukemias and lymphomas, brain tumors, kidney and adrenal tumors, and other, rarer tumors like sarcomas of bone and soft tissue. It was for this reason that Nadia and Judy and John Hannan entered my life in early November 10 years ago.

Nadia's "story" (or at least her "cancer story", as if her story began with her cancer . . .) remains as fresh in my memory today as it was the first morning I met her. Halloween. ..candy corn..her jaw "popping", a visit to the pediatrician, an x-ray and then a "CAT" scan", a call from her pediatrician to our office for an appointment the next day—and an adorable, slender, very bright 8½ year old little girl who didn't quite get—to me at least—what the fuss was all about. I remember, too, her parents, Judy and John, as I reviewed the CT scan that they had brought with them, a scan that showed a "textbook" example of the most common type of childhood bone cancer, osteosarcoma, only to be surprised the next day when Nadia's MRI was thought to show a rhabdomyosarcoma, only to be surprised when the biopsy a week later showed that her CT scan hadn't read the textbook and Nadia's tumor was actually a Ewing's sarcoma . . . .

Ewing's sarcoma, named after the renowned former Chair of Pathology of my illustrious institution, James Ewing, who in 1921 first reported the still-classic description of 7 children with characteristic bone tumors and the potential role of radiation therapy in their management. Ewing's sarcoma, a tumor that is diagnosed each year in fewer than 350 children and teens and young adults in the entire country, but a tumor that we see in nearly 30 new kids each year in our practice. Ewing's sarcoma, a tumor for which a clear role for chemotherapy was not established until 1972, yet a tumor for which modern chemotherapy (an oxymoron if ever there was), combined with surgical removal or irradiation of the primary site, is curative in more than two-thirds of patients. Ewing's sarcoma, a tumor for which we have finally begun to peel back the mysteries surrounding the post-natal genetic mishap, the translocation of portions of two normal healthy genes that normally "reside" nowhere near each other (one, EWS, "lives" on the long arm of chromosome 22; the other, FLI-1, "lives" on the long arm of chromosome 11) to create a hybrid "cancer gene", that is the first necessary step in the transformation of a once-normal but still-not-fully-characterized cell into a malignant, metastasizing cancer cell—but a mishap that we know almost nothing about "why" it happens when it does or who it does or does not happen to.

Once her diagnosis was confirmed, Nadia's treatment was, in my world, pretty "standard". Three rounds of intensive multi-agent chemotherapy, followed by complex reconstructive surgery to remove her tumor and create a new jaw bone from an "expendable" bone in her lower leg, followed by 4 more rounds of intensive multi-agent chemotherapy, followed by monthly check-ups and periodic scans for a year, then check-ups (still with periodic scans) every 2 then 3 then 6 months until, finally, once yearly visits mostly to say "hi" and catch-up on life . . . and make sure that nothing bad from that now longer-ago bad time becomes manifest as a "late effect" of her treatment. From the outside, from my side of the desk, using the criteria that "we" use to "objectively" assess a patient's tolerance to this therapy, she seemed to do "OK"—certainly nothing out of the ordinary that ever made me think that she could not "get through this". (Her mother's side effects and ability to withstand this treatment was more difficult for me to quantify, but her pain and suffering were there, hidden in plain sight, for an eye that was discerning enough to see.) I could sense but never know what happened after Nadia left the hospital, when she was at home, with her mother, with her father, with her siblings, with her friends. Nausea and vomiting. Hair loss. Low blood cell counts with the attendant need for transfusions of blood and platelets to ward off fatigue and prevent bleeding, and antibiotic infusions to treat infections from the relentless onslaught of her own germs when her body's immune defenses were at their nadir. Too many to count needle pokes to administer medicines to help her blood cell counts better withstand the withering effects of the chemotherapy. Narcotic pain medications to try to control the horrific pain of mouth sores or the throb of swollen healing tissues after surgery. Anger. Resentment. Rage. . . . and, in time, over time, cure and healing, though in what order and over what time and to what degree is a story still being told.

Judy Hannan has written a riveting, gut-wrenching, soul-shaking account of her beautiful daughter's descent into the hell of my world, and of her and Nadia's slow, painstaking recovery from the unspeakable horrors that we committed against her body and her soul in our efforts to rid her of her cancer. There are no chapters on "caring for your puking 8 year old when she comes home from the hospital after her first day of chemo" or "what to do when your 8 year old needs to have surgery to remove half her jaw" in the parenting handbook that new mothers and fathers receive when they bring their newborn twins home from the hospital. There is no standard operating procedure for how to help your older daughter or younger son or husband understand why you are short-tempered and exhausted and can't be there for them because you are spending every waking minute of your day caring for your OTHER child, the one who could die, the one who you are spending all night with waking up to go to the bathroom, giving anti-nausea medicines to, monitoring for fever, all the while not eating because your stomach is tied up in knots, not answering the phone because you just don't want to be bothered by the platitudes of your well-meaning friends and relatives who want to help, really they do, but are just clueless . . . .

For a doctor who cares for hundreds of children each year, Judy's account was a well-needed slap in the face, a reminder that it must always be about the child, about the family. That the "agenda" should, indeed must, always be set in response to what the family and child need and want, when they need and want it, not what the doctor thinks they need, when the doctor thinks they need it. For a doctor who cares for hundreds of children each year, Judy's account was also a poignant reminder that long after cure has been achieved, long after the fear that the cancer will ever again rear its ugly head has finally receded into a distant vestigial memory, healing is still taking place, indeed healing must still be taking place. Judy's, and Nadia's and John's and Max's and Frannie's courageous willingness to open up their ordeal to the outside world will resonate with all families whose lives have been touched by the tragedy of childhood cancer—and will also help remind them that Bat Mitzvahs and boyfriends and proms and college are dreams that should be held onto tightly because they can come true.

Every summer since 1997, my wife and I have vacationed on Martha's Vineyard, a place for which we and the Hannans share a deep and mutual love for its natural beauty and restorative tranquility. Our arrival at the check-in desk of the Woods' Hole ferry terminal is like the rush of intravenous narcotics hitting my brain. Frequently, we have seen Nadia or Judy, sometimes from a distance, sometimes at an event we both attended. My wife, a social worker who is far smarter than I can ever hope to be about the realm of human interaction, would frequently chastise me when I would want to say hello: "Lenny, leave them alone. They are on vacation. They don't need to see you. They live with this every day." Sometimes I would listen; sometimes I would not. Several years ago, shortly after we arrived and were taking in the beauty of our view from the deck of our rental home, I glanced to my right at some movement that I saw on at the house across the road and saw 3 teenagers frolicking on the lawn—Nadia and Max and Frannie. This time, there was no need to say anything. This time, there was merely the satisfaction of seeing a beautiful young woman, a tall slender teen who now bore only a faint resemblance to the slender adorable 8 year old I had met in November 2000, simply enjoying her life, a life that was, to be sure, different than what she or her loving family would ever have wanted for her or for any child, but a life that was very much worth living and loving. Nadia is now at college. Her future is bright. The scars on her body continue to fade. The scars on her soul have made her into someone different, not necessarily better, but different, as have the scars on the souls of her parents and her siblings. Although more research dollars are desperately needed to identify more sophisticated biologically targeted and less toxic therapies so that every child with cancer will be cured with as few short- and long-term adverse sequelae as possible, only when science discovers how to prevent these mutagenic translocations in the first instance, will these scars never again mar the lives of innocent beautiful children.

—Leonard H. Wexler, M.D.
Associate Attending Physician
Department of Pediatrics
Memorial Sloan-Kettering Cancer Center
New York, NY

Foreword

When God decided to test Job's faith, his first action was to afflict his children. God understood, as anyone who has experienced the serious illness of a child understands, that there is no greater test a good parent confronts than when a child faces death.

I know, for I too have been through this devastating experience. I wish I had had Judith Hannan's book when my child was diagnosed with a serious illness many years ago. Everything changes, and it never stops. Life is put on hold. Samuel Johnson once observed that nothing focuses the mind quite as clearly as an appointment with the hangman. Johnson obviously didn't have a child with cancer. Nothing can make a parent focus more single-mindedly on any issue than a child with a life-threatening illness and the steps that must be taken to maximize the chances of survival, both physical and psychological.

I have discussed this issue with several friends who have lived through life-threatening illnesses suffered by their children. Some, like me, try to become super scientists, reading everything they can get their hands on, conferring with every expert they can reach and micromanaging every medical decision. Others leave these matters to the doctors and devote themselves to showering the child with love and support. Still others find it difficult to engage either scientifically or emotionally. Every parent is different as are the needs of every child. Illness among children does not come with a one-size-fits-all instruction manual. The first priority, of course, is the life of the child, but not far behind is the psychological welfare, both short and long term, of the survivor of childhood illness.

One common reaction among parents of deathly ill children who have made it through a serious illness is to try to bury the difficult memories by not thinking or talking about the traumatic past. With cancer survivors this is especially problematic, since the threat of recurrence is ever-present, and past may become prologue. Healthy vigilance must be balanced against unhealthy obsession with every possible symptom. Life is never quite the same. Normalcy rarely returns. The battle never ends. The scars, though sometimes invisible, remain.

A seriously ill child tests the strength of every individual and every relationship. Some endure, even thrive, while others weaken or even shatter. There is no way to prepare for the challenge, because it almost always comes out of the blue. But experience shows that there are better or worse ways of confronting the inevitable tensions that accompany the illness of a child.

There are several stages a parent goes through during and following the diagnosis. The first stage involves immediate panic, overwhelming frustration and a sense of helplessness. This may be followed by intense involvement in the treatment process. Then there is the treatment itself—often surgery followed by radiation and chemotherapy. Finally, there is waiting—a year, five years, ten years—before one can be relatively confident that the treatment has worked. During this waiting period, it becomes difficult to concentrate on anything else, as your child seems cured, but you know there is the lingering fear of recurrence. In my situation, I could not focus on long term projects. I needed short deadlines that did not allow my mind to wander. But wander it did, to my child's future, to whether I was subtly treating him differently because of his encounter with illness, to every minor symptom that might signal a recurrence.

In trying to deal constructively with these complex issues, I looked for books and articles that could provide guidance to those of us who were inexperienced with childhood illness. I found little that was helpful in the literature. The best advice came from other parents who had been through similarly trying times.

Judith Hannan has performed a valuable service by publishing this remarkably honest account of the crisis she and her family went through as her daughter—now a brilliant and beautiful young woman—dealt with a rare form of cancer. She takes us with her on her journey through the valley of the shadow of death and then back to the sunshine of life. Tears of remembrance came to my eyes and will to the eyes of other readers who have been through similar crises. Judith's willingness to share intimate feelings and to discuss difficult moments is a gift that will help so many, as it has already helped me, to deal with the past as well as the future.

—Alan M. Dershowitz

Judith Hannan

MOTHERHOOD EXAGGERATED

I

Discovery

AN ALLEGORY

Once upon a time, there was a soul whose tiny embryonic form was not thriving like those of the brother and sister with whom it shared the womb.

The doctor said, "It won't survive beyond the first trimester."

The soul was frightened. "I want to come into the world, too," it whispered.

Such was the goodness of the stronger soul named Nadia that she could see tears flowing in salt water. "Don't worry," she said. "You can come with me."

The soul was grateful. "I promise not to stay too long—just enough time for me to taste Mama's milk, feel the lightness of air, know how colors explode and water sparkles."

Nadia protected her extra soul the way most children secure treasures in hidden places and thoughts in locked diaries, away from the prying camera, the probing question.

For the nameless soul, living only created longing. "I can't leave now. Not before experiencing the vastness of the sea, the first day of school, one more kiss from Mama."

The soul became greedy, taking up more space in Nadia's being. Running around in search of a place to hide, the soul's internal combustion would cause Nadia's fever to rise. The soul dashed into Nadia's jaw bone.

"See me, Mama," the soul cried. "Please see me," she begged.

But all Mama heard were Nadia's annoying hums. On Halloween, the soul cracked Nadia's jaw. It had gone too far.

1

Nadia has a fever. Naturally, I don't think a little bug or even Lyme disease. The new scare on Martha's Vineyard is deadly tularemia. What if that's what Nadia has?

— journal entry, August 15, 2000

Butterflies were scarce on Martha's Vineyard in the summer of 2000. Every day I would check the meadow outside my window. The summer before, the flowers would take flight each time I passed. Now they remained as immoveable as the queen's guards.

On Labor Day morning, as my family prepared for our return to New York, I searched one last time. Nothing. Who would want to come out to play on such a leaden, gray day? The sky was too heavy for my head.

I struggled to look up. One more search.

I cannot explain my desperate search for butterflies. My need for this symbol of renewal is primal, connected to my certainty, since her infancy, that something horrible would one day happen to my daughter Nadia, who now lay in bed with a 101-degree temperature.

Then, out of the northern sky, over the rooftop of my house, they came. Hundreds, maybe thousands of them—dragonflies—pushed by the wind or perhaps beating a hasty retreat from an advancing cold front. They dusted the air like ashes.

The dragonflies uneased me. Their flight was erratic, their purpose in such numbers seemed sinister. I resisted being borne back to New York on their wings.

There were two pieces of clinical evidence that summer that hinted that cancer was developing in Nadia's body, two pieces of a jigsaw puzzle whose meaning would only be revealed when seen as part of the whole. An athletic and determined eight-year-old, Nadia dragged her way at a plodding walk through the 3.1 miles of the annual Chilmark Road Race. A week later, she came down with the first of three fevers that left nearly as fast as they came. By the time we boarded our plane to return to New York at the end of the summer, the second fever was gone. (The third would come in late September.)

I've always felt panic in the face of fever. I've handled my children's broken bones, the croup, asthma, and anaphylaxis with more confidence than I have ever coped with a fever. Now, with no other symptoms to deal with, I brought Nadia tomato soup on a tray with a vase of flowers, hiding my anxiety behind an uncharacteristic level of fussing.

My sense of foreboding lifted once we were back in New York. Nadia had an easy transition back to school, and I had a more neutral perspective on her third fever. But outside of school, Nadia started to become unsettled.

For the first two years of her life, Nadia slept as if in a state of tormented limbo. She began her nights with a brief period of what resembled deep and satisfying rest but then spent hours moaning and squirming as if confronting a great fear. Anxious to banish whatever was causing Nadia such anguish, I went to her throughout the night.

Her eyes were always closed; she showed no signs of being awake, and I never found the source of her misery.

As Nadia grew, whatever haunted her in the dark vanished, and I began to get a better look at the daughter I would be raising. What defined her was her strut: on her way to her closet each morning to create a crazy couture of bright colors, sparkles, and contrasting patterns; off to the very important business of nursery school; into new groups of children where she typically identified the most dominant with whom to match wits; and, just as assuredly, away from those same friends when their bossiness offended her sense of justice.

In these scenes, I was always behind Nadia, following her lead. As she entered third grade, though, I saw in her a faint wobble, like a top that has just lost its momentum but has not yet begun to topple. Her emotional limbo, fueled by some underground source of dissatisfaction, returned.

I found it increasingly difficult to interpret Nadia's wishes. If I thought I knew anything, it was that gymnastics was her passion. But now, even as Nadia proclaimed her devotion to the sport and insisted on joining a team, she balked at going to practice when I picked her up in the car after school.

"I don't feel well." "My stomach hurts." "I have a headache." "I want to go home."

"Close your eyes and try to rest," I responded. "We're almost there." Or "Let's just get there and see how you feel." Or as my frustration grew, "Listen, Nadia, this was your idea. Do you want to do this or not?"

Early in the season Nadia would stay for the whole practice. Within a few weeks, she would quit halfway through. Ultimately, she refused to go inside the gym at all.

"You can't just sit outside. You made a commitment," I moralized.

"But I don't feel well," Nadia answered.

"Every week you don't feel well?" There had to be something more. "Is there a problem with the coach or the kids?" I asked, trying to make my voice more sympathetic.

Nadia just looked at the ground. "I don't know," she shrugged.

I stared at Nadia as if she were an anagram I could decipher; she kept her eyes down, refusing to engage me any further until I gave in and we went home.

Two years before, Nadia had also begged to play the violin. I admit that I doubted her sincerity. Her twin brother Max had already been playing the cello for a year. I had majored in music in college and reveled in the bond that Max's cello was creating between us. Nadia, who as an infant cried and kicked if I tried to nurse Max at the same time as her, now didn't like being left out.

Nadia enjoyed her group classes, always volunteering to demonstrate a skill or answer a question, but her private lessons made her squirm, as if she felt overly exposed. So when she asked to take a leave of absence from the violin and instead join a swim club with her best friend Gaby, my response was ambivalent. Gymnastics, violin, swimming—which was the whim and which would hold Nadia's interest?

Nadia continued her violin lessons while I waffled. They were disastrous. Whereas her posture had always been so proud and perfect, so representative of Nadia herself, now she slouched through her lesson with the violin hanging like a droopy branch under her chin instead of held firmly between her jaw and shoulder. It hurt, she said, but I just figured her heart wasn't in it anymore.

I didn't share the depth of my confusion with my husband John. I told him what Nadia did or didn't do on any given day; but while I wanted to try to get to the heart of Nadia's dissatisfaction, John wanted only to remove those things that made her, or any of the kids, unhappy. I imagine he would be great at the game of curling, whisking his broom as fast as he could to steer his stone in the right direction, and sweeping away any possible imperfection on the ice that would impede its progress. When the kids were young and John made them chicken soup, he would pick out all the dark meat they hated before serving it. I believe in serving the whole meal and letting them sort out their likes and dislikes. They're going to have to do it on their own eventually—not pick out chicken bits but sift through life. For me it's about the exploration. It's great to have a father who wants to give you what you need to be happy, but what if you don't know how to find out what those things are?

After twenty-five years of marriage, I felt I didn't have to talk with John about Nadia because I knew how the conversation would go:

Me: I'm worried about Nadia. She's become so whiny about going to gymnastics.

John: Well, she shouldn't go then.

Me: But she says she loves gymnastics. There has to be something more to it.

John: I don't know, Judi. If she doesn't want to go, I don't think you should make her.

Me: I'm not *making* her, not really.

John: Well, what do you want me to *do?*

Me: I don't want you to *do* anything. It's a problem that needs figuring out, not fixing.

John: Look. It's not so complicated. If she's unhappy, then don't make her go. There's nothing more to figure out.

Except why is she so unhappy?

If Nadia had ever shown any doubt about what she wanted before this, I could have accused myself of expecting too much self-knowledge from an eight-year-old. What I never considered was that there could be a physical cause behind her growing malaise before gymnastics practice or her sudden difficulty with the violin. I told Nadia she could take a leave of absence from the violin and join Gaby for a few trial sessions with the swim club. I also allowed her to drop the gymnastics team in favor of a weekly lesson with a former coach closer to home.

In the meantime, Nadia had developed the habit of humming when she wasn't talking and even in the pauses between words. It wasn't a song; she hummed just one note.

"How was school today, Nadia?" I'd ask.

"Hmmm. It was okay, hmmm, only we didn't have gymnastics, hmmm, because there was a fire drill, hmmm."

"Nadia, that humming is annoying. Stop it."

"I can't, hmmm. My ear feels funny, hmmm, and humming is the only way it feels better, hmmm."

Nadia had just had a cold, so I assumed her ears were blocked and I continued to nag her to be quiet.

Looking back, I wonder if I made a mistake in not taking Nadia to the doctor at this point. But what would I have said? My daughter had had three quick fevers from which she rebounded easily, she couldn't run the entire three miles of a road race, she hummed, and she said it hurt to play an instrument she had lost interest in. I tell myself she still would have had cancer, but maybe her scars would have been less, her odds for survival, which we couldn't be sure of at the time, greater. I do know it was the last time I was ever able to assume that any departure from perfect health was normal in Nadia.

Moreover, I was experiencing some peculiar behavior of my own. Ever since our return from the Vineyard, I couldn't sleep in my own bed at night. I would fall asleep easily enough next to John but awaken after midnight when I felt my body insisting that it sleep in the family room. Not just in that room but on a specific couch against the south wall with my head at the east end and my feet at the west. But as soon as Nadia was diagnosed, my need to sleep there vanished.

It is Halloween when the cancer finally shows itself. Nadia is still dressed in her angel costume after an evening of trick-or-treating when she asks, "Mama, can I have just one more piece of candy?"

"Just one," I answer.

Sounds of rummaging in her bag of treats, unwrapping, slurping, and then the trick: "Owee, my jaw cracked."

I glance up. Everything seems to be in order. The pain is already gone. But Nadia notices a change when she brushes her teeth before bed. "Mama, why is one side of my face different from the other?"

I look and see the lump. I am more curious than concerned, as if I have been given a puzzle to solve. It is still thirty-six hours before we first hear the word *cancer* from a doctor. Nadia will have one more gymnastics session with her new coach, one more swimming lesson with Gaby before her violin will be put away permanently, before she will be stripped of her wings and confined to a chrysalis woven of chemotherapy. I am the one who will grow wings, not the ethereal ones of Nadia's costume but the earthbound, blood-and-guts ones of the dragonflies. If I can fly like them, I will learn what I thought I should have already known but have always struggled with—how to be Nadia's mother.

2

What good will a brush with death do for this empathic, generous, strong, patient, and determined little girl?

—journal entry, November 3, 2000

February 19, 1992. Nadia did not want to be born. She had to be urged down from her comfortable position high in my uterus to follow the path of her twin brother Max, who had already battered his way from my womb. Nadia emerged with no sign of struggle, but her body was rigid, her arms and legs stiff and extended, the air acting on them like an electric current. *I will not be easy to raise,* her body challenged, as if she knew the battle was not in the birthing but in the living.

Even though I didn't believe in reincarnation or past lives, I sensed in Nadia a soul that had come to me through the ages rather than conception, as if she had found in my womb a place from which to reenter the world. Nursing, smiling, sitting, walking, talking, putting a puzzle together—Nadia mastered all these tasks and milestones early and with an unusual absence of frustration, not as if they were new challenges but as if she were being reminded of what she had already known. She did not want me to help her learn ("I do" were her first words) but just to be a witness. I watched in awe, but being a bystander made me feel distant from Nadia. It was like the difference between playing chamber music, when I would use my flute to engage in conversation with other players, and listening to an ensemble without gaining access to the intimate dialogue among the members.

Nadia didn't ask for my protection either. At her first-year checkup, the twelve-month-old observed her pediatrician warily, her eyes never leaving him. She knew what was coming. When the inevitable shot was given, her face assumed a look of prideful indignation that seemed supernatural, and I had to look twice to make sure she hadn't turned Dr. Murphy into a toad or vaporized him completely.

When Nadia was four, she jumped into a swimming pool without the floaties she always wore on her arms and sank to the bottom. As I dove in to pull her out, she pushed herself to the surface, paddled a few strokes to get to the wall, and then turned to me with calm curiosity, wondering what I was doing in the pool with all my clothes on. She didn't need me to save her.

I should have been happy to have such a spirited and capable daughter, but her intensity blinded me to the little girl within. When she was two, Nadia took my hand, turned my face toward hers, and said, "When I was your mommy, I used to give you your pacifiers."

"You were a good mommy," I answered.

I let the fantasy that Nadia could actually be my mother, who had died ten years earlier, seduce me. When I had a headache, I would only pretend that I didn't want Nadia to see me incapacitated. In truth, I hoped that she would come and find me because I knew she would try to rub the pain away. Her touch felt so familiar, her fingers long and strong like my mother's, finding the same places on my head to stroke. I did nothing to clarify for Nadia which one of us was raising the other.

I was not the only recipient of Nadia's empathy. One summer when Nadia was not yet three, a friend of mine came to visit on a chilly, damp day. Seeing her give a slight shiver, Nadia toddled off to get a blanket, spread it on my friend's lap, and gently tucked in the edges. She made so many of these gestures that I stopped seeing them, but I never failed to notice her response to the pain of others, particularly that of Max and her older sister, Frannie. When the kids were little, I would bring all three to the pediatrician's office together for their check-ups. Nadia's hurt from a shot would cause a quick burst of tears, but seeing her brother and older sister cry from their injections would pierce her heart. Long after I had dried Frannie's and Max's eyes, there was little I could do to stop Nadia's elephant-sized tears or to erase the red blotches from her face.

She was particularly protective of Max, who was still wrestling his way into childhood. Nadia was the focus of all his frustration. As a toddler, he bit her; and when he got older, he teased and belittled her. Nadia would come to me deeply wounded. "Why is he doing this to me?" she would ask.

I would tell her not to react to Max, not to cry. What kept him interested was her reaction, but Nadia did not know how to respond strategically. She voiced her pain. She had no idea how to fight back because defending herself meant attacking someone she loved. If I intervened, she would scream at me to leave Max alone, as if I were a dangerous interloper and she Max's true caregiver.

As I continued to search within Nadia for something that needed my care and nurturing, I became focused on her flaws—hubris and stubbornness. As preschoolers, Max and Nadia would go to the playground, where Nadia would race to the monkey bars and swing herself from end to end and back again. "Max," she would remind her brother, "you can only do it one way." At age seven, Nadia would see Frannie struggling on the trampoline at the gym and say, "I can do that; that's easy."

When I would say, "Nadia, stop boasting," she would look surprised, as if she had no idea how arrogant she sounded. I think she was addressing her comments not to Max and Frannie but to me. They were another way for her to say, "Mama, look at me."

When Nadia was five, her favorite book was an illustrated version of the lullaby *Hush, Little Baby*. She insisted we add it to our bedtime routine, which already included a chat about the day and a series of songs such as "Dona, Dona"; "Hine Ma Tov" (Here Is Good); and a few Peter, Paul, and Mary favorites. Every night, I would read the book through once and then sing it to her. One night, twice was not enough. Nadia wanted a third reading. "No, Nadia," I said, "it's time to go to sleep."

"Just one more, please?"

"No. I'm going to turn out the light. Give me a kiss goodnight."

I tried to bend toward Nadia's face, but she pushed me away. "No, Mama, no. One more time. Please. I promise I'll go to sleep then."

"You'll go to sleep now," I answered and without kissing Nadia goodnight I left the room.

Nadia followed me out of the room, her arms holding the book out toward me.

"Go back to bed," I told her, not daring to glance at her sad little face.

But from her room, Nadia continued to plead with me. "Please, Mama, just one more time."

"No," I called from my room. "Go to sleep."

The crying went on for another fifteen minutes. Finally, I heard a tired and beaten voice call to me, "Mama, you never gave me a kiss goodnight."

I went in to kiss her, to stroke the tears away, to give her an extra hug. I told myself I had done what a mother is supposed to do—set limits. I should not be feeling like someone who had just broken a majestic horse used to running free.

Nadia's strength kept me at a distance; her flaws gave her an exaggerated vulnerability. She defied any notion I had of what a mother needs to do to raise her child. But I was most unprepared for Nadia's questions about death. She had discovered much earlier than I the trick that had been played on her, on all of us, that she was born only someday to die. She would often imagine what it was like to be dead and would tell me how bored she was going to be when she died with only herself to talk to. I didn't lack in understanding; I have the same concerns about death and was relieved that the subject had never come up with Frannie.

Frannie, three and half years older than Nadia, gave me little practice talking about such serious subjects because she embraced a more lighthearted approach to life. Frannie is the daughter I waited four years to conceive, years also spent recovering from the death of my mother from breast cancer. Frannie was the one I could dress in my mother's name and nourish with her love of the sea. The ocean of Martha's Vineyard became our magical place. During our playful sessions of dancing at the water's edge and searching for sea life at low tide, my then five-year-old daughter would ply me with questions about my life. She made my memories her own—reciting the story of my first punishment at school as if it had happened to her, telling how my kitten, Mahitable, was killed by a dog as if she had been there, crying in loneliness at the grave of my mother, the grandmother she'd never met.

"Frannie," I'd ask, "can you see Grandma dancing out beyond the waves?"

Frannie would smile her *be tolerant of mommy* smile. But the next time we went she'd ask, "Do you think she's out there today?" In our imagination we would paint pictures of Grandma's life in the sea.

A trip to the ocean with Nadia when she was five was very different. For her, even a day of recreation was about accomplishing concrete tasks that I could witness and praise.

"Mama, look how deep I dug this hole."

"Watch, Mama, I'm going to jump over the waves."

"See my castle, Mama. Do you like it?"

"Nadia," I'd interrupt, "look at the ocean. Can you see Grandma dancing beyond the waves?"

"Mama, she's not really out there."

"I know, sweetie, it's just that if she could be someplace, it would be here."

I had more fun pretending with Frannie, who has inherited an Irish twinkle from her other, very much alive, grandmother. Frannie's youthful belief in the fantastical, her sparkle and ready giggles drown out the melancholy minor melodies that flow through my veins.

As a little boy, Max was like the impish leprechauns of Frannie's imagination. At the beach, freed from the restrictions of New York City sidewalks, Max twirled, zigzagged, and cartwheeled his way across the sand. No matter where he was, Max sang—he sang the rounds and folk songs he learned in school; he sang top-forty hits heard on the radio; he sang the melody from whatever cello piece he was working on. When he studied Beethoven's *Ninth Symphony* or Berlioz's *Symphonie Fantastique* in his music class at school, he sang those, too. With singing came dancing—jigs, jazz, hip-hop, languid improvisations, energetic jumps and leaps. Unlike Nadia, Max did not insist that I watch him, but it was impossible not to.

With Max, I could pretend death was not such a scary subject. On a trip to Ireland to visit John's aunts, uncles, and cousins, which we made when Max was six, he became fascinated with graveyards. On the bus, we played "I Spy a Graveyard." We walked through ancient country cemeteries, and I bought Max a miniature Celtic cross. I promised him that when we got back home I would take him to Jewish cemeteries. I did, however, draw the line at allowing him to decorate his birthday cake with tombstones.

"I want to be dead so I can live in a graveyard," Max said.

"I'll miss you," I responded, hiding my anxiety as if trying to fool a lie detector. "I won't be able to see you when you're dead." Even the mother in the children's book *The Runaway Bunny,* who was able to find her baby anywhere he could think to hide, wouldn't have been able to see beyond life.

Max told me not to worry. "I'll come see you," he said. "I promise."

I bit my tongue, but Nadia never held back her words. "Max, the only one who can see you when you're dead is yourself. Right, Mom?"

Where did she learn that from? I wondered. She sounded so matter-of-fact, but what she said was far more terrifying to me than Max's naïve desire to be dead. I managed a weak "I suppose so."

By age seven, Nadia had expressed her anxiety about what death is more directly. "I don't want to grow up," she said.

"Why not, honey?" I asked. After watching her work so hard to master one skill after another, I had assumed she was eager be older.

"If I grow up, I'll die. I don't want to die. What will I do lying there forever all by myself? I'll be with all the kids, and you'll be somewhere with the adults." Nadia's tears ran freely; I swallowed mine as I, too, imagined with unbearable clarity my beautiful little girl so alone and beyond my reach. Would she ever stop asking these questions for which I still had no answers?

"Don't worry, my love. We will both die as old women and will be together always." This was less than two years before cancer would make such pat responses impossible.

Only rarely did I know exactly what Nadia needed me to be. But one summer, when she was five, I had an answer.

I was alone swimming in the ocean. On the shore I saw what looked like a little piece of the sun fallen to earth and running across the sand. It was my Nadia in her yellow summer dress. In a flash she was naked, sleek as a seal, dog-paddling her way to me. I had given her the gift of the sea after all. During the few seconds it took her to swim to me, I thought my heart would burst in anticipation of receiving her more completely than when she had emerged from the salt water of my womb. When she reached me, she asked me the latest in her series of questions about death: when will I die, when will she die, what happens when you die?

"Mama, couldn't you please just live forever?"

"I tell you what," I answered, "if you live forever, so will I." Nadia smiled and snuggled closer. We were a sea mother and her sea baby, living forever.

Nadia's vulnerability was clear. Finally, I was the mother in this exchange. I pressed my face into that wonderful tender spot on the back of her neck, trying to memorize the feeling for the next time, when what I should do or say wouldn't be so obvious. I wished for immortality, for the time to get it right.

3

It was only a week ago that I innocently
brought Nadia to Dr. Murphy's.
It seems like another dimension now.

—journal entry, November 7, 2000

Cancer: hard-shelled, pinching, bottom feeder. To kill it, we become barbarians. Cytoxan, vincristine, doxorubicin, ifosfamide, etoposide—these chemicals poison patients into living. We operate and radiate. We cause nausea, hair loss, sores, pain, weakness, heart damage, deafness, bleeding bladders, malnutrition, infection, transfusions. This is reality to me now, but it wasn't always.

Despite having a mother who died of breast cancer when I was thirty, I found that the hard truths about treatment were as shadowy as the disease appears on X rays. As a child in the late 1950s and early 1960s, I remember learning simultaneously about the Holocaust and the evils of smoking and lung cancer. Both meant death, both conjured images of devastated bodies; but as morbidly fascinated as I would be, I was unable to imagine either.

My mother did not allow me to see the fine print of her cancer, which struck just as I was leaving Boston to set out on my adult life in New York. Even on my prolonged visits home, I saw little. I saw the row upon row of pill bottles but never knew what each one did or its name. I could feel the fuzzy baldness of my mother's head, listen to her muted (for my sake) complaints of tiredness or nausea, but I knew no details of her chemotherapy program. I saw drains and bandages following her mastectomy, could see the prosthesis that more often than not sat disembodied in her dresser drawer. But I never saw the scar, nor was I allowed to witness her fear.

"Hi, it's Judi. How's Ma?" I'd ask my father on the telephone.

"Oh, she's okay. Now."

"Now? What do you mean *now?* What happened?"

My father would relate the latest complication from the most recent round of treatment—fever, the risk of infection from low blood-cell counts, fluid in my mother's lungs. I got clinical facts but not the feelings. Nothing about the suffering, the fear, the danger.

Part of the reason behind this lack of communication was practical. My parents lived in Boston, I in New York. My mother was the only one in the family who was comfortable on the phone, and she only took calls when she was feeling well. So most of the communication was in my father's control, and he thought it was his responsibility not to burden me or intrude on the life I was building in New York with John, whom I had married the year before my mother's diagnosis.

I didn't know how to ask for more information without feeling as if I were adding to my parents' stress. Perhaps they would have to choose their words too carefully so as not to upset me or maybe my questions would siphon off energy they needed to cope. If they got impatient with me, I would feel even more left out. But my passivity also came from fear. I learned quickly that no news could easily mean bad news. It was easier to hear it after the fact.

In the early 1980s, about six years after my mother's diagnosis, we planned to celebrate Chanukah at my sister Joanny's house in Baltimore. My mother and father arrived the night before I did. When I got off the train, my sister met me and said we were going straight to the Johns Hopkins Medical Center.

"Why?" I asked.

"Mommy got a fever last night and had to be admitted," Joanny answered. Both she and my father, whom I met at the hospital, seemed surprised that I hadn't known my mother was there. Still, I never challenged them to admit that the only way I would have known would have been if they had called me.

My mother's cancer remained a cold fog. Only in her last year did it lift enough for me to see the devastation it wrought. I had gone to visit her two months before she died. She asked me to sleep in the room with her, in order to give my father some relief. I lay awake all night listening to her raspy breaths, got her stewed fruit when she was hungry, saw the exhaustion overtake her after just two bites. I laid out her clothes the next morning, helped her tie her shoes. But already my mother began to retreat. She could not look me in the eye, could not bear to see in them the reflections of her own dependence on her "baby girl." She was not going to allow me to be nurse anymore. And while caring for my mother helped me through the terror by giving me something to do, I had no idea how to help beyond my simple ministrations of that night.

A few weeks later my mother arranged separate goodbye visits for me and my sister. She was convinced she only had a few more days to live. She had fallen in love with the human voice in song, so for my visit I brought her two recordings of arias and lieder. She listened to them while staring out the window—or perhaps she was looking inward, where my eyes couldn't go. I also brought her the program from a benefit concert I had organized at the 92nd Street Y, where I worked at the time. It was the premiere of *A Song For Hope,* a commissioned choral work by Elie Wiesel with a score by David Diamond. She kept the journal open to the page with my name: Judith Hannan, Director of Development, a position to which I had risen from office assistant. Again, my mother kept her eyes trained on the window; maybe this time she was searching for the rest of my life.

I did not anticipate the day of her death, nor was I there for it. My father did not call me when he knew my mother was dying but waited until after her heart and breath had stopped. The details he related were familiar. My mother had had trouble breathing that morning. She went to the hospital for oxygen and to drain her lungs. Only this time she had had enough. She pushed the mask away. "No more," she said.

I was at a closing dinner that night for one of John's deals, the merger of two oil and gas companies. He was in charge of the affair, and my parents knew how important this evening was to him. My father reached me at the restaurant. There is no greater example of how detached I had been from my mother's illness than my father's next words: "I'm sure Mummy would have wanted you to stay at the party."

Even after death, though, my mother still had a secret. On the day of her funeral, I was getting dressed in what I still saw as my father *and* mother's room when

John came in. "I just asked your father where the cemetery is," he said.

"Where?" I asked.

"He said she's going to be cremated."

"What?" I cried.

I went out to the living room, not sure what I wanted. I wasn't against cremation. I saw my father, my sister, my aunts, my cousins—they all knew.

"I thought she told everyone," my father lamented.

"No, she never told me," I whispered, realizing that what I wanted was to feel sorry for myself but I couldn't do this in front of my father's grief.

I returned to the bedroom and sobbed to John. "I was the only one she never told," as if distinguishing myself as most pained was just as good as being someone my mother confided in.

Because there was so much of my mother's illness that I didn't see, my response to her death remained that of a child—grieving over *my* loss without acknowledging my mother's mourning during her final days.

I had gone back to see my mother two weeks after our goodbye weekend, just a few days before she died. She had surprised herself by remaining alive. But I had come uninvited; she wasn't happy to see me. There was not enough left of her to be my mother. I felt as if I had intruded on a woman I was never supposed to know. I resented her lack of happiness in seeing me. More than a year earlier, she had asked me not to have a baby until after she died. My sister had a daughter, and we could see my mother trying to fill up on Rachel as if this connection could sustain her after life. Our goodbye weekend was supposed to be the last topping up. My mother's pain at having to say goodbye again, at realizing that there would be no end to her desire to know my life, must have competed with the pain in her body. When I open myself to her pain, I can see that so much of her not telling was part of her grief at no longer being able to protect me.

But that compassion—the lack of which stemmed from what I could not see, either by my choice or the choice of what others chose to share—was not yet fully formed when we first discovered Nadia's cancer. I was still too angry about all I hadn't been told to question the roots of my family's silence. As I grabbed for some knowledge that might have helped me, the elusiveness of my mother's experience was like trying to recount a dream—it's all there until you try to relate it to someone. As I sensed the cold tentacles reaching for my daughter, I refused to acknowledge the menace they represented. I was not ready, yet, to act as if I knew what I was dealing with, and so Nadia will not always find in me the mother she needs. Only when I fully understand the roots of my resistance to being fully informed will I soften.

A cancer diagnosis is not an overnight phenomenon. I imagine they all begin with variations on the same theme. "Don't worry," the doctor says. "I'm almost certain it's nothing, but why don't we run some tests to make sure?"

No one seems overly concerned at the pediatrician's on the morning of November 1, 2000. Assuming that the swelling in Nadia's jaw is unusual but benign, I chat with Dr. Murphy, who has been our pediatrician since Frannie was born, while Nadia expresses her impatience by way of exaggerated sighs and appeals to go home.

"It's definitely the bone, not a gland or muscle," says Dr. Murphy as he and the colleagues he has called in feel Nadia's face. There are enough of us present for a tea party, and we are appropriately festive.

"I'm glad I brought you something interesting," I joke. "What do you think it is?"

"Well, it's hard to say without taking an X ray but I'm 99 percent sure it's nothing."

He sends us straight from his office to see a maxillofacial expert at the Mount Sinai Medical Center. If there is undue urgency in his voice, I don't hear it.

"Would you like me to call John?" he asks as Nadia and I get ready to leave his office. A little voice in my belly that I don't allow to escape through my lips wonders, *Why would you want to do that?* John only joins us for serious medical emergencies, like the time Frannie broke her foot or Max suffered one of his anaphylactic reactions to the peanuts he is allergic to. I rarely include John in more routine matters. Our roles were traditional, a reflection of what our parents modeled and of the different nature of our ambitions. John had ambition from the start and found his identity in his career. I would find mine years later in motherhood.

John grew up in the working-class environs of Elmhurst, Queens, where he was raised in an Irish immigrant household. His goals were always clear. First, get an accounting degree. Then work for a couple of years to establish his professional credibility. Next, get an advanced professional degree from an Ivy League school. Last, become an investment banker.

I met John during the first week of our freshman year at Adelphi University in Long Island, when he came to visit my roommate, Sharon. I was sitting cross-legged on my bed going through a pile of orientation handouts. After Sharon introduced us, I went back to my papers. John wasn't here to see me, and I was too shy or unskilled to insert myself into their conversation. But John appeared to take a great interest in me; with my waist-length, dark-brown hair and eyes he said were soulful, I was, he later told me, the girl of his dreams. But John was not the boy of mine. His red hair sprang from his head in all directions except down; he was pale and freckled and so thin that his chest was concave.

John commuted by car from home and would often drive me and Sharon to the Roosevelt Field Mall or the grocery store to get supplies for our room. Sharon always got the front seat. She liked him. I thought I already had a boyfriend, Peter, who lived in Brooklyn. He was the sort of dark, bad-boy character I made a point of liking. We had met a year earlier in Israel, where his mother had sent him for the summer hoping it would stop his slide into delinquency. I never found out if her plan worked. Although I had chosen a school in New York to be closer to Peter, he broke up with me that fall.

It became hard to ignore John as only a means of transportation. He worked a subtle seduction by giving me a level of attention I was unused to in boys. Then, on one trip to the mall, he asked me sit in the front seat of the car. A week later, I asked him if he wanted to go see the Paul Butterfield Blues Band in Brooklyn. I was drawn to the rough earthiness of Paul Butterfield in high school; I never fully rebelled against the upper-middle-class suburban homogeneity of my childhood town of Lexington, Massachusetts, except through my taste in music. When I saw a poster announcing Paul Butterfield's concert in Brooklyn, I knew the only way I could get to see the band would be if someone drove me. I didn't consider this to be a date with John, but, of course, it was. I had never made the effort to see the group before, no matter how much I claimed to love them. By not calling it a date, I wouldn't have had to take it personally if John had said no.

After our first date, which included a fender bender

and picking up a hitchhiker, John took charge of our second one. He took me to Le Cave Henri Cinq, a French restaurant that was as similar to the diners I was used to eating in as French roast coffee is similar to Sanka. I wore a form-fitting, floor-length black and maroon dress; John wore a blazer, tie, and slacks, an outfit that should have been a mismatch with his hair but wasn't. For John and me, the date fit our definition of romance perfectly. He was the gallant knight to my maiden. In fact, though, he was a less-than-well-off boy trying to impress, while I began internalizing the notion that John was someone who could take care of me.

But once we got back to campus, we reverted to being college kids. John was hungry again so we drove to White Castle, where he got a sack of burgers that he ate in the car while we listened to Van Morrison on his eight-track tape player.

By the middle of our freshman year, John took me to meet his parents and three sisters. The table was laid with platters of meat, potatoes, and vegetables. I was a slow eater and only liked small portions of food on my plate at a time. When I realized after a few minutes that I hadn't had any broccoli, I looked up to find that it, and all the other food, was gone—inhaled, it seemed. Then John's mother started crying, accusing me of taking her son away from her. John said, "Mommy!" and the sisters rolled their eyes and laughed. But John's mother knew her son very well; he had already fallen in love with me.

By the end of our freshman year, John and I had become a couple. My sister was getting married that June, and my mother was concerned about John's mop of hair being in the family pictures, so she made him get a haircut. I drove John to the salon because he was too nervous and too busy making his way through my pack of cigarettes to take the wheel himself. John saw his hair as a necessary limb, each snip a dismembering. That he agreed to the haircut showed his devotion to me. That I only laughed and didn't tell my mother she was asking too much showed my immaturity. I couldn't side against my mother, and I had the childlike expectation that John would understand and be the one to make the sacrifice.

But I didn't fall in love with John because I could depend on him or because he adored me. It was his genius. I have always fallen in love with genius. I just had never associated it with business before.

In my family, genius was associated with creativity, either artistic or scientific. My father was a genius not just because he had a high IQ but because of his inventions. I would go to his lab on occasion, where he would teach me about the vacuum tubes he designed that made radio and television possible. He showed me a machine that transmitted high-quality photographs over the telephone line. He demonstrated a sonar system he had invented called the boomer, which could chart what lies beneath the ocean floor. He explained how a nuclear clock worked. I didn't know these would all be precursors to modern technologies. I only understood they came from my father's brain.

My mother's side of the family contained the musical geniuses. Two of her sisters, a violinist and a pianist, both stifled their careers for their husbands. It was my cousin Bobby who was chosen to be the family prodigy—debuting at Symphony Hall with the Boston Pops at age thirteen.

My mother made it a requirement that my sister and I take music lessons. I began playing the flute when I was eight. I studied with a teacher across town, Mrs. Porter. For seven years, my mother drove me each week for my hour-long lesson, where she either waited in the car or did her shopping at nearby Wilson's Farm, often bringing back my favorite candy, Molasses Puff, which I would melt in my mouth, no longer caring if my lips and fingers were sticky now that my lesson was over.

One of my treasured possessions is my *Altès Célèbre Methode Complète de Flûte,* which still contains Mrs. Porter's handwriting and the gold and silver stars she gave me and which still sings to me of those hours when Mrs. Porter made me feel like a true musician, one of the best she ever taught. But the conductor of my school's orchestra was Mrs. Porter's opposite. After holding one of the first-chair positions for two years, I decided to switch to band, just to see what it was like. When I found it didn't suit me, I returned to orchestra and, without explanation, was demoted to second flute, replaced by a girl who had just moved into town. Jana was the ideal teacher's pet, truly puppy-like in her devotion. I had betrayed the conductor by joining the band, and I was being punished.

When I began applying to college, I announced my decision to study music. I had left Mrs. Porter two years earlier and had been attending the Longy School of Music in Cambridge. My senior recital generated no standing ovation, nerves having overtaken me, nor did my announcement. My mother, whose studies to become a psychiatric social worker had made her particularly perceptive, knew I had given little thought to the matter but had simply chosen music because it was familiar. I don't remember if my father had any response; I didn't know it at the time, but my departure for college would be hard on him. The most stinging response came from Bobby's mother: "Judi, it's a very hard life. Just look at Bobby."

I didn't want to look at Bobby. We were always looking at, hearing about, or listening to Bobby. But she and my mother ended up being right. I loved to play the flute and I was good, but not good enough to get into the competitive music programs. I didn't put in the hours of practice. The weakness of my technique thwarted my musicality, as if I knew my thoughts but didn't have the skill to communicate them.

There was no instrumental program at Adelphi. I majored in music education, found playing opportunities in a community orchestra, and studied flute outside of school, first with a local teacher and then with John Wummer, former first flutist of the New York Philharmonic. Teaching, I learned, required the same kind of confidence needed to be a performer. My best lesson plan would be on the physics of sound, which I worked out with my father in much the same way we had worked on my science projects together when I was a child. But Adelphi wasn't barren of inspiration. I discovered opera, the intricacy and soul of Bach. I learned to analyze scores, a skill I would put to use on airplanes to calm my nerves.

And I underwent my most powerful musical and even spiritual transformation. Every music major at Adelphi was required to sing in the annual performance of Bach's *St. Matthew Passion*, held at the Cathedral of the Incarnation in Garden City, New York. For me, everything about the experience was harrowing—the brutal story, which, as a Jew, I found so foreign; the gothic gloom of the cathedral; the anguished Jesus on the crucifix; our entrance from the basement via a narrow spiral staircase, up which we progressed slowly enough to trap us in its well, where the light from above and below couldn't penetrate. Even the music, with its dissonances and tears, could drown out its own glory. A hired orchestra accompanied the chorus each year, and I looked down at them from my wobbly stance on the risers, craving the silver light of my flute.

After the first year, I approached the head of the music department. Lawrence Rasmussen was a large, imposing, formal man with eyebrows bent in a perpetual scowl. He ruled rather than ran the department. He had favorites, and I wasn't one of them. But my desire to play the flute was a hunger, so I approached him to ask if, the next year, I could be in the orchestra during the *Passion* performance. He said no; every student had to sing. I backed down, trembling. When I was a junior, however, Mr. Rasmussen surprised me by inviting me to play second flute in that year's performance. A year later, I was moved to first chair, replacing the woman who had been my teacher.

"Buss und Reu," is a beautiful musical conversation in the *Passion* between the alto soloist and flute. It was perfect for me, requiring musicality more than technique. The soloist was Adelphi's voice teacher and Mr. Rasmussen's wife, with whom I had studied but who had not befriended me. I was beginning to learn that musicians required a lot of adoration, which I wasn't providing. I had no idea how I could ever speak intimately with this woman.

We had two rehearsals together. I was competent; Mrs. Rasmussen was patronizing. But on the night of the performance, the melody entered me, and I wove it with the voice as if spinning fine silk. The duet transformed us into friends, family, lovers. The cathedral vanished—its stone, its crosses, its tortured Jesus. At the end I was just music, not body or breath. Then there was silence, and then a deeper silence. I struggled to return myself to the physical world around me before the next movement began. I swaddled myself in the knowledge that John, my mother, and father were in the audience, and gradually I felt my limbs and lungs once again return to my conscious control.

I graduated a few months later with no opportunity to repeat this moment. I didn't want to live my cousin Bobby's life of sacrifice and constant practicing and, ultimately, of failure. I wanted to build a home and a family. The business school at Adelphi had a graduation banquet. John reaped many awards and honors. I wasn't just proud of him in the way he was of me after the *St. Matthew Passion.* I basked in his glory; I was the girlfriend of the genius. A month after graduation, we married.

After graduation, John implemented his plan. He worked for two years at Arthur Andersen, went to Harvard Business School, and began his career as an investment banker at Kidder Peabody. I became a drifter, a jellyfish with no practical skills, waiting to see where the tide would take me. I worked as a billing clerk, a switchboard operator, a data entry clerk, an office temp. Eventually, I wandered into a career as a fundraiser—beginning as a secretary, putting children on hold after each promotion. We didn't have our first child for thirteen years. After Frannie's birth, I continued to work full time, then part time, soon no time, then full time again. The addition of Max and Nadia removed any conflict I had about working. I could finally claim a calling. But choosing to stay home while John worked long hours and traveled meant a growing gap between the time we each spent as parents. I became the keeper of the knowledge, the secrets, the routines, the lives of our children.

It wasn't that John didn't understand the magic of childbirth. On the day Frannie was born, while I was warehoused in a room for that morning's new mothers, John ran up and down the stairs to look at Frannie. "She's beautiful," he would say before dashing off again. "She's still there," he would say on the next visit, not quite believing in her permanence. But he was not a modern dad. He didn't change diapers or get up in the middle of the night; he didn't take temperatures or administer medicine. I bought the clothes and played airplane with spoonfuls of pureed peaches. I went to the park and to birthday parties. I chaperoned dances and walked safety patrol.

John swooped in at the end of the day with love and hugs and boisterous greetings. "Frannie! Max! Nadia!" he would yell. "How are my babies? How's my Judi?"

His entrance jarred me from my daytime single motherhood, as if I had been immersed in Bach's *Suites for Unaccompanied Cello* and someone had put on the Rolling Stones without asking or warning me. I tried to hide my irritation from the kids because John was so happy to be at home and with us. But when John gave us all his inevitable head rubs, I would duck my head as if avoiding raindrops rather than love. I needed a slower transition.

During Nadia's treatment, John's now forced upbeat energy was hard for her to tolerate, and I still wonder if I influenced her intolerance. I was never very good at filling John in on what he had missed during the day, at seeking his advice, at including him as a partner in raising our children. In the same way that distance had affected my communication with my parents during my mother's illness, John's virtual residence in a world so different from mine meant that keeping him abreast of the details of the children's lives required much more sharing than I was accustomed to. I didn't want to exclude him from the kids' lives, but I was worried about any encroachment on my identity as a mother.

I wasn't alone in my lack of communication. Other than telling me when he might be home and, maybe, the company he was trying to do a deal for, John told me nothing else about his work. At a business dinner, I would be mute while others, including spouses, discussed a buyout or a merger. When I told John that my ignorance made me feel stupid, he would prep me a little more before the next dinner but would forget before each future occasion unless I pressed him.

His questions about the children were also general. *How were they? Did they have a good day?* To answer him fairly I had to raise topics he didn't always understand, such as separation anxiety. John has never experienced it; I have combated it since my first move away from my mother's side to go to nursery school.

Frannie, like me, screamed every morning when I left her at nursery school. I was never successful at getting John to feel how this twisted my gut—how the guilt I felt at leaving her and at wanting to get away did battle with each other. "I don't get it," he would say. "She's only a few blocks from home, and it's only for a few hours. Is someone being mean to her? Are the teachers not nice?"

"It has nothing to do with distance," I said. "She's still in a new world. No one's being mean to her. She likes her teachers."

"Then I still don't get it," John replied.

I assumed that a man who met daily with the CEOs of major corporations, who could add up a list of multidigit numbers in his head almost as fast as he could read this sentence, would never be able to understand how it felt to be stuck in a play-sized chair with a bunch of three-year-olds who ask you to take them to the bathroom because they assume you're a teacher rather than a mother with a very clingy child who must be pried from you slowly.

How many times did I have to repeat the names of the kids' friends, the topics of the reports they were working on, where they were going on a field trip, something they had said just a minute ago, while John was in the room but not listening?

I'm not about to explain all these dynamics to Dr. Murphy, so I give him John's number. I know this call will send John into a panic. In retrospect, I can see that of course it should have, but, at the time, I am just worried about how I will diffuse his anxiety. One of the companion obligations of being in charge of the kids is feeling it is my responsibility to manage John's reactions to events in their lives, to protect him and myself from any sign that he can't handle a situation. So I behave as if I am still feeling in control. Once I get my marching orders from Dr. Murphy, I brandish this control as my shield.

Nadia and I arrive at the hospital first. I keep an eager eye out for John. I am getting bored of entertaining Nadia; since I don't believe there is anything to worry about, I wouldn't mind relinquishing responsibility. We have exhausted Nadia's repertoire of hand games, and I am numbed by the details of the Halloween costumes worn by Gabu, Em, Mar-Mar, and Luce-Goose (Nadia's friends Gaby, Emily, Marlena, and Lucie).

Nadia is called in to see the doctor before John arrives. After taking a brief history and feeling Nadia's mandible, the doctor recommends an X ray called a Panorax, which will take an orbital picture of her jaw. It is one of many tests we will come to know well.

The Panorax machine will circle Nadia's head. It will take less than a minute. She enters the room, dons the protective lead shield.

"Now, be sure you stand very still," the technician says as she and I leave. The door closes. I watch through the window. Nadia's back is to me. She stands so straight and still, taking responsibility through this simple act of perfect cooperation. Nadia is unreachable now. Later, I will recognize this as the point at which my journey and Nadia's separated, as it must for all mothers and daughters—but, for us, too abruptly. We will remain side by side; Nadia in her boat and me in mine, our vessels the same size, color, and shape but never again the same. I am grateful that she can't see me, to observe the tears that sense this separation, even as my brain keeps trying to convince me there is nothing to worry about.

John arrives while Nadia is still in the room. I am relieved to see him, not because I want to share my thoughts—they are too nebulous and would take far too much effort to convey—but because his presence distracts me from Nadia, gives me something else to focus on. John and I stand close enough for the fabric of our clothes to touch but with our bodies erect. As we watch Nadia, I tell John the little bit that has happened so far. I can see in the set of his features that he is scared, that he wants me to tell him what I think the doctors are looking for. But I want to act as if there is no problem so I stick with the details of what a Panorax does and how it works. I fall back on science in the way my father would have; knowing facts is comforting.

The first picture isn't clear. Another Panorax has to be done. I call the gymnastics coach to cancel Nadia's lesson.

The second picture is clearer but no more edifying.

"We can see here that this tooth in the back has been pushed sideways," the doctor says. "There's some kind of shadow, but we can't really tell from this what it is."

The doctor, a glorified dentist really, remains focused on Nadia's teeth, trying to explain the anomalies but coming up empty-handed. *Forget the teeth,* I seethe; *it's not her teeth.* Finally, he admits he doesn't know.

"I think it would be best to arrange a CAT scan before the end of today," he says.

But radiology is very busy. It is hard for them to fit Nadia in.

"Perhaps first thing tomorrow morning," the keeper of the schedule suggests.

John takes over. "No. Today," he insists.

A time is found, 6:00 P.M. Nadia, John, and I walk the few blocks to our apartment to fill the hours before we have to return.

"She has cancer," John says when we are alone in our room. "What else could it be?"

"How do you know? Didn't you hear him? He still says the odds are 99 percent that it's nothing to worry about."

"How can you believe that, Judi? What are we going to do?"

"Well, I'm not going to get all upset yet. I'm going to wait for the CAT scan."

It's easy for me to dismiss John's pessimism. His is always the voice of doom, the one that cries, "Watch out," and "Be careful," at every robust action of his children. His constant anticipation of the worst was bound to hit the mark at some point. But why now? I can't accept that his parental intuition is more acute than mine. That would make him the better parent, able to know what I don't, despite spending less time with his children.

John has a more sympathetic listener in his mother, who had come in from Long Island a few days earlier for a visit. "Please, God," she says in her Irish brogue, "I pray everything will be okay."

"Everything's fine," I say, bristling at what I believe is my mother-in-law's unnecessary appeal and her certainty that God exists in the first place. "You're all jumping the gun. Why don't we just wait and see what the CAT scan shows?"

Then I run to find my children, to see them doing normal things—calling friends, sneaking snacks before dinner, trying to get away with watching TV instead of doing homework, or, in Nadia's case, being absorbed in a new work of art that requires her to dump all her supplies onto the playroom floor. *Normal* for Nadia means not wanting to be pulled away for a return trip to the hospital.

"Why do I have to go now?" she gripes. "I'm tired, and I haven't even had supper yet."

"Because this is when your appointment is," I say through tight lips. "Now get your spelling book and math worksheet so you won't have to do them when we get back."

The scan lasts for only a few minutes. Nadia and I giggle as the technician replays the tape for us—a technological flip-book of Nadia's skull—sure, I guess, that we don't have a clue as to what we're looking at. John stands off to the side, the first of many times we will position ourselves this way. I don't try to draw him over to Nadia and me. I'm not sure he would have been able to have this little bit of fun anyway. His thoughts are too dark.

The fog snakes around my legs. I have twelve hours left to fool myself.

4

I don't let Nadia see me cry or witness my fear and helplessness, so how can she know how deeply I hurt for her?

—journal entry, December 2, 2000

The call from Dr. Murphy comes early the next morning. It is Thursday, November 2, exactly thirty-six hours after Nadia's jaw had cracked. "The chief of radiology looked at Nadia's CAT scan. He is concerned enough to recommend a biopsy as soon as possible. There are two places you can go, Columbia Presbyterian or Memorial Sloan-Kettering. I've talked to the doctors at Memorial, and they want to see Nadia right away."

"What do you mean, right away?" I ask.

"Today. Now."

"Today?" I whine. "Can't I let Nadia finish her day at school? She was so happy to go back after yesterday."

"No. I know you want to protect her, but you have to override her wishes right now."

This is a new Dr. Murphy. No more joking about the kids' latest antics, tantrums, or complaints. No more leading me to believe that *I* was in charge, that *I* knew what was best for my daughter.

"You'll be getting calls from Dennis Kraus, a surgeon, and Leonard Wexler, an oncologist, to set up appointments. You'll need to bring Nadia's CAT scan, which is here at the office."

I want to challenge Dr. Murphy, tell him it's too early to admit defeat, but I don't. I'm too afraid that he will tell me what he already knows.

Within thirty minutes, both Dr. Kraus and Dr. Wexler have called me personally. Appointments are arranged for a few hours later in the day. I know I called John at work. I must have called him twice, once after talking to Dr. Murphy and once after scheduling Nadia's appointments, but I don't remember what either of us said. I didn't want to think, only to do.

My feet on autopilot, I walk from my apartment to Dr. Murphy's office three blocks away to pick up the oversized manila envelope with my baby's pictures. The route is so familiar that I can almost convince myself that this is just another errand, as if I were picking up school health forms. When I find Dr. Murphy, his voice is softer now but still certain: "Judi, because of what they've seen, the doctors have reason to be very concerned. You need to prepare yourself for a cancer diagnosis."

"This is too surreal," I say, looking anywhere but at him, as if that would prevent his words from finding me.

"It's going to be okay. Surgery, chemo, and she's going to be fine."

"How do you know that?"

"Because I've seen it, over and over again. Either way, it's going to be okay."

At least he doesn't say he's 99 percent sure.

On the way home, I wonder how words such as *chemo* and *oncology* and *CAT scan* could have entered my life.

These are not terms that belong to me. I don't understand how I can be holding these films of my daughter as if I were carrying a file home from work, or why the trees are still growing right side up, or why my body is still working when Nadia's is in peril.

Thirty-six hours, three blocks, four phone conversations—parcels of time, space, and action in which I had felt safe coping with the minutiae of my life—are now units that can no longer be trusted.

I go home to change clothes. This was a trick I had used just two days before, when I'd gone to have a mammogram. Newly washed hair, nice clothes, a pair of earrings, a clean bill of health. It had always worked before.

John picks me up at the apartment and we leave to get Nadia at school. I had called to let the teachers know we were coming. John waits in the car while I go in to get Nadia. I find her in the lobby—alone, confused, angry.

"What are you doing here?" she accuses, ready to bolt.

"I'm sorry, sweetie, but we need to take you to see some more doctors."

"No. I'm not going. I went to the doctor's yesterday. Why can't I stay in school? Why can't I go later or tomorrow? Why can't I just stay here with my friends? Why?"

"Because, Nadia, the doctors have some more questions about why you have a lump in your jaw, and this is the time they can see you."

I want her to accept all this with maturity, to understand the world of medicine and schedules.

"Come on. Get your coat on. Daddy's waiting outside in the car," I tell her too abruptly.

"Can we stop at Ciao Bella's for an ice-cream cone?"

"Not now, Nadia. We can't be late."

"But I'm hungry."

"Please, just get in the car. We'll get you something later."

Time was not the issue. Ice cream on the way to the doctor's office sounded like a bribe, and bribes were for when terrible things were happening.

Nadia opens the door to the car. She doesn't see the strong set of John's face so asks him, "Please, can I get an ice-cream cone first?"

"No." His answer is curt. "We can't be late for the doctor."

John has his own form of blinders. His fear will not allow him to tolerate any deviation from the goal of getting to the hospital any more than a tightrope walker would take his eyes from the focal point that is keeping him balanced. Ice cream would be for after.

Seeing Nadia's shoulders slump, I hear the cruelty in John's and my words. I know I have handled this all wrong. Still, I am unable to change my mind. I convince myself that I am showing Nadia that I am a strong mother, as if this were no different than her asking for one more reading of *Hush, Little Baby.*

Nadia could not find in me or her father a mirror for her own feelings, so her confusion festered, morphing into frustration and fury. "How do I know you're upset?" she demanded as the days of doctors' appointments and tests dragged on. "I never see you cry."

From the moment Dr. Murphy first said the word *cancer,* all I wanted was to shield Nadia from my inner roiling. If she could feel the weight of my pain when I got a headache or of Max's and Frannie's pain when they got shots, how could she not stagger from the rush of tears that poured from my eyes nearly every moment I was not with her. I was no longer the daughter who was angry at not witnessing her mother's experience in all its vibrant hues: the purple of panic and pain, the reds of regret and rage, sienna for sorrow, amber for alone. Now, I was the mother who wanted only to protect her daughter from her own toxic rainbow of emotions.

But I didn't just want to protect Nadia; I needed her as a defense against my terror. When she was out of the house at school or a friend's, my imagination would suck the vitality from her. I could not conjure the sound of her laughter or see her gobbling her lunch or being the last one out in dodge ball. In her physical presence, I indulged myself in her aliveness, used her energy to keep me safe from my own emotions. I needed her to prove to me that the strength of her soul had not wavered.

5

There is no drama in this new hospital. Kids with cancer just being kids—sometimes they're happy, sometimes not. They eat french fries and chicken fingers, wear tee shirts featuring their favorite sports team, and play with Game Boys. They toddle and sit on Mom's lap to be read to or given a bottle.

— journal entry, November 12, 2000

New places, new people, unknown rules of conduct—these have long been the sources of my greatest distress. At age six entering first grade, at nine going to sleepaway camp for the first time, at nineteen leaving for college, I used to think my problem was simply homesickness—an often-debilitating case to be sure, but the diagnosis seemed to be clear. But I didn't just miss my mother, my room, the smell of my father's woodshop; I missed my sense of belonging.

John was not the first person I attached myself to as a means of defining myself. Second-born, I had a tough time breaking in on the relationship that had formed between my mother and my sister. My sister Joanny was busy and bossy; no playpen was big enough to contain her because, for her, the issue wasn't about how much room she had but about being told what her boundaries were. She siphoned off my mother's attention, demanding to be heard. Even her bedroom door was louder than mine, giving a more satisfying bang when she slammed it. Mine whooshed like the door of an airtight Volkswagen Beetle.

I found my perch next to my father, a literal perch in his basement workshop, where he expressed his creativity not through inventions but by transforming wood into beauty and function—guitars, tables, cabinets, a hi-fi console, even a boat. Only I entered into my father's solitude in this way; my mother and sister were either not interested or not invited. I learned the purpose of every tool, the quality of various woods, how a flat plank can be formed into a graceful curve. I had small chores but never made anything of my own.

Our partnership extended to auto mechanics, nature walks, observing the night sky, and visits to my father's lab. I learned how to mix cement, split wood, drain water pipes, use a soldering iron and a calking gun. My father showed me how to solve algebraic equations and develop my own photographs. He helped me build a rudimentary computer from a RadioShack kit. Depending on what project my father was sharing with me, I wanted to be an oceanographer, an astronomer, or a physicist. I invested my identity in his, not so that I could be like him but because the investment bound us together.

Adolescence weakened our bond. I wasn't going to tell my father about the crush I had on his best friend's son or how upset I was when my friend Ruthie's mother commented on the new jiggling of my chest while I was jumping rope.

At this point, particularly during the upheaval of the 1970s, most teenagers were rebelling. My sister was now slamming the front door and the car door and her foot onto the gas pedal as she fled the restrictions of home. But when I had to leave the house, my instinct was to drive to Aunt Essie's house for tea.

Some people need to wear certain clothes to convey an identity. I needed to wear people. To rebel properly, I had to attach myself to other people, such as my neighbor Ann. Ann was a year older. Her embrace of the anti-establishment movement shamed me into skipping school, hitchhiking around town, and allowing her to fix me up with guys who wanted me to be as uninhibited as Ann was. With Ann's courage, not mine, I defied my parents one night to meet the boy I was going out with. Barry was a drug dealer who took particular pleasure in drawing good girls into his web. I had allowed myself to be trapped.

My mother said, "The decision is yours, Judi, but I can't approve and I don't think you should go."

Even as I walked out the door to meet Barry, I was agreeing with my mother. I didn't see Barry for much longer.

I wasn't Ann. I couldn't be her, and I felt as if I disappointed people by being myself—for instance, my tenth-grade biology teacher. Mrs. H was known to be one of the cool teachers, the kind who shares too much and wants to be your friend outside of the classroom. Ann had taken her class the year before. Mrs. H had been to Ann's house; Ann had intimated that they had gotten stoned together, and Ann had told Mrs. H all about me, making me sound like an Ann clone. When Mrs. H finally met me, she freely expressed her disappointment. "You're nothing like Ann," she said. "You're so aloof. I feel like I can't get to know you."

But I wasn't being aloof; I was being small, uncertain, quiet. Unattached to someone else's identity, I merely looked aloof.

My lack of self-definition continued at college. When I walked through the student union, I felt like an intruder. Every person—whether a student, a teacher, a bookstore cashier, or a security guard—gave off a sense of citizenship that I never felt, not even by the time I graduated four years later. I had no idea how to join clubs, study groups, or classmates for a movie. My right to enter the library came not from my status as a student but as the girlfriend of John whom I was there to meet. Even today, at age fifty-two, I have dreams that I am going to a new school where everyone else already knows each other. I either go to the wrong floor, entering a classroom where everyone is older, or wander the building looking for the bathroom, afraid to ask directions. In my waking life, I still imagine that everyone, from social peers to colleagues to shopkeepers, engages in a constant evaluation of my appropriateness. My past membership in the National Society of Fund Raising Executives, my participation in a chamber music group, or the first suit I purchased with my brand-new credit card, all made me feel less like a fundraiser, a musician, or a well-dressed woman. I was still looking for Mrs. Porter's gold stars. So perhaps it is no surprise that motherhood has defined me so completely. Being a mother means attaching yourself to another person, seeing yourself through a relationship.

Nadia, however, is my opposite. She walks through her world with her chin up and accords herself full-citizen status in every place and situation. She's at ease at school, eager to burst in on any conversation, free at age five to jump naked into a hot tub with a group of bathing-suited nine-year-old girls, to make an unfaltering entrance into the center of a friend's *bat mitzvah* party where she knew no one else. Nadia is always the first to ask shopkeepers where a particular item might be, to hail inattentive waitresses, or, as she did on a trip to Spain, to use her rudimentary and garbled Spanish to ask directions or order ice cream.

But on November 2, 2000, our first day at the Memorial Sloan-Kettering Cancer Center (MSKCC), Nadia is not bold. She is being ripped from her third-grade life, and she instinctively resists any association with this new place. It will be up to me to navigate this new world for her.

Our first trip to MSKCC is like arriving anywhere new. A plane takes you down through thick clouds, a train moves you through a dark tunnel, a bus pulls up to the rear of a terminal while you paint images in your head of this foreign land soon to be revealed. Of course, during my twenty-five years spent living in Manhattan, I had driven by the full square block MSKCC occupies between York and First avenues and 67th and 68th streets, but I had never really seen it. MSKCC is a mutant Brigadoon, emerging from invisibility only when it is your actual destination. Approaching it now I think, Don't look—don't look for the coffee shop, the magazine stand, the park bench in a patch of sunlight, the neighborhood Blockbuster or the drugstore. We won't be spending much time here. Just get us in and get us out, back home, where I can relegate all this to nightmare.

I can't avoid looking, though, when the elevator doors open on the fifth floor to reveal the Pediatric Day Hospital (PDH). We are the pale new arrivals at the beachside resort, catching a glimpse of a sliver of its life. We are not yet part of this world.

How much of the scene Nadia notices is hard to tell. The children are bald and connected to IV poles via tubes that disappear under their shirts. Some limp or have an arm in a cast. Some are skinny, while some show the bloating effects of steroids. I see it because I know what to look for, like a teenage girl sussing out the cute guys at a dance. An innocent would see kids doing what kids do. They play games, piece puzzles together, race toy cars. They sit on the lap of a mother or father for a bottle or a story. They laugh or cry, ask for food, or whine that they want to go home.

Nadia and John start the first of what will be countless games of cards—Spit, Black Jack, War, Gin Rummy, Solitaire—while I check us in. Today, their game is subdued; but when we return over the coming days with an expanded entourage of family and friends, the slap and shuffle of cards and the cries of "21!" and "I win!" become quite boisterous. We have to remind ourselves that this is not a place for so much fun; Nadia is not yet an official cancer patient, and we imagine we are an affront to those who are suffering.

"Nadia Hannan to see Dr. Wexler," I announce to the receptionist.

"Does she need a stick?"

"A what?"

"A finger stick. A blood test."

"No," I say firmly. I don't know exactly what the sticks are for, but I know they have something to do with kids being treated for cancer. Doesn't the receptionist know that Nadia is not being treated for cancer?

When the doctor calls us into his office, I am confronted with a problem I hadn't anticipated. What are we to do with Nadia while Dr. Wexler talks to us?

After introducing himself to all three of us, Dr. Wexler turns to Nadia who is slouched against me with her head down. "Nadia," he says, "I'd like to talk to your mother and father for a few minutes. We have a wonderful volunteer who'd love to play with you. Do you think you'd like to go to the playroom with her?"

"Mama, will you come?"

"No, Nadia. I have to talk to Dr. Wexler first. Then I'll come meet you."

"I don't want to go without you," Nadia sobs.

"Please, Nadia. I'll be out as soon as I can."

"No. You come."

Nadia has never had trouble separating before. When she started nursery school at less than three years old, the only backward glance she cast my way was to make sure I was leaving. This is yet another difference between us. My own preschool days were filled with tears and stomach aches as I begged my mother not to leave me. How I longed for her to hold her tearstained face to mine and say, "Hush, my love. I'm going to miss you too, but you'll be okay." I forgot this yearning when Frannie began nursery school and I left her sobbing in the arms of her teachers. I felt as if I couldn't get away fast enough. She would be safe; she would calm down and have a great day. My sympathy would only make things worse. But turning my back on Frannie was all about what I wanted, which was to walk away with a clean conscience.

Now in the hospital with Nadia, my program again leaves no room for sweet-voiced attention to her needs. I just want her to let me go. I can tell Dr. Wexler the story better than Daddy can, I want her to understand. I'm your primary parent; I should be the first to hear what the doctor has to say. Daddy's the one who thought you had cancer. If he goes in there first, then he'll be right, and I'll have relinquished all authority to him.

According to Nadia, though, my only responsibility as her mother is to be with her.

"Okay, I'll go with you," I huff. "Come on."

As we join the volunteer to set up the Monopoly board, pick our pieces, and count out the money, I ask

Nadia repeatedly if I can go back to the doctor now. I imagine all the information John is getting before me, the head start he has on establishing a relationship with the doctor. I can't imagine that I will get the same attention and detail during a second telling.

Meanwhile, Nadia becomes so angry and contrary that she refuses to play, overturns the board, and turns her back on the volunteer, thus making sure that I have to stay with her. This, I tell myself, is just Nadia being manipulative. I recognize her actions like an old friend. My face can still form the pout, the simper, the little-lost-girl look I had perfected as a child when I wanted attention. I find comfort in this comparison. Nadia is just a little girl, like I once was. I am so ready to see my own faults in Nadia that I don't see the truth—that my daughter has the right to play the victim now, to be helpless and demanding and crave ice-cream cones. She has the right to need her mother, to trust me to stay with her long enough to take a few turns around the Monopoly board. I am afraid to be with her, though, afraid of her dependence on me, afraid of how I might fail her, afraid of seeing her die. If I were getting the facts now, the ones that John was getting, I would know what I was dealing with. I didn't recognize that this was precisely my father's strategy during my mother's illness. By worrying more about the "what" than the "who," I have denied Nadia the most basic ingredient in the compact between mother and child.

6

I am becoming more terrified by the moment, both about what will happen to Nadia and about my ability to take care of her. My weight has dropped to 108 pounds—that's five pounds lost in two weeks.

—journal entry, November 16, 2000

When John emerges from Dr. Wexler's office to switch places with me, I avoid looking at his face. I am in no mood for the terror I know I will see there. I direct my attention only toward Dr. Wexler. A yarmulke rests atop his reddish hair. His face is slightly round, his eyes kind but direct. When he sits, he is relaxed but completely focused on me. He could be any number of rabbis I have known, except that there is no divinity in the news he will be delivering. I was wrong to think I would get anything less than the full story. I was wrong to think the facts that Dr. Wexler will dispense will be comforting.

Even though Nadia has not yet had any additional diagnostic tests, Dr. Wexler prepares me for a certain cancer diagnosis. He tells me that what Nadia most likely has is an osteogenic sarcoma—the most common type of bone cancer in children and occurring within the cells that form the bone itself.

Dr. Wexler talks to me like I am a child; I listen with the gape-mouthed, unblinking expression of a five-year-old being read to. The doctor is a good storyteller. I hang onto every word about treatments and side effects and prognosis. So this is what my mother had to contend with. This is what Nadia will face.

The doctor will recite the same tale many times on subsequent visits. The more vivid the details become about chemo—including a particularly toxic substance called methotrexate that is so poisonous that it must be antidoted as soon as it is given—the less vividly I can imagine the reality that awaits us.

Back at home, I can't avoid looking at John's face. I see the terror but also see that he has arrived at tragedy faster than I have.

Because I don't possess John's drive, I don't always understand the stress of possessing a vision of the perfect life. Early in our marriage, John was often derailed. At that time Ivy League schools were not chasing after Irish-Catholic scholarship kids from Queens. Nor were the investment banks where John craved to work. Each disappointment—the first round of graduate school rejections, the summer internship spent in a Frito-Lay truck studying the company's distribution system in Texas rather than in New York on Wall Street with his peers, another round of rejections after getting his MBA until one firm finally deigned to hire him—caused John to retreat into blackness. He would glare at me if I tried to offer words of comfort. As I was to learn, John is a pessimist in the short term and has to find his own way to hope.

He was so invested in his concepts of the ideal job, lifestyle, and home that even small events, such as my dog's shredding of a new rug, sent him first into a rage and then into despair. "It's only a rug," I said, but the issue was about so much more than the carpeting. No matter how hard John worked, he could never make life perfect. He certainly couldn't make it so for Nadia. Still, despite the potency of my own sadness, I didn't expect him to give up so soon.

I was already feeling distant from John before the doctors' visits, the tests, the storytelling. This was only the second time in what was then our twenty-seventh year of marriage that we hadn't fit into the roles we had defined for each other. This doesn't mean that during all those other years we were a perfect couple. But the ways in which we were imperfect, the perhaps not so healthy needs each one of us had, matched the giving strength of the other partner.

After the fight about the rug I began a slow distancing from John. Perhaps if he hadn't been working so hard or if we had shared more friends or even if we had lived in Boston near my family rather than in his home city of New York, I wouldn't have felt so much like an ice floe drifting away from its glacier. I knew John loved me, but I was struggling with my response to how he showed it. His love came in the form of boxes—shiny blue, rippled white, elegant velvet, rich leather, gold-embossed, satin-lined. Like so many oysters enfolding their precious gems, the boxes held my husband's adoration. In the beginning, I would open each box as if greeting a tiny new lover, caressing the contents, allowing them to adorn my body and lift my heart. But the boxes started coming too quickly. I began to feel promiscuous. I didn't know what to do with so many lovers.

I began to feel as if our love for each other was unequal. I didn't know how to reciprocate. To assuage my sense of inadequacy, I erected a defense—a not very original or imaginative one. I visualized John as the stock investment banker in a Hollywood movie—stiff-collared, club-joining, Ivy-choked. I stripped him and his gifts of emotion. I played the role of the investment banker's wife, allowing myself to be a showcase but all the while feeling smug because, even while I found John's success thrilling, I still kept my soul.

"It's too much," I said, when the next box arrived. "I don't know what to do with all these gifts."

So the gifts changed into declarations of love that came with pieces of whimsy or symbols of who I am—a fountain pen made from driftwood, a painting of a solitary woman by the sea, a stone painted to look like a butterfly or a seal. These gifts were asking for nothing in return. They came from the man I never finished coloring in: the Irishman in love with windy nights by the sea, the street kid chewing Sen-Sen in his Cuban-heeled boots, the frustrated drummer, the moody sentimentalist constantly rummaging around in his soul. My gift to John was to soften, to fall in love with him more deeply and more maturely than I had when we were college kids.

Twenty years later, John's rummaging was unearthing a growing restlessness. Fun was beginning to replace work as a priority. This wasn't a classic midlife crisis. He wasn't tired of me or looking for a younger trophy wife. He wasn't questioning his career. But after working since boyhood, he was ready for some extended pleasure, which led to an extended search for what would make his life most meaningful. Rock concerts, wine collecting, traveling, and parties were followed by yoga, meditation, and a spiritual awakening.

I didn't resent John's departure from his usual behavior. I had had a little mini-crisis myself before our children were born, which primarily had involved upgrading my look and going out dancing with friends from work. While I trusted that John's restlessness wouldn't last forever, I judged him. It was the wrong time in our children's lives for his self-indulgences. I, said in my internal voice, was going to be the responsible parent. My challenges to his freedom sounded like lectures. I said, "You should," or "Don't you think," or, echoing my mother, "I don't approve, but it's your decision." Our lives diverged. The night that Nadia's jaw cracked, the space between us was still expanding and it felt to me as if John were reluctant to abandon his playtime.

So when we arrive back home after our meeting with Dr. Wexler, we don't know how to be together. We have never both been in need of solace at the same time. When my mother was diagnosed with cancer and when she died, John was sad but not grieving. He could put his arms around me and keep me company as I mourned. Now I am furious at him for accepting Dr. Wexler's tall tales. Even if he were able soothe me, I will not let him.

John feels the need to do something; I feel the need to escape. Separately, we each go out for a walk. Our paths cross by accident. We have both been crying. We slip into each other's arms. For a moment, in this public place, we are a unit of grief. Our embrace grows cold quickly. I can't convince John that it isn't his responsibility to mend this problem, and he can't help me because he has no hope to share.

For the next few days, we bicker over details as we translate what we have learned for his mother or my father. We disagree about the chemo schedule and how long the entire treatment will take. So there, I think when my version turns out to be right, I am back in control now. It makes no difference that no one yet knows what kind of cancer Nadia has.

I am certain, though, that Nadia will never get mouth sores, fevers, transfusions, a feeding tube. I have to feel this way if I am going to believe I can handle the stress—this confrontation with my daughter's mortality and with my own.

My strength, my sanity, hadn't been tested since I went away to college and discovered that my confidence and independence had wilted without the scaffolding of my family and their familiar routine. The separation anxiety I experienced as a child returned tenfold. John became my transitional object, what my teddy bear was supposed to be when I was little. But as cuddly as my teddy bear was and as attentive a caretaker as John proved to be, neither was effective in the face of my anxiety.

The first manifestation of my anxiety was disordered eating—not the deliberate starvation of anorexia but a lack of interest and hunger that I wasn't completely aware of. I had had a similar attitude toward food as a school-phobic five- and six-year-old. Each morning, my mother would place a plate of scrambled eggs in front of me. When she left the kitchen, I would run to the wastebasket and bury the rubbery yellow mess in the trash. So desperate was I to remove all traces of my food that moving to a house with a garbage disposal felt like a miracle until I realized the attention the noise of the machine would attract.

I have no memory of what the dining hall looked like at my college. I began school weighing 122 pounds. In the late fall of my freshman year, when I had dropped to 112 pounds on my way down to 97, I began having fainting spells. I passed out on the floor of the local deli and in music class. As I regained consciousness, my body stiff, sounds and sensation came back to me in slow distortion. Strangers touched me, not knowing that their every stroke made me feel as if I were being pulled like taffy. "You have to eat," they said, praising themselves for their concern. I retreated. Only on rare days did I venture far from the dorm room to which I had exiled myself. These were the moments when the inanimate objects around me didn't appear to be moving, when the ground didn't dip and rise under my feet, when the bed I had just arisen from—dead metal and lifeless ticking—didn't shimmer and shake.

The shower was the worst. When I closed my eyes to rinse my hair, my little stall became a flight simulator mimicking a ride through a thunderstorm. It rocked and pitched. I couldn't tell up from down. So I sat down, pressed my buttocks and the backs of my legs against the cool floor tiles. I wedged my shoulders into the corner. I kept my hand on the wall. In this way I remained oriented. When I was ready to return to my room, I made sure the coast was clear before walking down the dormitory hallway, weaving from side to side, hugging the wall to brace myself against imaginary air turbulence.

I chose my classes based on whether the grade depended upon tests or papers. Papers meant I didn't have to leave my room so often to go to class. I learned that if I kept moving my body, I wouldn't feel the world lurching around me. In chorus, I swayed and bounced, not in response to the songs but to keep from becoming so off-balance that I would fall off the risers.

My most important coping strategy became John. Despite his ambition, John is a gentle man. He could have been different. If he had patterned himself after his father, a heavy drinker who was often bitter and played little role in raising his son, his drive might have turned corrosive, stripping him of his humanity. Instead, John identified not only with his mother but his three sisters—two older and one younger—and absorbed their unwritten covenants of caring. He was both prince and provider, doted on and devoted to filling the needs of his family, at first emotionally and ultimately financially.

I wanted to be a normal girlfriend. I promised myself that the next time John wanted to go to a movie or a concert or into Manhattan for the day, I would go. But the outside world was too big; going from my room to Manhattan felt like going from the tightness of the womb into the open air, where it would be so much harder to figure out where I was in space. John tolerated my broken promises to go out. Instead, we watched television in the dorm lounge, went to the campus bar, and, on good days, to the local diner. He brought me to his childhood home on weekends, where I was embraced by his family. On the rare occasions I made it to the movies, he knew enough to tell me, when I gripped his arm, that a brain tumor was not making the theater go dark; simply the lights dimming in the theater.

Years later, when I asked John why he stayed with me—after all, this all took place very early in our relationship—he said I wasn't that bad. I used to get angry at him for saying that. It felt like a dismissal of what I had gone through. But I see how he has put that time into perspective. There were moments then when I could love him back—by making love, by typing his papers, by going with him to the beach in winter, by taking pictures of him with his wild hair, his freckles, his fringe jacket, and ripped jeans, by placing the picture on my desk and smiling back at it.

My mother thought I should transfer to a school closer to home. I refused. At the time, I saw staying put as a matter of pride. Moreover, home was changing, and my visits there were not the soothing, refueling experiences they might have been. Yes, I could still lay my head on my mother's belly so that she could massage the constricted muscles of my scalp and neck, but the release never lasted long. There was a growing tension between my parents. Their bickering, my father's restlessness, the hollow sound of the grandfather clock ticking time to the beat of the tension told me their world had shifted. Each time I left to go back to school, I felt like a loose thread, unraveling more of their marriage. Eventually, they would separate, my father returning home only when my mother was diagnosed with breast cancer.

I began to eat again because I was too much of a hypochondriac to starve myself. Fear of unconsciousness, so like what I imagined death would be, motivated me. I had enough sanity to get by, but not on my own. I was like an abandoned dog that has lost the comfort of domestication. So I married John, a benevolent caretaker, who could provide home, hearth, and cupboard, who would stock the kitchen with all my favorite foods before going on a business trip, who agreed to live in Queens because Manhattan scared me, who drove me nine hours to Pittsburgh to see my sister because I was afraid to fly.

I designed my world to accommodate my fears. Rather than pursue professional opportunities that would have taken me too far from my apartment building, I chose a job as a billing clerk. I could drive there; I used no subways, bridges, or tunnels; I could work on the ground floor; I never needed to travel for business. In the supermarket I masked my twitches and fidgets by rocking my cart as if the lettuce were a baby in need of soothing. I walked my dog on the same route every day, knowing where I could stop undetected to duck my head below my heart when a dizzy spell came on.

By practicing with bite-size pieces of life, I learned to live more fully. It's hard to practice flying, though. Three years after I graduated from college, my sister Joanny moved to Michigan. I visited her once, a white-knuckled flight that was to be my last for several years. When the birth of her baby couldn't overcome my fear, I enrolled in a class called "Freedom from Fear of Flying." The most significant result of the class was not that I started flying again but that I had unearthed within me a resolve and a determination I had kept hidden even from myself.

The day after our meeting with Dr. Wexler, as I walk Nadia into the room for the MRI he has ordered, see the cylinder, feel the claustrophobia, anticipate the noise of the machine, realize the likely news this test will deliver, I feel those long-dormant anxieties limping alongside me like a phantom limb. The technicians are efficient but slow enough to allow Nadia to take in her surroundings. She lies down; we cover her with a blanket, adjust her headphones for the *Harry Potter* tape she has brought to make the next hour and a half pass more easily.

I look into the tube and see that it is shorter than I had expected, and wider, too. Not bad. Then they reach for what looks like a box which they start to put over Nadia's head.

"What's that?" she screams.

"We need it to keep your head still," the technician answers.

"I promise I won't move. Take it off!"

"But . . ."

"Take it off," I command.

The lid comes off. I wipe Nadia's tears, calm her breaths. We examine the contraption, the mirror she can look up at to see me. "It's like Max's periscope," I say.

The lid goes back on, and they start to slide her back into the machine.

"No," she cries. "Not yet."

They bring her out.

"Maybe you can reschedule this for another day," the technician suggests, as if we have a choice, as if the tumor will wait until Nadia is ready, as if two extra days is enough time for an eight-year-old to mature.

"No, we'll do it now. Just give us a minute," I insist.

I turn my attention to Nadia who is uncovered once again. "Nadia, love, we're going to put this over your head again, but we won't do anything else until you're ready. Now just take some deep breaths. Our day here is almost over, and once we're done, Daddy is going to take you and Gaby to the movies. Keep taking deep breaths and think of Gaby. You'll be all right. No one is going to start until you say so. Just breathe; in and out. That's my girl. Are you ready?"

She nods. We begin. Rather than stand at the end of the table where Nadia can see me through her mirror, I station myself where I can touch her. We never lose contact. The noise of each cycle—three to seven minutes each for a dozen rounds—is deafening, the rhythm and cadences of the giant magnet a magnified version of the distorted voices I used to hear in semi-consciousness. I peer in often, then with less frequency, to check Nadia's eyes, the only part of her face that I can see. They're calm; at times they close.

She's right; she never moves, not even when my beeper, which I had forgotten to remove from my belt, is pulled by the powerful magnetic force, flies out from under my sweater into the magnetic tube, and starts crawling up Nadia's chest, stopping at the base of her neck when the cycle ends. I am proud of Nadia and proud of me. I got her through it.

That night in bed, when my soul is no longer so pregnant with Nadia and the umbilical cord has released its hold on me for a moment, I challenge myself to see how long I can lie without moving my head. One minute passes. Before I get close to two, I realize I've barely been breathing. My shoulders are tensed up by my ears; my fists are clenched. I start again, focusing on my breathing. My throat tickles; I cough. This is stupid, I think. I am not in an MRI. But can I really help Nadia if what she is being asked to tolerate is something I have trouble imagining doing myself?

7

Here is the worst thought I had yesterday. I don't want Nadia to be innocent anymore. It's too hard looking at her being so incredibly happy and knowing how much everything is going to change for her.

—journal entry, November 7, 2000

When Max and Nadia were little and weighed only a few ounces apart, they nonetheless felt completely different when I carried them. Max was firm and compact. He sat high in my arms, the way a bird might poise on your shoulder in the split second just before taking flight. But Nadia relaxed her full weight against me. She was going to get the most out of the opportunity to nestle, be close, let someone else do all the work. Imperceptibly, she would sink; without thinking I would hoist.

Of course, I never told Nadia how much easier it was to carry Max. Siblings, especially twins, never take kindly to such comparisons. Nor could I ever say that Max seemed so much easier to understand. He was happy or sad, afraid or secure, good or bad. His questions were straightforward and easy, the answers he sought brief and focused.

"Am I going to die?" he asked at age five, as I ran with him in my arms to the doctor's office following an unexpected allergic reaction to an as yet undiagnosed soy allergy.

"No, of course not," I answered.

His question lightened my load. Even though I couldn't guarantee to myself that I was right, the subject was out in the open.

With Nadia, I had always struggled. If she woke up in the morning and something wasn't quite right, I might take an entire day to figure out the problem. She'd whine or cling or cry, and I'd ask, "What's wrong, Nadia?"

"Nothing. Leave me alone."

"Well, if nothing's wrong, why are you so unhappy?"

"There's nothing wrong," she'd insist, even as she flew into her room, slammed the door, and flung herself onto her bed in tears. Only after many hours of gentle probing would I learn that her friend at nursery school was mean, or the movie she'd insisted on watching because her brother and sister wanted to was too scary, or some part of her hurt and she didn't want to tell anyone but me.

Sometimes I would never get to the bottom of the problem. We all knew that sitting for a family photograph would cause Nadia to cry, but we could never figure out why the eye of the camera bothered her so. We knew she loved to talk but were always surprised when she would run from the dinner table if we asked one too many questions about a story she was telling. She shied from the intensity of one-on-one instruction for an unknown reason that had nothing to do with a fear of failing.

I wondered if it was easier for Nadia to live on the surface of her thoughts—if underneath there lurked questions with answers as mysterious and frightening as the ancient sea creatures that troll the darkest depths of the ocean. Did she always know that there was a fatal force hiding within her that would be exposed if she examined herself too closely? Did she think that if she didn't stir things up, it would go away?

It has been a week since the lump appeared in Nadia's jaw, and she shows no interest in talking about it. She never asks what the doctors are looking for or why she's having more tests—a diagnostic bone scan and CAT scan of her chest to follow the MRI, baseline hearing and heart function tests to help to measure any future damage caused by chemotherapy. All Nadia asks is, "What are you doing here?" when I pick her up at school for an unscheduled appointment, and "When can I go home?" when tests and doctors' visits go on for hours, and "Can I at least sleep at Gaby's tonight?" when she learns all her other plans have to be dismantled. She never talks about the other children she sees at the hospital; she never sees through my calm veneer or notices my red-rimmed eyes.

I want to shake her, drag her down to my depths where I am desperate for company. I shield myself from John's tears because his sorrow scares me; it heightens the sense of tragedy and I assume this means he can't help me. My father's grief adds to my sadness; I feel a burden to soothe and protect him. The concerns of my friends about how Nadia is doing or how I am holding up require a response I have no energy to provide. What I want is for Nadia to be my partner in anger and fear. It would be so easy to bombard her with words like *cancer* and *tumor* and *chemotherapy* and *round blue cells* and *survivability,* to attach them to her like a cement block and sink with me to the most chilling scenario we can imagine—her death.

Of course, I do none of that. But my frustration is starting to show. I have stood by Nadia for all of her scans, held her hand while she screamed during each IV and blood test, absorbed her fury. We are nearing the end of all the various ways medicine has of looking inside the body when Dr. Wexler says Nadia needs a flu shot.

Of all the procedures Nadia has been through, a flu shot is not only the least painful but also the most familiar. But Nadia has reached her limit. I have, too. She dashes from the IV room, where the nurse is preparing the shot. I scramble after her. I grab her arm, but she keeps pulling away. I tackle her; take hold of her top half while a nurse holds her legs. We carry her back into the room while a second nurse shuts and locks the door. My adrenalin-enhanced grip holds Nadia as she screams, "Get off me!" The shot is given. I release my hold, looking at my hands as if they have been possessed. I know the monster that inhabited me is gone but Nadia doesn't. She glares at me, closing the door on any apology I might offer. Not in my worst moments of bad mothering could I have ever imagined doing what I have just done to my daughter. We go home in silence.

But I have to start telling Nadia something. Unlike the curious and inquisitive girl she was before October 31, she now asks no questions beyond her angry appeals. I recall all those child-rearing experts who advise never to answer a child's question with more than what she asks for. She'll let you know when she's ready for more information, the professionals insist. But what if she never asks in the first place?

I unburden myself gently of the knowledge I have been carrying for Nadia. "You have a lump, and it's always important to know why a lump is there, what it's made of. Some can keep growing and cause damage to your body. The doctors need to find out if yours is one of those kinds of lumps."

Only after a meeting with Dr. Kraus, the head and neck surgeon, to review the results of the MRI—when Nadia is again asked to go play with a complete stranger and again refuses—does she ask her first direct question: "When are they going to do that thing where they take out a piece of the lump?"

She speaks so calmly that I forget I have never told her about such a procedure. Which of the five doctors, which nurse, which receptionist, which parent had she overheard?

"It's called a biopsy, Nadia. They're going to do it in about a week."

"Is it going to hurt?"

"Not at all. They're going to give you anesthesia, which will make you sleep."

"What if I wake up?"

"You won't, honey. There's a special doctor whose only job is to make sure that doesn't happen."

Fear doesn't command Nadia's attention for very long, particularly when she is not at the hospital and we are talking about something a week in the future. At eight years old, Nadia wants to accept the promises her mother makes. For now, she finds it easy to hold on to her familiar life, and being able to talk openly to her makes me feel relieved, lighter.

I can't remember if John part of this conversation. We had never discussed strategies about how to have important discussions with our children. I initiated most of such conversations but I was opportunistic rather than proactive. For instance, I was the one who had the conversation with Max about puberty. We were in the car together, and a commercial came on the radio about some shaving product. Poor Max was trapped as I talked about how his body was going to develop. My talk with Frannie about my aunt's drinking or the alcoholism in John's family was prompted by her first drinking episode. Usually, I asked John to punctuate my conversations by talking to the kids himself. But I rarely knew if he did because he didn't report back. If I asked, I would receive a vague "yeah" or "I will" in response.

Most of my conversations with Nadia were similarly opportunistic. By now she and I had established tunnel vision. She seemed to be trying to regenerate her umbilical cord and attach herself to me for her survival, and I was locked onto her. During those first months of diagnosis and treatment, caring for her felt like being asked, day after day, to rescue a child who had been struck by a car outside my window while I was washing the dishes. The adrenaline rushed, my focus narrowed, the world around me disappeared. This left little room for John.

Closer to the day of the biopsy, I told Nadia more about what the doctors were going to do and what they were looking for. I didn't use the word *cancer*; but I told her that if the tumor was the type that keeps growing, she would need medicine that would probably make her feel sick. She would wake up with an IV line called a Broviac in her chest so that it would be easier and painless for her to get her medicine.

The procedure is scheduled for November 10. That morning, John asks Dr. Kraus, "If the tumor is benign, Nadia won't need a Broviac, right?

"That's right," he answers, but he will not give John the comfort he seeks. "We're not gods, but I do have to tell you what's most likely." Dr. Kraus is tall; I have to tilt my head up to look at him. His expression is always kind; each greeting is warm and embracing. We are from the same generation, yet he radiates assurance. Nadia was always relaxed with him, and only after a year into her remission did I realize he was the only person who had never had a reason to cause her pain—without anesthesia, that is.

I want Dr. Kraus to be a god. He continues, "Nadia has the classic signs of an osteogenic sarcoma."

All I can remember from my first conversation with Dr. Wexler is the good news that the cure rate for osteogenic sarcoma is 90 percent and the terrifying news that, to survive, you need to be given a drug so powerful you have to counteract it almost as soon as it is given. I never ask Dr. Kraus what the classic signs of this cancer are. They would become irrelevant anyway.

The separation I felt from Nadia on the day of her Panorax is nothing compared to what I feel as I see her being wheeled into the operating room. I had thought she was asleep, but when I bend to kiss her forehead she mumbles, "You've ruined my ride; I was just about to fly."

I am glad Nadia is so hard to sedate. I see it as a sign of her fighting spirit. When she finally succumbs, I remember a bedtime scene three nights before. Nadia had insisted that I stay with her until she fell asleep. I was perched on the edge of her bed, anticipating my escape, until Nadia entwined her wiry limbs through my own exhausted ones and insisted, "No, stay with me."

But now Nadia wants to fly, and I don't want to let her go. I know it is only the drugs making her feel that way. Still, I feel the familiar pang of rejection, similar to all those times she had pushed me away with the words, "I do," when she wanted to do everything on her own.

The operating rooms at MSKCC are on the second

floor. Family waits in the main lobby on the first floor. It is a very public space. Being there feels like being in an airport waiting area when you know there is a good chance that the plane you can't avoid boarding is going to crash. I have Nadia's North Face jacket, which I cling to, burying my heart in it, refusing to let anyone take it from me, as if this can excuse me for leaving Nadia in the operating room with those strangers, all alone.

The doctors *weren't* gods. The tumor was not an osteogenic sarcoma, but it *was* cancerous. They just didn't know what kind of cancer yet. The Broviac had been put into place.

Broviac is one of the ugliest sounding words in the English language. For me, it became a synonym for *your daughter has cancer and we're going to pierce her, create a barrier that you will feel every time you hug her, see every time you bathe her, imagine in every dream you have.* A Broviac is an IV line surgically implanted into a main artery of the heart. It has a single length of tubing approximately eight inches long that then splits in two for another eight inches. At the end of each tube are caps, the shape and size of pencil erasers, to which syringes and IV's can be attached. The toddlers at the hospital called these their "tubies" and screamed, "No tubies, no tubies!" anytime a nurse came near them. They had just discovered their hands and feet and had no idea their Broviac was not a part of their body and that a needle inserted there wouldn't hurt.

All of Nadia's chemo medicines, her blood, her antibiotics, her transfusions went in and out of this central IV line. She would not end her treatment with tracks on her arm like a junkie. But even as the Broviac makes treatment easier and less painful, it is a breach in the body's armor—a penetration through which germs and bacteria can enter, threatening to cause more damage than the cancer itself. It requires constant maintenance. Changing the dressing covering the site of the implant was to be my first chore as a mother caring for a child with cancer. This dressing needed to be changed three days a week for the next seven months. These were the steps:

First, remove the dressing. Open sterile kit containing supplies. Put on surgical mask so mother's germs won't poison child. Wash sweaty hands. Put on gloves. Peel off old bandage, which will pull at delicate skin and make it red, sore, and itchy. Check the site for inflammation. Throw contaminated gloves away.

Second, clean and rebandage. Open sterile field, like an oversized napkin, touching only the edges of the paper. Put sterile gloves on shaky hands. Do not brush hair from eyes, scratch an itch, answer the phone, or touch anything outside your germ-free area until task is completed. Open the three alcohol and three blood-red Provodone swabs contained in kit. Place on sterile field with gauze and Primipore bandages. Clean site three times with alcohol that stings. Wash with Provodone. Let air dry. Be sure that child doesn't breathe on site, dogs don't come over to play, and siblings stay far away with their sneezes and coughs. Cover with gauze, then bandages. Remove mask made damp from nervous breaths. Sigh deeply.

Third, secure the tubes. Loop and tape tubes to chest so they don't hang and pull. Attach to undershirt with safety pin showing so next time you have to change the dressing, you won't whip the shirt off with the tubes still attached and cause unbearable pain to child. Throw garbage away. Resume living.

Twice a week, the caps had to be changed and the lines flushed with Heparin, a blood thinner, so that if we actually got through a few days when the Broviac neither gave nor received fluids, it wouldn't get clogged with clotted blood.

Nadia and I arrive at the hospital on the Monday after the biopsy to perform our first dressing change in front of a nurse practitioner. Nadia strides through the doors that day, already making the transition to MSKCC citizen. She asserts her control by calling for the elevator and pressing the button for the fifth floor. She hops up onto the examination table as if mounting a vault at the gym.

Before changing her dressing, I practice on a dummy. Then I turn to my daughter. She unbuttons her shirt, undoes the safety pin, and peels off the old dressing herself. But when it is time for me to be in charge, Nadia begins to get nervous. "Are you sure you know what you're doing?" she asks. Perhaps she had seen my hands shaking so much that I couldn't get the needle into the dummy's caps to inject the Heparin.

But Nadia and I both survive my ministrations. The nurse tells me I am a natural but in more than one hundred changes, not one was pain-free for my daughter, although usually the hurt was minor. I saw many parents negotiating with their children when it was time for a dressing change, so I assume I was not the only one causing discomfort.

Worry about the Broviac, however, will come after I tell Nadia she has cancer, and that will have to wait until she recovers from the effects of sedation. Waking up is not nearly as pleasant for her as going under. She rouses slowly and, in her confusion, becomes agitated. I realize how foolish I was to think she could have ever anticipated what it means to have a biopsy or a Broviac. Indeed, it will be a full six months before Nadia tells me that she thought all they were going to do for the biopsy was remove the tooth that had been knocked sideways and that her IV line was only going to stay in for a few days.

Unable to metabolize the anesthesia, Nadia vomits and is unable to eat or drink. So what was supposed to have been an outpatient procedure results in her first hospital admission. I pretend to be disappointed, as if not even getting through the biopsy smoothly is an omen. But I also take shelter in the hospital, where I can practice my nursing skills before being let loose on my own.

That evening, when Nadia feels better, I tell her she has the type of tumor that will keep growing, which means she has cancer. Her eyes open, big and round. I mistake them for an open doorway ready to receive me and all my carefully rehearsed words.

But the next morning, I ask, "Nadia, do you remember our conversation from yesterday?"

"Sort of."

"Can you tell me in your own words what I said?"

Silence.

"Do you want me to tell you again?"

I am met with a shrug, a turning away. Once again, I find myself wanting Nadia to react like an adult, which means I want some acknowledgment that she has heard me and understands. I tell her again that she has cancer. Silence still.

I don't push. Even though the doctors know the tumor is malignant, the pathologists will need a few more days to identify the precise form of cancer. Without that knowledge, there is no treatment plan, and without a plan there is no point, in Nadia's view, of discussing anything. She returns to school; she wastes no energy on waiting and wondering.

I dread the ringing of the phone, the call that will extinguish the fantasy I still cling to—that, under closer scrutiny, Nadia's tumor will be benign. Or else I will be told that they've never seen a cancer like Nadia's; they can't type it and so can't treat it. Instead, after five days of waiting, Dr. Wexler calls to reveal that the stringy blue cells seen under the microscope are from a rare bone cancer called Ewing's sarcoma.

"Are you sure?" I ask when John and I find ourselves back in Dr. Wexler's office that afternoon, two lost children who have learned that the story they were told the first time wasn't true.

"That's a good question," Dr. Wexler answers. "The pathologists had to make certain because the chromosomal abnormality we usually see in Ewing's is different in Nadia's case but, yes, we're sure. None of this changes Nadia's chances of being cured, however."

"What are those chances?" I ask, as if I could possibly forget the 90 percent survivability rate for osteogenic sarcoma.

"The average cure rate for Ewing's is 70 percent," Dr. Wexler begins.

"But that's ..."

"I said average. Nadia's age, the fact that the tumor was found early, that there is no sign of its having spread—all bring Nadia into the 90 percent range."

I don't feel much relief. In the ten days since the doctors first said osteogenic sarcoma, the name had become familiar. This Ewing's is a stranger I don't trust.

Next comes a description of the treatment protocol. There would be two phases to Nadia's chemotherapy. In the first, three agents—cyclophosphamide, doxorubicin, and vincristine—would be administered in three cycles, three weeks apart, to shrink the tumor. "Local control" they called it, like containing a riot of cells gone mad. Cyclophosphamide (trade name Cytoxan), derived from mustard gas, blasted the crowd of cells during their resting or nondividing phase. Doxorubicin, called an antitumor antibiotic, is derived from a fungus and invades cells during their dividing phase. Vincristine also attacks cells as they divide, but it comes from the much prettier-sounding periwinkle plant. Because cyclophosphamide can cause bleeding of the bladder, Nadia would also be given a protective drug called mesna. The greatest concern with doxorubicin would be long-term heart damage.

Following these three rounds of chemo, Nadia would have surgery to remove whatever part of the tumor was left. Surgery was not our only option for the total removal of the tumor. Ewing's sarcoma is also responsive to radiation. I had felt fortunate that we had choices. The decision about which one to choose, however, wouldn't be made until after the initial rounds of chemo, when scans would tell us how Nadia's tumor had responded.

The purpose of the second phase of chemo, after the surgery, would be to wipe out any cancer cells that might have traveled throughout Nadia's body. Ifosfamide, which functions similarly to cyclophosphamide, and etoposide, an enzyme from the mayapple plant, would be used for two rounds, then the original combination for one round, then one more of the second combination. While receiving chemo, Nadia would spend her day at the hospital and would go home at night with a battery-operated pump that continued to infuse chemo, the mesna, and hydrating fluids to wash the poisons from her system.

In the past, treatment for Ewing's lasted for a year, with more rounds of chemo but at lower dosages. The new protocol called for condensing the cycles. This more potent brew could not be given to adults, Dr. Wexler said;

their older bodies simply couldn't handle it. If Nadia started at the end of November, by May 2001, she would be done.

So there would be none of the dreaded methotrexate used to treat osteogenic sarcomas, but now I had to worry about bleeding bladders, heart disease as well as nausea, vomiting, hair loss, infection, mouth sores and death—always death. Still, I clutched at the fiction that Nadia would bounce back after each round. I created a mental chart of how many days of school she would miss, crossing off only the days she had chemo plus one or two more when her counts might drop.

Now that Dr. Wexler has given me something to tell Nadia, I don't know what to say. The night before our meeting with him, Nadia and I had fought. While I had called only family and our closest friends about her diagnosis, I had done nothing to contain the news from spreading. Among the cards and letters of support John and I had received that day was an envelope for Nadia from a ski instructor we had befriended. When I handed it to her, she asked, "Didn't Frannie and Max get a letter, too?"

"No, just you," I answered, assuming Nadia would know why.

"How come she only wrote to me?" Nadia wanted to know.

"Because she was thinking of you and wants you to get well."

"You *told* her? Why did you do that? Does everyone know?"

"Nadia, I had to tell people," I started to answer. But I couldn't figure out how to make her understand why. People saw the disruption in our lives; our sadness was a physical presence that couldn't be ignored. I had to give it a voice. To Nadia, though, who could control so little in her life right now, I had undercut the one aspect of her experience she had power over: who should be told and when.

When we return home from our meeting with Dr. Wexler, I find a package for Nadia. Inside is a silver-beaded journal from a friend of mine and John's who had survived breast cancer. She included a note telling Nadia that she could use the book to keep a record of her chemo treatments, how she felt, her blood counts, etc. I find the words abrasive—this woman is trying to share too much of her own experience. Nadia looks offended, her privacy once again intruded upon, but the note provides a good segue for me into telling Nadia what we had learned. I tell her that the type of cancer she has is called Ewing's sarcoma, that she will be getting drugs to kill the cancer cells and that they will probably make her feel sick.

After two minutes, as I get more specific about what might happen, Nadia starts to fidget. I think she is getting scared. But she is only bored. "Okay, Mom. Can I go play now?" she asks.

"Sure. Go on," I answer in relief. I should have known that, at eight years old, Nadia is able to anticipate the future only if she could relate it to her past.

Nadia is to begin chemotherapy four days later, on November 20. I pretend to prepare, studying the treatment regimen for the sentence that says, "Nadia will be fine," making arrangements for Frannie and Max, calling family. On November 19, I receive an e-mail from Dr. Wexler saying he hoped we were doing well in spite of what the next day would bring. I realize I have no idea what that will be.

On the first day of chemo, as the first drops of Cytoxan cut the ribbon of Nadia's brand-new Broviac, we play hangman. She chooses "tumor," "chemotherapy,"

"Memorial Sloan-Kettering." This is extraordinary, I think. She knows now. She gets it. But when I try to talk that night about another girl who also has cancer, Nadia blurts, "I don't have cancer. I have a tumor."

"Okay, Nadia, you have a tumor."

On the third day, Nadia is visited by Louise, a thirteen-year-old patient of Dr. Wexler's who had finished treatment for Ewing's two years earlier. She can do what I haven't been able to. She tells Nadia her own story. To my ears, it sounds like this: "When I learned cancer, cancer, cancer, cancer, cancer. Then cancer, cancer, cancer, cancer, cancer. My mom thought cancer, cancer, cancer, cancer, cancer, cancer." Her words are as raw as freshly scraped knuckles, but she relays her mishaps with humor. "The school nurse mentioned something to me one day about my cancer and I said, 'What cancer? What are you talking about?' My mother hadn't told me yet because she was too afraid."

"One day my mother was changing my Broviac dressing and couldn't get the tape off so she went to cut it with a scissors but she cut the tube instead. That was bad," Louise says, but she's smiling, a master of slapstick comedy.

Nadia can't help but laugh. She glances at me and in her eyes I see that Nadia has accepted that this girl's story is her own, too.

Yes, I think, the rest will be easy. I can carry Nadia now. She'll look at all the other kids with bald heads, ask me if she will lose her hair, and I will be able to divulge the final secret that I have been dragging around with me.

Except she never asks. I hold the weight of her ... what?—denial, innocence, fear,—like a dead stone in my belly. Once chemo starts, I have to tell her.

I choose a quiet moment when the vincristine-induced stomach cramps have eased. "Nadia, there's one more thing we have to talk about." She's ready to flee. I convince myself that she has to know about her hair, that I am not telling her just to relieve my burden.

"What?" she demands. She won't look at me but stares at a painting on the wall—fat rectangles of earth tones stacked and aligned like stones.

"Did you notice that most of the kids at the hospital don't have much hair?"

"No." She isn't going to let me off that easily.

"Well, the reason why chemotherapy helps kill can... I mean, tumor cells is because it attacks all the rapidly dividing cells in your body." Nadia has had enough science to follow this and seems almost interested. "Hair cells divide quickly so that's why hair falls out."

"So you mean I'm going to lose my hair? No, no, no," she sobs. "I don't want to lose my hair."

"Of course you don't, sweetie." Absentmindedly, I stroke her shoulder-length bob. It's a reflex, the way I have always consoled my children. Then I flinch. What will I do a month from now?

"They say it's easier if you get it cut short before it starts to thin. Maybe we could get it cut today."

No response.

"Mom, why do artists get paid so much money just to paint a bunch of stripes?"

Nadia's had enough. I'm happy to talk about art. I still don't know what has sunk in. At the hairdresser, she agrees to a chin-length do, despite my pleas to go shorter because I can imagine what Nadia cannot.

8

No matter how many people I have around me, the burden is mine. The truth, though, is that I don't want to become dependent or even an equal sharer. I think I want my mother, but haven't I become stronger without her?

—journal entry, December 30, 2000

"Now. Push *now*." The command filtered through the air vents on the labor and delivery floor of the Mount Sinai Medical Center. The year was 1988; I was in labor with Frannie.

"Ahhhhhh. It hurts."

"Push," I heard again, from another room. Another voice moaned in response.

What is this pushing? I wondered. I had gone to every Lamaze class, hung onto every word. No one had ever said anything about pushing. Whatever this was, it hurt and I was not going to do it.

"Okay, when I say push, just keep trying to get that baby out until I tell you to stop."The voice came from behind my right ear. It was my turn now.

How had I missed this part? Even if my mother had been alive, there wasn't much she could have done to prepare me. In her day women gave birth in twilight. What a romantic way to describe being knocked unconscious, to have your baby delivered by forceps, like taking a chicken from a pot.

I thought I knew how to be a motherless mother. During her last years, my mother had devoted herself to getting me ready to survive without her. She died before her work was finished; all I was able to learn from her about motherhood were the lessons I could glean from her own life. For years I thought I had learned enough; but as I struggled with Nadia's illness and all the issues of passivity and anxiety it raised, I realized my version of my mother was too narrow and incomplete—like a musical composition with only one theme, no harmony, and no modulation. In fact, my mother's history had many movements, and they didn't always seem to have been written by the same composer.

My mother's life opened in Revere Beach, adjacent to Boston, to the sound of waves and carnival rides and to the scales and etudes of her two oldest sisters practicing their instruments. Here, a unifying theme was introduced—my mother's love of the ocean, the one place she was guaranteed to feel free.

She was the daughter of Eastern European Jewish immigrant parents. In addition to her two oldest sisters, she had a third sister much closer to her in age who became her best friend. But when my mother was six, she began living her life in a minor key. Her mother was stricken with the first of two strokes, which had left her dragging a dead-weight leg and speaking to people in an unseen world. At the end of a day at school, my mother received no maternal embrace. Instead, her mother's arms encircled the hot-water heater to which she spoke Yiddish, as if its warmth represented a life.

I need to pause here to feel the mood of the music more fully. My aunt Alice had told me that, in the days after the stroke, my mother was forced to remain outside the closed door as most of her mother disappeared forever. Alice took over the care of my mother and my aunt Essie. My mother raised my sister and me to judge Alice harshly. We were told she was shallow because she obsessed too much over how to get a white silk shirt she had seen in *Women's Wear Daily* and always wore high heels and makeup and dyed her hair. My mother wanted us to see the reason behind Alice's vanity; it was all to please her men—her father, her husband, her son. *Seduce* would be a more accurate word—to wield power in the guise of devotion, the same power she wielded over my mother, poor Francela.

So when Alice told me about my mother's being alone and confused, I allowed the wrong theme to take precedence. In the quiet I allow myself now, I wait to hear my mother's melody. It comes to me as a lone viola, and I can weep for a six-year-old child.

My mother felt like a six-year-old for many years. She and Essie tiptoed through their childhood. They did not have Hebrew lessons or music lessons, unlike their older sisters. I imagine Essie studying voice and my mother—whose nickname was Tzippora, little bird—the flute.

I tried to change the key of my mother's life back to major. I imagined her when she was eighteen and just married. I found a picture that I thought was proof of her happiness. She was at the beach with my father; her bikini-clad body was perched on his shoulders. Her long, curly, dark-brown hair waved in the ocean breeze. My father's muscled arms gripped her legs to his chest. They wore matching grins. The picture is in black and white, but it is alive with color, with the expectation that being a wife and mother will be a joyful experience. I became locked into what I thought of as the truth of this picture. Even when I was eighteen and still felt my childhood, I could look at a photo of my mother at the same age and see her as an adult—launched on her marriage, two years away from motherhood. Can a child look at her mother in any other way?

I have been forced to open my ears to the dissonance between image and reality. Not only was my mother young, but she had never tasted independence. She had had no other boyfriends before my father and hadn't lived anywhere other than her parents' home. She never went to college. She never worked. And she was the baby of her family. With no mother and no experience to learn from, she couldn't have known much about being a woman, a wife, a mother.

Before Nadia's diagnosis, if one of the children were sick, I imagined my mother's voice guiding me: "Okay, Judi," I remembered her saying in my childhood, "you've had your morning in bed. It's time to come down to the kitchen now." I used to think this was to make me tough, to keep me from self-pity. But now I wonder if she spoke that way because she had never had the experience of her own mother stroking her forehead or murmuring soft words when she was sick.

I have always been enchanted by another picture of my mother. In this one she is posed in profile. She has just had a nose job, her hair is bobbed, she's wearing lipstick. My mother was looking for Audrey Hepburn, Jackie Kennedy glamour—those waiflike characters with soft voices and European elegance. Cigarettes, held between her long fingers, kept my mother's collar bones protruding like bird wings from the olive skin of her slender frame. The bone of my mother's nose, though, was more pottery than porcelain, more bulb than bird. In its smaller version, it became the focus of the many portraits my father took of her. So it was easy not to notice that something was missing from her smile. Somewhere between the picture on the beach and this one, between then and the two babies, between then and the move my parents made to the suburbs, my mother realized she had no vocabulary to define herself.

My mother began a disappearance of her own, not the sudden one of her own mother but one whose beginning was barely detectable. Perhaps it had already begun when I entered nursery school. Perhaps my anxiety at being separated from her came from my little-girl intuition, which told me she wasn't quite the same when she came to pick me up as she was when she dropped me off.

My mother's life began to play like a warped recording of Handel's *Water Music.* She ached to see the world, but she always found herself at places my father loved, camping at Lake George or skiing in New England. If my mother had thought my father loved the sea like she did, she soon learned he craved the mountains, even more so after he fell in love with skiing and an old stone house in Hill, New Hampshire. She negotiated a trip to Paris and Greece and saw Rome with her sisters a year before she died. I remember her return from Greece. She brought back musical recordings to which we would dance, our arms around each other's waists, our feet moving in synchronized, serpentine steps. I wished she would go to Israel and Turkey and Russia and bring back more songs.

I was in the third grade when the signs of my mother's unhappiness became more apparent. I was finally eager to go to school because I had a new teacher, Mr. Miller, who was teaching me how to play the guitar. "I learned a new round today," I said to my mother one day after school. "Will you sing it with me?"

My mother was at the kitchen sink, where she stayed hunched over a moment too long. When she turned, I saw an unnamed pain in her eyes. She did not sing well; she was not perfect. I thought I was the reminder of her failure, the source of her tears. Like a circus monkey dancing to the music of the organ grinder, I began my tricks, waiting for the clink of my mother's happiness to fill the heart I passed around.

Then my mother stopped getting out of bed in the morning before we went to school. She was in the bed in the afternoon, too. When I got my period for the first time, she didn't get up but yelled through the adjacent bathroom door to tell me where the Kotex was. She wrestled with a box of hair dye, which she kept unopened under the sink in the bathroom. She had learned from her nose job that external changes didn't reach inside, but she was searching for something to cover the gray in her soul. At dinner, my mother's eyes would glaze over. Through her eyes, I saw my mother vanish.

By the time I was eleven, my mother disappeared for real. I had returned home from my friend Ruthie's house crying. "Mummy . . . ," I began. I wanted to tell her that Ruthie had said she wasn't my friend anymore. She had made me leave. I wanted my mother to hug me and tell me how sorry she was that Ruthie had hurt my feelings. I wanted her to say, "I love you, Judi."

But I stopped after calling her name because she hadn't heard me. She was examining her face in the bathroom mirror. When she finally turned to me, I could see that her eyes did not know me; they did not know the woman in the mirror.

I could no longer hear the score to my mother's life. I had to listen to it in reruns. Later, I learned about the months of psychiatric treatment she had already been receiving; later I heard about the medications that made everything worse; later I heard how my mother had saved herself from electric shock therapy by getting a cold. After my mother was admitted to a nearby psychiatric hospital, I dreamt that I went with my father and sister to visit her. I could see her looking out through an open window. My father and sister could reach this window, but I could not. No one would lift me up and my mother wouldn't look down.

After the aborted electric shock therapy, some instinct in my mother told her to run. She entered McLean Hospital's outpatient program. My father retreated. He kept a journal recording all the facts of my mother's depression so that his scientific, analytic mind could try to cope. He did not know how to talk to his children.

I have no memory of the time my mother spent as an outpatient, how it felt at the end of the day to have her back home—this person who had become so fragile and foreign. Now it was my turn to tiptoe; if I stayed still and wasn't a burden on anyone, my mother could get better.

My mother did get better, a process that remained a mystery to me but one I think I would have asked about had she lived longer. She entered college as I entered high school. On late afternoons when she was at school, I searched her possessions for answers to who she was. On her dresser, I found the blue velvet jewelry box with the few pieces of practical embellishments and the even fewer glittery fancies now sunk to the bottom of the tray. I ran my hands over the lingerie in the top drawer, bypassing the cotton items for the unfamiliar luxuriousness of the lacy strapless bra, the sheer camisole, the silk negligee. I had never seen my mother wear these and tried to imagine how she felt when she wore them.

I skipped the tops, pants and skirts in practical mix-

and-match neutrals and lingered over three pairs of stiff kid-skin gloves awaiting the warmth of my hands to soften them. I unfolded the scarves, mostly in muted earth tones to match my mother's sensible wardrobe. But there was one in blue and turquoise that I wrapped around my neck remembering the story my mother told me about Isadora Duncan.

Underneath the scarves were two black and white portraits of me and my sister, which my mother had commissioned from a local "artistic" photographer. They intruded on our young faces. These were the extra copies that no aunts or grandparents had asked for.

I trailed my fingertips over the items on the bedside table—the familiar white princess phone, the box of tissues, the clock radio, the new psychology textbook, the yellow highlighter, the course syllabus. I couldn't bear to look at my mother with her books and papers, couldn't tolerate the sound of her voice when she talked about an upcoming test or a favorite teacher, or, as her psychology studies advanced, when she told me she knew why I left my own homework to the last minute because she had just learned about the fear of success—or was it failure?—in class. I didn't understand what it meant to her, at age thirty-five, to be going to college, to be establishing a career. This woman was no longer anyone's baby. Now I imagine that I can hear the strident strings of Stravinsky's *Rite of Spring* emerging in this movement of my mother's life.

Soon it took more and more of my mother's will to keep up with this music. Somehow I had missed the perversity of her effort to compose this new melody for her life, only to discover she had a limited number of years to play it. I was too busy feeling left out of her life.

When I was on a visit home from college, my mother

invited me to her new office. This meant a trip to Boston, lunch at Bailey's, the possibility of woman-to-woman intimacy. I entered the office as if stepping into a trophy case. I saw my mother's diploma from Boston College's Graduate School of Social Work on the wall, the warm light, the slightly worn upholstered chairs that facilitated the transfer of anguish from client to therapist. I ran my hands over the yellow legal pads. I imagined the sound of sharpened pencils filling up pages.

"Aren't you lucky to have all these supplies? Could I bring a pad of paper home, sort of as a memento?"

"That would be stealing, Judi. We have our own paper at home."

There wasn't much to talk about at Bailey's. "What time do you think you'll be home tonight?" I asked.

"About six. Do you think you can start dinner?"

"Sure."

What part of my mother's life would I draw from to care for my own children? Should I be the stern moralist, the tiptoer, the fighter, the pragmatist, the woman who swayed her hips when she danced, or the one who had found her freedom at the sea? By the time of Nadia's crisis, all I knew was that the perfunctory care my mother had given me and my sister when we were sick would be inadequate for a child with a life-threatening illness, a lesson I had already learned by way of Max.

At eighteen months of age, Max suffered his first potentially fatal allergic reaction to peanuts. At age three, an asthma attack sent him to the intensive care unit. By the time he was eight, Max had already made ten trips to the emergency room, four by ambulance, as more foods became toxic to his system. These were acute episodes, a quick shock to the status quo followed by recovery, a few wasted hours that I spent on guilt. Then Max would return to school and his friends. To keep Max safe and me in control, it helped to mimic my mother's pragmatism. I read food labels, talked to his teachers, and became as familiar with medical protocol as any doctor or nurse who treated Max. But I learned more from Frannie about patience and how to humor a sick child, when all I wanted to do was run away because I had no protection against Max's suffering.

My mother died not only before she finished raising me but before she finished raising herself. If she had lived longer, she would have given me different lessons. During her last few years, the tone of her life modulated. In it, I could hear the strains of Barber's *Adagio for Strings*; her themes were about grief, but they piled upon each other with both beauty and a tension that released at their shimmering climax.

When I was twenty-seven, my mother came to care for me after I had a hernia operation. Her breast cancer had already returned. But she bathed me and changed my dressings and stroked my forehead. She came for one day but stayed for three, telling me she had to leave then or she would never be able to separate from me.

This was the blueprint I had to follow. If I didn't, I would become the third generation of mothers who had failed their daughters. I didn't yet know, though, if the blueprint would be enough for me.

As Nadia's diagnosis became clearer, I called to tell my father, my sister, and my close friends the most recent news. I caught in their sadness my first glimpse of the choice I would have to make—to ask them to be strong for me or to keep myself from becoming dependent on anyone else. I remembered a dog I had had when I was a teenager who injured himself. The more comfort I offered, the farther away from me he moved, until he had retreated to the farthest corner of our lawn, where he spent the night. I had that same need to withdraw. I could have asked for relief, for help with Frannie and Max, for someone to run errands, but comforting words and other well-meaning gestures were enervating. So I created a mental backyard to which I could retreat, with only enough room for Nadia and me.

This included caring for the Broviac. I was the only one whom Nadia would let near it, and I never insisted that she let me share that burden with anyone else. I was the only one who could give her the shots that would boost her white-blood-cell count. I was the only one whom she would allow to stay with her overnight in the hospital. Ideally, I was the one after surgery to squirt saline down her tracheostomy and mop up the postsurgical blood and mucus she coughed up.

It wasn't as if I didn't have other options. There was John's older sister Maureen, a nurse. In the early days of my marriage, the only relief I had found from my self-imposed isolation was visiting Maureen, who was at home with her new baby. I called Maureen to be with me when I first had to change Nadia's dressing at home. I wanted Maureen with me when I walked into the recovery room after Nadia's surgery. I needed Maureen to stay with me at the hospital for two nights after the operation.

There was also Margie, who had been my children's babysitter since Frannie was two weeks old, and who was now also a nurse. Margie was Nadia's preferred maternal substitute. She would spend nights at our house when Nadia was receiving chemo through the portable pump that infused her drugs around the clock. Often, she slept in Nadia's room so I could be spared a night of listening to the pump's endless cycling. Margie bathed Nadia because she knew how to do it without causing her any pain.

Margie relieved me when Nadia was in the hospital so that I could go home. My first urge was to take a shower; I needed to decontaminate to make the transition. But there were no typical family evenings. Often, Frannie wasn't at home. She would be at the hospital herself to spend the evening in the playroom with Nadia. If she were home, she was usually sick.

One night, I tried to escape from the responsibility of caring for Frannie. The floor in our bathroom has radiant heat, and I needed its warmth to penetrate my exhausted body. But Frannie followed me in, sneezing. "I don't feel good," she complained.

"I'm sorry, Frannie," I said.

"Can't you make me feel better?"

"No, Frannie. I can't. It's just a cold. Take some Tylenol if your sinuses hurt or you have a fever."

This was not the response Frannie was used to. I was usually ready with the thermometer and at least a "poor baby." But Frannie wouldn't leave me. She curled up against me, yet all I could think about was her germs; would I be passing them along to Nadia?

John was home most evenings; he visited Nadia after work so that he, Max, and I could have dinner together. (Max was too young to visit Nadia as an inpatient, although we did sneak him in on occasion.) John and I found little to talk about, so Max became the focus of these evenings. We listened to him talk about school or laughed at his imitations of Fat Bastard from the Austin Powers movies. After dinner, he practiced his cello with me or asked for help with his homework. He loved to cuddle, but just as I was relishing the feel of his body, he would ask questions about how Nadia was feeling, when she'd be home, what her roommate was like. I'd feel myself returning to that other life down on Sixty-Eighth Street.

My own family came to visit—my father and his wife, Donna, from New Hampshire; my sister Joanny from Baltimore; my aunt Essie from Massachusetts. It was hard to find roles for them. I was so wrapped up in Nadia that I didn't know how to incorporate them into the routine. They were most valuable at helping with the logistics of Max's and Frannie's routines or going to find a special food that Nadia was craving or a just-released video she had begged for.

John's role was the most complicated. He had responded to Nadia's diagnosis by seeking every doctor friend we had to tease out words of reassurance. He threw himself into organizing Thanksgiving, which we hosted annually for my family and his. Would we have enough room for everyone? How many tables should we rent? Was there anything special I wanted to serve this year? All of this energy threatened to pull me from my backyard.

Nothing about John's behavior surprised me. He likes action and big gestures. When we moved into our house on Martha's Vineyard, he spent the first month going to artisans' fairs and gallery openings, filling up wall space so fast I had to tell him to stop. Decorating our house was a process that I wanted to last for years. Every morning, he greets me and the kids with big hellos and hearty hugs, whereas during one summer, which I spent living with an aunt, we had an agreement that she wouldn't talk to me until I had been up for at least an hour. I was happy when John became a devotee of yoga; I thought it would be a quiet, peaceful pursuit for him. But in typical John fashion, he practiced for up to two hours a day, five to six days a week. When he wasn't doing yoga, he was talking about it. John was the noisiest yogi-in-training I've ever met. I chafe at the idea of living my life so publicly, even if just in front of one person, which is what marriage demands.

When it came to the nursing aspects of Nadia's care, however, John made no move to take over. He accompanied us to the hospital each morning when Nadia was getting chemo, but he still had his work, his connection to an old, familiar world. I was jealous of this anchor in his life, as if his sorrows and fears were able to sit patiently outside his office door until it was time for him to go back to the hospital. I never thought about how lonely he might have felt in his normal life, how hard the transition must have been for him.

At the end of the day, John came to pick us up, breezing in with a robust, "Hey, Nadia, how are you?" He bent over her bed to give her a kiss.

"Go away," Nadia said, curling into a tight ball.

"What's the matter with her? Is she okay?" he asked, whispering over her head.

"She's fine," I hissed. "She's just tired." I don't know why I didn't say the truth: that John's boisterous entrance, meant to be uplifting, was too loud; that Nadia couldn't stand people breathing on her because the smell made her sick. I had figured out these things without being told; therefore, I thought John should know them too. I couldn't be sympathetic, even though I knew how rejected he must have been feeling.

"Is there anything we should be giving her?" John asked.

"No."

"Should I get the doctor?"

"No! She's just tired."

"Stop talking about me," Nadia burst in, shutting us both up.

But when Nadia felt well, John was the entertainer, taking her to the game arcade, FAO Schwarz, or a nearby amusement park. I was glad for the relief, but eventually I started to sulk. How come he got to have all the fun with her? I ignored the fact that I hated arcades, shopping, and amusement parks. It had never been my job to take the kids there. All I seemed to get to do with Nadia when she was feeling strong was to nag her about her homework.

When Nadia was feeling good, when she was out with John or at school and there was no distraction from my self-pity, I allowed myself to fantasize about my mother being alive. She would have been sad about Nadia, like me, but I wouldn't have had to soothe her or interpret for her as I had to for everyone else. She would have had the strength to care for *me*. Nadia would have found in my mother the one other person she could have depended upon, besides me. But where would my own strength have gone if my mother had been there? Would we both have reverted to old patterns of dependence and caretaking. My world was spinning for real now. I needed all my focus to stay still. I couldn't be distracted by dreams of my mother's fingers drawing tension from my scalp, of swaying to a rhythm only the two of us heard, of her surviving cancer and telling Nadia all she had learned.

I was stronger alone. It all came down to just me and Nadia. I had to prove to Nadia that I was there for her, that I wouldn't disappear.

I could not expect Nadia to come downstairs for lunch soon.

I couldn't find my mother's eyes. I couldn't set my lips like hers. The only heart beating was my own. I was pushing through twilight but coming upon dawn. I was the Mother now.

9

I have no moods of my own anymore. Like water that gets its shape from the vessel it is in, my moods are molded by Nadia. If she is happy and comfortable, so am I. If she is miserable, so am I. If she sleeps well, I can sleep well. Does she feel that burden?

—journal entry, November 24, 2000

What will an eight-year-old on chemo require of me?

On Monday, November 20, we arrive at the Pediatric Day Hospital (PDH) at 7:30 A.M. Our past visits had been confined to the central waiting area and the examination rooms. Today, after Nadia is weighed, checked for fever, and has her wrist adorned with a plastic hospital bracelet, we are told to proceed to the "bed area." This is an open room with twenty-five to thirty beds lining the perimeter. There is just enough room between each bed for a compact end table with drawers and one chair. A small, personal television hangs from the wall on a retractable arm. Curtains can be closed for visual privacy, transforming the large room into a nest of cocoons.

Natural light struggles in through three or four small windows lining only one wall. Nadia is shown to a bed under one of these bright patches, and I wonder whether the staff saves these coveted spots for new patients.

Chemo cannot begin before Nadia is adequately hydrated. As the nurse hooks up an IV bag of fluids to Nadia's Broviac, I think, Finally we are underway. An hour later, I watch the first drops emerge from the inverted bottle of Cytoxan (cyclophosphamide). They move as if reluctant to make their journey. Now the month of May—the end of treatment—might as well exist in another dimension rather than be a time that we can reach by passing through a finite number of days. Not knowing what to expect minute by minute is unbearable. I stare at Nadia, waiting for her to explode or disintegrate, to undergo some grotesque transformation before my eyes

The curtains do nothing to screen out the sounds of nausea, fear, and conversations that the desperately ill are having about dying. Nadia is halfway through her day of chemo when I pick up the middle of a conversation between the girl in the bed next to Nadia and her social worker. The girl is perhaps nineteen. I come in on these words: "You know, you're out of treatment options."

"Yes, I know," the girl answers.

"Have you thought about what you want to do in the time you have left?"

"Well, I want to keep going to school for as long as I can."

"Good, you should feel better for a while since you won't be getting any chemo."

"I'm looking forward to hanging out with my friends."

"What about when you can't go to school anymore? Do you know who's going to take care of you? Are you talking to your doctor about palliative care?"

I am fascinated by this conversation, with the girl's

calm acceptance, with the fact that she has no mother or father there to make the conversation easier. Or maybe her parents would have made it worse. How could they not project their despair?

But I also don't want to hear anymore. I don't want Nadia to hear it. I turn the television volume a little louder, ask Nadia if she needs anything or wants to play cards. I fuss with the items on the bedside table. I try to make noise to block out the voice of the girl who is going to die.

By 5:45 P.M.; the PDH is closing. Nadia has been to the playroom, watched TV, slept. Now she is engaged with Gaby in a card game called Spit as she waits for a shot of Ativan, an anti-anxiety medication that relieves nausea caused by chemo. She seems little changed. Kytril and Vistaril also keep her queasiness at bay; a steroid has fueled her hunger. A little redness around the eyes, a little tiredness, a little stomach discomfort; that's all I see.

The nurse attaches Nadia's Broviac lines to a portable IV pump. She zips this into a backpack along with the vincristine and doxorubicin, a heavy bag of hydrating fluid, and the mesna to protect Nadia's bladder, all of which will be infused continuously for three days. On this first day, Nadia insists on carrying the backpack herself; she will not always be able to do so. The nurse hands me a piece of paper with instructions about what to do in case there is a problem with the pump.

As John, Nadia, and I leave the hospital, fear clings to me like the smell of the Provodone soap in the bathrooms, following me into the car, where I waver between worries that first Nadia's pump and then her body will undergo some catastrophic malfunction. My instructions say, "To ensure that your pump is working properly, please remember to check it **at least four times** after you leave the hospital." I place the backpack on the floor by

Nadia's feet and listen to the whirring of the little machine inside the way, as a child, I used to press my ear into my pillow at night to listen to my heartbeat, knowing that if the sound stopped it meant I was dead.

I look at Nadia; still there; still whole.

I listen for the pump; still cycling.

I read my instruction sheet again: "The pump should be checked when you arrive home, before bedtime, during the night, and the following morning."

I look at Nadia again, listen for the pump, strain to hear any high-pitched alarms, check the lines to make sure there are no kinks. We're only halfway home, and I have already checked for problems four times.

I am absorbed in these repetitive thoughts and motions when we pull up to our apartment building. Routine actions don't register—the doorman opening the car door, looking for bags he can help carry, reaching for the backpack, preparing to walk away with it, unaware of its connection to Nadia's body, of the searing pain that would rip through her chest from the yanking of the IV lines on her Broviac.

"No," I blurt, startled by the realization that my familiar world can hold so many unforeseen. "I'll take that," I say.

Nadia takes one step out of the car. I follow with the backpack. "Move in front of me," she says before we enter our building's lobby so I can block the view of the tubes protruding from under her shirt.

At home, Nadia wants to use my computer, so I set her up in my office with the backpack again at her feet and leave her there. I check the mail, get a snack, moving from room to room in my apartment, getting farther away from Nadia. I allow the familiarity of home to relax me. I don't forget about Nadia, but I'm not actively thinking of her either when, after ten or fifteen minutes, I hear her screaming. I race down the hall. "What is it, Nadia?" I ask, expecting that now that I have let my guard down I will finally see a pool of blood, a face twisted in pain, a crumpled body.

What I see is fury. "I've been calling you and calling you," she accuses. "I have to go to the bathroom, and I can't carry the backpack anymore."

"Oh, Nadia, I am so sorry. I wasn't thinking." Or I was thinking but, for one minute, I wasn't thinking about Nadia. I was thinking about how much I loved my home and my books in my bookshelf, which I hadn't added to since Halloween. I was thinking about what I would do first now that I was free. I had forgotten I wasn't free, nor was Nadia, who was anchored to the floor with a bag full of chemotherapy drugs.

I want to fix her fury and helplessness with a hug, but affection won't get Nadia to the bathroom. She needs expertise more than love. I lean in to apologize anyway. The Cytoxan has affected her sense of smell; I am no longer a person but an odor that she must push away or vomit on. I try not to take this first of her many rebuffs personally, but the feeling of rejection comes just the same. I remember my mother complaining about how sensitive her nose had become when she was on chemo. *She* never pushed me away. I am angry that Nadia, who always seemed to protect all of us, has not tried harder to spare my feelings. I feel like a bumbling fool around her now, as if my daughter has surpassed me in maturity because, at age eight, she is having an experience that I, at forty-eight, have only half-witnessed in my mother.

By the end of the third day of the first round of chemo, with no dramas materializing, I begin to breathe more easily. The pump will be disconnected in less than eighteen hours, a task I am instructed in how to perform at home because the PDH will be closed on Thanksgiving. Before we leave, the nurse warns me that the effects of the vincristine, severe stomach cramping and constipation, come later. A mother whose son is in the bed next to Nadia's advises me to be aggressive with all of the medications I have been given to ease her nausea and pain. "Don't wait for something to happen. Assume it will."

Her advice goes counter to what I see before my eyes and to how my mother mothered me—downplaying our illnesses, aches and pains. Nadia is urging me to follow her to the elevator faster, eager to get home. I will wait and see what happens.

I put Nadia to bed at 9 P.M. She sleeps calmly until midnight when she cries, "Owee! Owee!"

"What's the matter?" I begin the words in my sleep. I can't seem to drag myself over to her bed from the mattress on the floor of her room where I sleep to watch over not Nadia but the chemo pump.

"My stomach hurts."

"Do you want an Ativan?" I ask.

"I don't know. Owee!"

I get the Ativan. "Where does it hurt?"

"I don't know. Here." Her hand circles around her navel. "Do something."

"Do you want me to rub it?"

"I don't know. Will it help?"

If she doesn't know anything, what can I possibly know? I rub. Circle after circle. Each time I stop she demands more. The pain builds. The mother's touch can't heal. We endure an hour of moaning, of cries, of Nadia's wrath at my helplessness. Finally, she vomits. Instantly, she is fine. I wash her face. We return to bed.

An hour later: "Owee, it still hurts."

"Let me get you a Vistaril."

The pattern repeats itself. After another sixty minutes Nadia cries, "Can't you give me something?"

"There's nothing else, honey."

"It hurts, it hurts."

I rub.

This is nothing like my first taste of motherhood, when Frannie was an infant and I nursed her in the darkness of midnight. I was smug in our world of just the two of us; even the light from an apartment across the street felt like an intrusion. But I am not smug now living alone in Nadia's world of pain. I want to wake everyone in the house. "See, see!" I want to holler. "This is what I have to deal with while all of you are safe in your beds!" I am astounded that Nadia's cries haven't roused everyone.

Everyone, besides John, Frannie, and Max, includes my father and his wife, Donna, as well as my sister and brother-in-law. They have come early for the Thanksgiving weekend, thinking there must be some way to help us. I can think of nothing that they could do right now except stop asking me if there's something they can do.

I don't think it's odd that we never considered different plans for Thanksgiving, which we were hosting in a home we had at the time in Pound Ridge, New York, an hour north of Manhattan. We have always invited family and friends to our home for this holiday. I thought Frannie, Max, and Nadia would lose confidence in me if I told them I couldn't handle it. Besides, Nadia had worked for days on an activity schedule for the weekend, including the singing of the national anthem from everyone's country of origin (even if that meant going back a couple of generations). Russia, Poland, Lithuania, Ireland, England, Scotland, Italy, Brazil, and America were all to be represented, with each respective group standing up to sing (with the aid of a few preselected recordings).

I was sure I could handle things. Someone else would be cooking and cleaning and organizing. I just had to be there. I forgot that people would want to talk to me, to ask me questions, to see how they could help, to cheer me up; that they would need help to get directions, to find the linen closet, to work the television.

An hour before dawn, Nadia throws up again and falls back to sleep. Quiet descends. Unable to sleep, I pace through rooms that still reverberate with her cries. At 7 A.M., I collapse on the couch in the living room, where I finally stop moving long enough to achieve a stillness more akin to paralysis than rest. Now I hear my father's footsteps in the hallway. I don't want to talk to him. As angry as I was during the night, I now resent having to spend my energy on trying to explain my exhaustion.

"You're up," my father says when he sees me. "I thought everyone was still sleeping."

"I've been up for hours," I answer, my voice flat. I take a deep breath, knowing I owe him more of an explanation. "Nadia had a bad night. Lots of stomach pain. She threw up a couple of times."

"Is she okay now?" my father asks. He is slight but, at age seventy-four, still muscular with a spring in his step left from his days as a marathon runner. I remember seeing him cry only three times. The first time was when I was three or four. We were in the kitchen in our first home in Lexington and just about to eat. My father was on the phone, which was also in the kitchen. I didn't hear or understand the conversation. I saw his head bow; and when he hung up the phone, I heard him making strange sounds, like choking or hiccups. His face was wet and his features scrunched. When I realized he was crying, I became afraid. His grief, which I ultimately figured out was over the early death of his sister, appeared to weaken him. It was like seeing him in a costume I wasn't sure he would ever take off.

The tears my father shed after my mother's death were not frightening. They were proof that he loved her, that that other costume he had donned during the brief separation he had sought from her had been tossed onto the rag pile of mistakes.

It wasn't until the day before Nadia's first round of chemo that I saw my father cry for a third time. As I recited the regimen, my father's head nodded in recognition of the names of the drugs I am sure he never wanted to hear of again, and in his liquid eyes I saw the co-mingling of past and current sorrow.

These tears were neither scary nor welcome. They made me want to protect my father, who seems at such a loss when there is no use for the imaginings and calculations of his powerful brain, when there is nothing for him to fix. I remember my first traffic ticket for running a stop sign. My father asked me to draw a diagram of the street configuration and where the sign was. With this blueprint, he could understand how I had made such a mistake. He could draw a map of a rogue cancer cell. He could explain how cancer works. But he could not explain why his granddaughter has it.

I don't know how to ask for help from a father who has no answers. The droop I see in his shoulders now, the barely visible downturn at the corners of his mouth, the cloud that comes over his eyes have only one source—a sadness that breaks my heart.

I can't be needy now. I answer his question only with the facts. "Nadia's been sleeping for a couple of hours. She seems much more comfortable now."

I'm more confused about what I want to tell John or, more accurately, what I want *from* him. I could cry and be comforted. I could play the martyr and ask him what he thought he was doing by sleeping all night. My anger is stronger than my need for solace, even though I know that, had John responded to my silent middle-of-the-night plea for company, his presence would have been more annoying to me than helpful. Nadia would have rejected him as a caregiver, and I would have had no tolerance for his fretting over the meaning of every one of her hurts and gasps. I should have done more, before Nadia got sick, to connect John to the kids. We could have been more of a team. I'm not willing to take total responsibility, though, for his feeling like an outsider. He was as complicit as I was. This fact helps fuel my power now. If I ask for sympathy, some recognition of my self-sacrifice, then I will be weakened. It's as if I can recognize only two states of being: self-righteous pride or total dependence on another person.

So when John wakes up, I use the same words I had used with my father.

"Is she okay now?" he asks.

"I don't know," I answer, my voice aloof as I choose, as a small punishment, not to wrap my words in the soft cotton bunting of reassurance.

"Should we call the doctor?" he asks in alarm. "Do you think she'll be okay?"

"Let's just wait and see how she feels when she wakes up," I sigh. I have not given John any reassurance; and despite my dismissal of him as someone who can help, his uncertainty has made me less certain myself.

Nadia wakes up without pain. She eats a little. At 11 A.M., I disconnect the IV lines and tape up the Broviac.

At 11:30 we divide ourselves between two cars and

begin the drive to Pound Ridge. Nadia and I take the back seat of our minivan; she rests her head on my lap. Five minutes into the ride, her moans start. "Owee," she cries, over and over and over. Citrus smells used to make my mother feel better after chemo, so I give Nadia orange peels to hold against her nose. I try to distract her with a song, tell her to breathe. Instinctively, she starts a series of rhythmic pants and fixes her gaze on a point on the car's ceiling. She appears to lose awareness of where she is. The moans stop. My body is rigid with the same kind of fear I had as a child listening in the night for sounds of intruders or ghosts in my house. A jolt of the car, my brother-in-law (who is driving) asking for directions, a twitch of my own leg all threaten to break in on the sanctuary Nadia has built, calling her back to her pain.

Donna and Max play hangman. I have to stop myself from telling Max not to shout out his letters or Donna not to laugh when she finally figures out Max's secret phrase was "Spice Girls." The sounds of normal life are as dissonant to me as hearing Chopin's *Funeral March* played in a major key.

Nadia rallies during the last twenty minutes of the ride, joining the game of hangman. As the house comes into sight, I am overjoyed at the thought of freeing myself from my daughter. My aunt Essie has already arrived, and I anticipate collapsing on her shoulder, having a drink, then locking myself in my room for some gut-wrenching sobbing.

"Mama, can I watch TV in your room?" Nadia asks before I can even make it to the freezer for some ice. I should have known. Nadia loves her family, but the same instinct that drives me to withdraw drives her, too. She's not ready for the aunts and uncles and cousins and grandparents who have taken over the house. "You come, too," she adds.

I don't want to be alone with Nadia anymore. Being in the presence of her suffering is peeling away the layers of my sanity. But I agree, thinking she'll be asleep in minutes.

I lie on the bed next to her. "Why don't you close your eyes and try to sleep? You must be exhausted," I tell her.

"I can't sleep," she says. "My belly still hurts."

"Do you want to go to the bathroom?"

"No."

"Why don't you just try? It's been a while." I'm remembering (too late) the warnings that vincristine causes constipation.

"Fine, I'll try."

I hear her scream from the bathroom, find her hunched over in pain. "Mama, please make the hurt go away."

I call the doctor who is covering over the holiday and learn that we can expect another two days of cramping. She recommends stool softeners and laxatives, but they won't provide immediate relief.

I tuck Nadia back into bed. "Nadia, honey, I'm just going downstairs for a few minutes. Can I get you anything? Do you want Donna or Frannie to come sit with you?"

"No, I want you," she insists.

"I know, Nadia. I'll be right back."

"No, you stay."

So I stay, fuming at Nadia and at every laugh and snippet of conversation that drifts up through the floorboards. It's not just anger, of course. I, more than anyone, know what it feels like to believe that only your mother can make you feel safe. But now I am beginning to see things from my mother's side, how she must have wanted to pry me from her body every morning when I refused to leave her to go to nursery school, kindergarten, first grade, then second; how, when I left home for college and then married life, she must have cringed with impatience and frustration when I called her for help, as often as five times a day, with a problem I couldn't even identify. The conversations were almost always the same.

"I miss you," I began.

"I'm sorry, Judi."

"I don't feel well."

"What's the matter?"

"I don't know. I just don't feel right."

"Judi, I don't know how much I can help you. Maybe you should come home."

"No."

"Then you have to find a way to figure out what's going on."

Sometimes I would ask about Joanny. Sometimes my mother would put my father on the phone. Whereas my mother tried to push me to figure out what was wrong, my father just seemed confused. He told me he wished he could help me but he had no answers. Rarely did we speak about my classes or my music or about what I was doing that I enjoyed. Rarely did I ask them what they were doing. One reason I kept calling was to make sure home was still there since I was beginning to realize that my father's restlessness was making home unstable. How relieved my mother must have been when I finally hung up.

As Thanksgiving dinner approaches, Nadia, at last, falls asleep. I sneak away and sit through the meal, finding little relief in her absence. Only Frannie tiptoes up the stairs as often as I do to peek in on Nadia, sensing the injustice of our incomplete table. (It isn't until we return to the city three days later, and Nadia finds the program outlining the weekend's activities that she had written before chemo started, when she was innocent of its effects, that we remember the national anthems.)

Nadia wakes later that evening feeling fine and joins us for leftovers and late-night conversation, but the next morning she is as clingy as before. My sister is leaving, and I want to say goodbye.

"Nadia, I'm just going to say bye to Joanny."

"No, don't leave me."

"I'm not leaving you, Nadia. I'll send someone else to sit with you, but I need to go downstairs for a bit. Donna will come up. I'll be right back."

I don't come right back. I savor my liberation, stand out in the sun, walk the dogs, have a cup of tea. I know Nadia is fine. I hear no cries or moans. I am tempted to call her a faker.

"Well, Nadia," I say on my return, "I see you're just fine."

"It still hurts. I'm just not showing it."

Is Nadia being stoic? Is she exaggerating to get my attention? Could she actually feel better when I am not there? *Why can't you ever make it clear what you need from me?*

As a baby, Nadia's first words were "I do" punctuated by a turn of her back or a push against my intruding hand. But if I tried to leave her alone, she would call me back, saying, "Watch me, Mama." As a young child, she would choose to ignore me for hours until a hug that I might give Frannie or Max brought her running to me for her share. By age five, Nadia would go off on sleepovers like a veteran, but at home she would beg me to lie with her at bedtime.

Knowing that Nadia could handle so much without me (my mother's dream of independence finally realized by the granddaughter), I expected that she would—and should—be self-sufficient. I was always suspicious of her moments of neediness and assumed they were just attempts to get my attention. There were occasions when I left Nadia to calm her own fears at night, or turned away from yet another handstand she felt she needed to show me, or reluctantly relinquished my hold on Frannie or Max when she tried to break in on a hug.

As I read these words back to myself, they are sandpaper scraping my heart. It doesn't matter that I have a right to a respite. As long as Nadia can't leave her cancer in the room and come downstairs with me, the sun will cover itself with clouds and my tea will turn bitter on my tongue.

A rabbi once told me that if I wanted to deepen my practice as a Jew—for example, by keeping kosher or observing *Shabbat*—it wasn't necessary to change all at once. Choose one or two gestures—don't eat pork, light candles on Friday night. At first, the actions might feel stiff and artificial, perhaps meaningless. But if you keep at it, he said, these actions may grow roots of true faith. Maybe next you'll choose not to mix meat and dairy or to forego turning lights on and off during the Sabbath to see where these conscious actions, performed with skepticism and awkwardness, take you.

It is with the same lack of commitment that I now relieve Donna and lie next to Nadia on the bed. After a few minutes, I feel the familiar need to bolt. I fidget and sigh loudly, glancing at Nadia to see if my distress has made any impact. It hasn't, of course. My eye is still on the door and my heart is beating at the window, but my body stays—one second at a time.

I thought ill children were supposed to suffer their fate differently from adults; I thought they were braver, wiser, and more heroic. When I read *Death Be Not Proud,* John Gunther made me believe his son was almost perfect—unafraid to die and only sorry that he didn't have more time to complete his scientific work. In *Little Women,* Beth approaches her death with quiet grace and continued altruism. And in the movie *Simon Birch,* which Nadia saw repeatedly both before and after her diagnosis, a young boy who is stunted physically believes God has given him a purpose, which he fulfills before dying a hero's death. Until Nadia, children with cancer wore smiling faces and posed in ads for St. Jude's Hospital, the Make-A-Wish Foundation, or Ronald MacDonald House.

I had had these unrealistic expectations of my mother as well. Her end-stage illness coincided with the release of Norman Cousins' *Anatomy of an Illness,* espousing mind over matter and laughing as cures, and with the rise of self-help groups and the power of positive thinking. I was in the kitchen when my mother said, "I'm not going to survive this, Judi."

I looked at all the pills lining the kitchen counter and said, "So you're just going to stop trying? Just like that?"

"There's nothing else to try."

I would have felt foolish accusing her of not laughing enough, of being negative; that there was no way she would ever get better if she wasn't going to put her mind to it. But still I am surprised by what I now see as Nadia's bad attitude and by my lack of patience and grace. I feel as if we are failing some test of character while everyone around us is acing the class.

Prowling the hundreds of channels on cable TV as a distraction, I find just the opposite of us. The Discovery Health Channel has a feature about a girl, perhaps seven, with lymphoma. She has lived with her father since her parents' divorce. Her mother has remarried and moved to a different city to care for her ailing father and now has two more children, one barely out of infancy. With her two younger children in tow, the mother returns to be with her older daughter.

A sick child, an ill father, a divorce, two younger children, a move—could life get any more stressful for a mother? Yet, what strikes me most at the end of an hour showing the girl getting treatments, having her Broviac cared for, undergoing tests, talking about losing her hair or missing school—after hearing the parents talk about how their lives had been redirected—is that no one has to tackle the patient to give her a shot, no one flips over a Monopoly board, no one buries her head in a pillow so that she won't have to listen to what she is being told. There is no anger, no loss of control. Everyone, even the girl, is articulate and strong. The baby never cries no matter how many times he is shown accompanying the mother to the hospital or waiting for the mother to finish caring for her daughter. The middle child never whines, and the daughter never screams at her mother as if this is all her fault. The mother never loses her temper, never pulls her hair out, never looks at her brood and her life and wonders how she got herself in this fix anyway.

The whole experience has been sanitized, stripped of its tragedy and ugliness. It is like looking at a faded bruise, the shock, pain, and blood of the initial impact having dulled to a soft yellow.

Why can't our culture look at pain more honestly? Why must I sit chained to Nadia's side feeling like a freak because I haven't achieved a state of grace? Why must I look at my daughter, for whom my only wish is that she will stop hurting and live, and think that she'd never qualify for an entry in *Chicken Soup for the Soul* with its uplifting stories of brave children who overcome tragedy with the peace of Zen masters?

I know that little baby cried. I know that girl told her mother that she hated her for what was happening. I know that mother came close to cracking under the pressure. I know all this because I experienced it. I saw Nadia's despair the day she realized that third grade—when traditions abounded in a year-long study of the Middle Ages—would be her own Dark Age.

One of the projects she rushed to complete before she began treatment was the building of a medieval castle. Instructions had not yet been given out, but Nadia knew castles could be made out of anything. (Several years earlier, Frannie had made hers out of Milk Bones.) Nadia chose to give hers an Oreo theme. She spent a weekend working with the feverish enthusiasm of a chef given the very best kitchen to work in but required to turn out a dinner for five hundred in only a few hours. The castle she unveiled was a sprawling construction of precariously perched Oreo packages and boxes with a high outer wall surrounding a maze of inner passageways and rooms.

A week later, Nadia began chemo. In her homework package from the teachers was a list of castle requirements. As she read the list, I saw her body sag: each must have a moat, a drawbridge and four turrets; it could be no bigger than a desk top. Nadia glared at her castle—now looking ungainly and lacking all necessary architectural elements—as if it were scoffing at her attempt to maintain her life as a normal third-grade student at the Nightingale-Bamford School.

"I hate this stupid thing," Nadia said.

"All you have to do is make it smaller and add a few things," I countered. But I have always hated all these "creative" home projects schools love to assign and truly had no idea how Nadia should go about transforming what she had made into an official castle.

"Why should I bother?" Nadia answered. "I'm not even going to be in school when they put it on display."

Where, in the documentary, is the acting out of the siblings? A few weeks into Nadia's treatment, Max dragged a mattress into her room so as not to be left out when I slept there. Many nights were peaceful; on others Max found something to object to, like the sound of Nadia's chemo pump.

"I can't sleep with that noise," he said.

"It's just a whirr; you can hardly hear it," I answered, moving the backpack farther down Nadia's bed under the covers, trying not to wake her up. I couldn't believe I was trying to placate Max; but if I was successful, perhaps I could realize my fantasy of a perfect sibling union between him and Nadia.

"I can still hear it."

"Go sleep in your own room then," I snapped.

I didn't get an answer. A few minutes later, Max growled, "Turn that thing off!"

I couldn't, and he knew it. I was not interested in understanding his motives or trying to put myself in his place. I just wished he would be quiet.

In those first few weeks—in fact, during the full course of Nadia's treatment—I never saw another mother arrive at the hospital like I did, so dizzy and achy from lack of sleep that I displaced Nadia in her bed while she went to the playroom alone. The only clue I ever had that the rawness of my and Nadia's emotions was normal came during that first round of chemo, when the doctors and nurses were thinking of possible friends for her at the hospital. One girl's name came up but was immediately rejected. "Don't you remember, in the beginning, how mad she was? She'd pull the blankets up over her head whenever we tried to come near," said one of the nurse practitioners in the group that was treating Nadia.

Yes, Yes, I thought. Nadia needs to meet this girl. She was finishing her ten months of treatment for osteogenic sarcoma and had already earned her hero status. I, however, clung to the version of her as the rebellious and scared young girl she used to be. I repeated what the nurse said, "In the beginning," even as I watched the now smiling preteen posing with her friends and doctors for pictures that will make up a photo album. Memories can be made here that are worth preserving, I told myself. But we never take pictures of the anger, as if we need to hide the darkness. I was reminded of the way in which Baroque composers would end even minor-keyed pieces on a major chord, as if all the sadness or grief that came before could be erased in one final moment of harmony.

It's not that the documentaries are wrong; they just don't let us in on the process. Nadia and I were actors in our first read-through of a new drama. It would take some time before our characters would develop strength and certainty.

Nadia learned faster than I did. She had less to unlearn, more that she knew instinctively. She spent her first day of chemo trying to figure out what she was going to do for fun for ten hours. When the announcement came over the P.A. system calling all eight to twelve year-olds to Explorer's Group, Nadia ran to the playroom, not even knowing what the group was. As she went rushing off, my concern was with hospital protocol, with being helpful and cooperative for the nurses, with not causing trouble or asking too many questions. But all I had were questions. Why did the doctors suddenly pull the curtain around a teenage boy? What is the beeping sound that keeps coming from the IV pumps? Which bathroom can I use? How does the TV work, the bed operate? What time will they need Nadia back from the playroom? Can she eat whatever she wants? Why are some people wearing masks? Who are the refrigerator and microwave for? Are we supposed to have a social worker? Can friends come and visit whenever they want?

Instead, I employed the scientific method I became so familiar with under my father's tutelage. I observed, drew conjectures, predicted, and tested. I looked at the bed and its mechanisms and figured out how to adjust its various positions. When someone's IV beeped, I watched the nurse press different buttons and adjust IV lines and figured out the difference between a malfunction and a bag of fluid that had been emptied. The people wearing masks had colds. There seemed to be a steady stream of people coming and going, so I told family and friends they could come anytime. The curtain opened on the boy. A mother stroked his forehead, and a nurse removed a bedpan.

Before this first day of chemo, I searched for ways to keep Nadia as attached to her life at school as possible. But while I was talking to Nadia's teachers and hospital staff about setting up a closed-circuit television hookup to her classroom, she was wise enough to know that there was no way she would sit in a hospital bed and observe her friends going through their familiar routines and rituals to a background noise of IV pumps cycling and beeping, nurses being paged, patients being sick. It wasn't just about seeing what she was missing, though. Nadia did not want to be distracted from what she now saw as the necessary task of establishing her life at the hospital.

Nadia and I disagreed on what made us lucky. One

day, early in her treatment, she had been in the day hospital all morning getting a blood transfusion when her temperature started to climb in the afternoon. Her white-blood-cell count was low, so by evening she was admitted in case she was developing a potentially fatal infection. I saw only more separation from life at home and another day of school missed. But Nadia said, "I'm so lucky. I can use the playroom all day." That meant from 9 A.M. to 2 P.M., when it was open for outpatients, and from 2 P.M. through the evening when it opened to inpatients.

Each time Nadia had to be admitted for fever or surgery, I became a hospital resident as well. I would close my eyes and hold my breath as we stepped over the threshold into our room. Would we have a roommate? Who would it be? I always hoped we'd get a night or two to ourselves. But Nadia wanted company; every roommate was a potential friend, a playmate, a human connection that normalized the hospital experience.

I avoided other parents, even though I might have learned from them what the documentaries don't show. I didn't want to talk about blood counts or treatments or prognoses or doctors, buzzwords in every conversation I overheard. Each contact simply reinforced the perversity of this new PTA of which I had become a member.

Nadia and I looked for different qualities in the doctors and nurses. She sought out the ones who could make her laugh, who would ask her about her life at home and school. When Nadia laughed, I could laugh too; and when she spoke about gymnastics or her friends, her cancer got out of the way for a moment, and I could see my daughter behind it. But I also needed reassurance in a way that Nadia didn't since she got all of her comfort from me. I sought out the softer voices, the gentler smiles, those who saw that I was someone needing "treatment" as well.

We were fortunate that Dr. Wexler had a colleague, Dr. Paul Meyers, who also managed Nadia's care. Between the two doctors, Nadia and I could find the support we needed, even if those needs were different.

While I pined for the past, coped with the present, reached for the future, Nadia dealt only with what was directly in front of her. Once she accepted her circumstances, she cried only when she was in pain. She didn't dwell on the next round of chemo or on the fevers, hospitalizations, mouth sores, and restricted diet that came with neutropenia when she had a zero-white-blood-cell count. She went to school when she could, had play dates with friends, and even attempted to maintain her gymnastics skills by meeting privately with her coach.

Nadia wasn't asking me to watch her now, but I couldn't look away as I saw her grow beyond her anger. She was no longer upsetting Monopoly boards or running away from nurses or burying her head in a pillow every time I came to talk to her. Now she was ready to set down the roots of her survival. Reassured by her strength, I threw myself into the job of lady-in-waiting. I fetched and carried; ran errands for food, games, and videos; paged nurses; and doled out pills, salves, and tonics as needed. If this were a case of searching for faith, I was no longer an unobservant Jew who never celebrated the Sabbath but one who observed *Shabbat* seven days a week. But just as such fanaticism could strip this weekly holy day of its meaning, so had my newfound devotion to Nadia obscured my true role of mother, which was not just to take care of Nadia but to raise her.

What I needed was to find a balance between my just-deal-with-it approach and my current level of servitude. The initial strategy was more familiar, like a favorite accessory. It matched my mother's way of dealing with illness in herself and others; it mimicked the effect of her withdrawal from family when depression must have made my and my sister's problems too much to handle and it was in consonance with my father's aversion to asking others for help. The genesis of my second strategy was guilt; slavish devotion was the closest I could come to actually being Nadia. If she couldn't escape from her pain, I should at least be there to bear witness. But this was as uncomfortable as if I had spent my entire life in tailored suits and now decided to wear frilly, flowered dresses. It left me vulnerable to the sad-eyed stares of others, which threatened to draw me into the enervating quicksand of pity for me, the martyr, and Nadia, the victim. I was determined that Nadia would never see herself or her circumstances as tragic.

I also had concerns about the effect that money could have on Nadia's development. Cancer struck Nadia at the time when she was beginning to realize that the summer home, private school, and extensive travel she enjoyed were not available to everyone. Without attention, the combination of privilege and serious illness had the potential to instill in Nadia a sense of entitlement.

If my mother thought being sick was no excuse to rest in bed, money was the root of both moral and intellectual sloth. While my childhood was spent in middle-class comfort, it was seasoned with a Depression Era mentality. My mother never bought a skirt that didn't match a shirt she already had and considered the desire for two pairs of black shoes a sign of incipient shallowness. She told John she was proud of him but warned me not to be seduced into superficiality by his growing wealth. I dutifully lectured my own children about the difference between needs and wants, reminded them that what made their father outstanding professionally was his extraordinary work ethic, that his story could not be found in a bank statement but in the contrail left behind by the upward arc of his path. I demonstrated my attitude toward wealth by devoting my own professional and personal life to philanthropy.

Money, anyway, couldn't protect Nadia from cancer, nor did I ever see her receiving special treatment in the hospital because of it. Rather, our greatest fortune was living so close to MSKCC. Nadia was constantly surrounded by friends and relatives who gathered in the hospital playroom or by Nadia's bed. They brought what felt like a daily supply of gifts. Her abundance glared like a garish costume compared to the more modest belongings of many of the other children who came from all over the world, often with only one parent and no siblings, unsupported by their own community.

Perhaps out of my own self-consciousness as much as to teach a lesson in altruism, I suggested that Nadia weed through her presents and give all but her favorite stuffed animals, games, and art supplies to the hospital or holiday toy drives. A prize earned at Bingo that wasn't used right away was quickly recycled. Nadia had a greater gift to give, though—herself. She sought out the babies and toddlers who had no friends or siblings to play with; you could see the relief on the faces of their mothers and fathers when she entered the playroom.

Money could make it easier for Nadia to shed her cancer patient identity outside of the hospital, though. In the spring of 2001, our family went to Disney World. When we told the hospital's Child Life specialist about the trip, she asked Nadia if she wanted to contact Make-A-Wish. I knew the Make-A-Wish Foundation filled the dreams of any child with a life-threatening illness, but my gut response was to say no, that wishes like that were only for dying children and Nadia was very much alive. I told her that the foundation had needier children to serve, so instead we made a contribution. Just a few weeks after our trip to Disney World, Nadia secured more than a thousand dollars in sponsorships for her first annual Pediatric Cancer Foundation Walk-a-Thon, an event she walked, hobbled, and piggybacked her way through.

But what I ultimately had to groom Nadia for was a world in which neither financial status nor illness can provide easy assumptions about who you are. Nadia and I made a habit of stopping by a small candy store near the hospital. The owner, a Pakistani immigrant, knew us well. His smile for Nadia was always tender, his voice soft. One day, we entered the store in high spirits after Nadia had been freed from a long day at the hospital. She filled a bag with Jordan almonds, my favorite candy, as a treat for me. But when she handed it to me I dropped it. Although many of the candy shells around the almonds cracked, I didn't care because I knew they would taste just as delicious broken. The owner, however, wouldn't let us pay for them. I tried to tell him that dropping the almonds was my fault, but he insisted we throw the old candy away and fill a new bag. It would have been rude to reject his kindness. From his viewpoint, our life seemed to hold much suffering. I had a hard time accepting his generosity, though. As a compromise, I told Nadia just to take a few new candies to cover the ones we had already picked out. When we left the store, I explained to her that the owner's life as an immigrant and small store owner in one of Manhattan's highest rent districts was probably one of constant struggle—financially and perhaps socially as well—making his graciousness all the more meaningful.

These were important long-term lessons, no matter

what our means, but they were easy ones because Nadia was so uncomfortable about being singled out for special treatment that she refused a wheelchair or the preferred access that Disney World routinely provides to ill children. My most challenging job was to help her cope with the acute episodes of anxiety, sadness, or fear that arose throughout her treatment and afterward.

The summer before Nadia was diagnosed, she and I were on an airplane that hit sudden, severe turbulence. We had been listening to a classical music tape when the plane dropped, and I saw Nadia blanch. No great flier myself, I could have easily succumbed to the panic, the claustrophobia, the loss of control. I surprised myself by being able to stay calm for Nadia, but I needed to reach beyond reassuring words and hand-holding to help her. Over the headphones came the lively, jazzy strands of "Zuki Blues."

"Listen, Nadia, the plane's dancing to the music."

In our seats we began to shimmy and shake. The song ended, and the turbulence faded. I saw Nadia's flushed face and smile, and I leaned back triumphantly. My inspiration had come not from my mother, my father, nor Nadia herself but from me.

Could the lesson of this three-minute drama apply to a six-month struggle for life?

On the Monday following Thanksgiving, Nadia has recovered enough from her first round of chemo to go to school, once the morning stomach cramps pass. In the afternoon, I pick her up along with two friends. They begin their usual race home. Gaby and Emily pull ahead, and I am shocked to see long-limbed, athletic Nadia trailing and out of breath after half a block. She has to gulp before calling, "Wait up, guys."

I realize the foolishness of my magical thought, when cancer treatment was not yet fact, that Nadia could escape chemo's revenge. I long to ask how her day at school had been: Did you manage the stairs? Were you tired? Did you eat? How do you feel?

What I say is "Take your time. There's no rush."

At home, I leave the girls to their own resources and pretend that the giggles, thumps, and mess filling Nadia's room represent normalcy. I take little comfort in their joy. To me, Nadia's friends are energy suckers. I think she should rest, be still, conserve. I am relieved when Gaby and Emily leave.

The next day, Nadia's white-blood-cell count drops to zero. She's neutropenic; there isn't a single infection-fighting cell in her body. On Wednesday morning, she dresses but is in no rush to go to school. There are no specific symptoms, but I know icky when I see it. I take her temperature. Nadia is as shy of thermometers as she is of the cameras that she has always hated to pose for. They are too probing, might reveal something she doesn't want known. She is not happy with the result.

One hundred degrees. The doctors said to call if Nadia's temperature reached 100.4 because that could be sign of an infection. Should we wait or should we go? I know what Nadia's answer would be, but I can see the fever in her eyes; they are liquid and weak, as if they don't have the energy to see. This is the first round. I can't make a mistake.

I get high marks at the hospital for bringing Nadia in early. Her fever does creep up by late afternoon, and everyone is happy to start the IV antibiotics before her temperature has a chance to spike. They have seen the devastating effects of runaway infections. I haven't and only feel guilty.

"I guess we could have spent the day at home," I admit to Nadia. We learn early that even an additional six hours free of the hospital is a treasure not to be squandered.

"Why didn't we then?" Nadia asks.

"I'm sorry. I wasn't sure." I see Nadia's body tense, her eyes suddenly focus. She's ready to jump all over my self-doubting helplessness. "Nadia, I had no choice. I did the right thing. I'm sorry you're mad at me, but this is what I need to do to keep you well."

When we are admitted to the inpatient floor, I am grateful for the night we spent after the biopsy. We won't have to deal with the dual fears of fever and foreignness. Now we just need to play the waiting game—wait for Nadia's blood cultures to rule out infection, wait for her counts to come back up and fever to go down, wait for her hair to fall out.

I wake up in the morning in my reclining chair and turn, as I always do, to study Nadia's sleeping face for clues as to why or how or will she forgive me. This morning, a few hairs are stuck to her pillow, the corners of her mouth, the collar of her pajamas.

For a part of us that is so external, hair has a curious intimacy. With hair, Nadia is Nadia; without it, she is a category. I don't realize this until months after her chemo is over, when I spend hours studying pictures of Nadia from the summer before cancer, with her full and messy mane, as if trying to see if that daughter is the same one I have now. A surprise photo of Nadia bald made me gasp. From the distance of time I did not see my daughter but a girl who has cancer.

Waiting for Nadia to wake, I don't go far. I don't want her to see the hair without warning. She stirs.

"Good morning, love. Does your mouth feel better?" Nadia had sores because chemo attacks all fast-growing cells, including the ones in the mouth.

"A little."

"I'm glad." This is where I would normally stroke Nadia's head, but I refrain. "Do you remember Dr. Wexler said it would be about two weeks before you would start to lose your hair?"

"Yes."

"Well, it's just about that time. When you look at your pillow, you'll see some hair has already fallen out."

Nadia lifts her head and looks at her pillow. She reaches for her scalp and takes away a clump of hair. She looks at me and freezes. This is my "Zuki Blues" moment.

I run my hand over a section of Nadia's head. "Wow. This is weird," I say. "It's kind of cool." The hair comes off like dandelion fluff—no roots or resistance.

Nadia takes another handful. She thinks this might be fun but isn't sure if it's okay.

"Go for it. It's not like you're going to have a chance to do this again."

Soon there is hair everywhere—pillow, sheets, floor, clothes. If Nadia had gotten a shorter haircut, we wouldn't have had this mess. Then again, we wouldn't be having this much fun.

Nadia's hair is now thin on top. She has to go to the bathroom.

"I don't want to ruin the good time you're having, but you're going to look different when you see yourself in the mirror." My warning is useless.

"Mom, I hate it!"

I'm ready for her to lash out more, accusing me of deceiving her into believing that losing hair could be so festive. But she is quiet. The floor is swept. I change her sheets. We proceed with our day—playroom, videos, visitors, rest. The hair falls out on its own.

I wasn't there the day my mother began to go bald, but

I'm sure she never reacted to losing great clumps of hair with the same zest as Nadia did. I don't imagine many adults would have. I know what my mother would have said to me in her perfect social worker voice: by wanting to turn losing hair into fun, you are expressing your own denial of Nadia's experience. You are not allowing Nadia to examine her feelings so that when she looked at herself in the mirror, the shock of what she saw was made even sharper.

But Nadia needed to know that losing her hair, like flying in turbulence, did not mean that she was going to crash and burn. Laughter diffused her terror.

John is due later in the afternoon. I call to warn him about what he will see. I don't say anything about the hair-pulling scene. He wouldn't have seen the humor. When my mother made John get his haircut for my sister's wedding, he convinced the stylist to trim as little as possible, as if each cut were a lesion from which his entire being would seep. He didn't even look at the floor for fear he would see a piece of himself lying there, forever helpless and lost. Today, from the front, John has the receding hairline and gray shading of a fifty-year-old, but, from the back, his hair still falls in curls to brush the top of his shirt collar. I don't think he has ever fully forgiven me for cutting the waist-length hair I had at our wedding, which I now wear in cropped, silver-streaked layers.

John has avoided any conversation on the subject of Nadia's hair; he was not with us when I took her weeks earlier for a cut. Indeed, when John arrives, it is only for Nadia's sake that he doesn't let his feelings show, although I can tell from his slowness to enter the room and the distance he keeps that he is mourning the loss of her hair. Nadia is just happy to see him; her somber mood of that morning has passed quickly.

The next day, good news: Nadia's counts are up. We get to go home. Her hair is still falling out. I am proud I remembered to bring a scarf.

At home, the fun resumes. Nadia's giggles and snorts bring Frannie and Max running to her side. They are fascinated at all the hair she is still losing. Nadia is on stage now and starts pulling and laughing.

"What are you doing?" Frannie shrieks.

"I'm pulling my hair out. It's a once-in-a-lifetime opportunity."

"You're crazy," Max laughs.

John doesn't understand, but he manages a smile.

Just before dinnertime Nadia calls, "Mom, come see what I made you." At my seat is a bowl of downy tresses. Nadia is beaming. "It's angel hair pasta."

10

Friends keep telling me how Nadia's cancer will bring us all closer. The words make me want to gag, like being made to eat liver because it will make you strong.

—journal entry, November 17, 2000

Nadia's laughter over her hair allowed us to sit down to dinner as a family—five connected people, not four plus one with cancer. Of course, one did have cancer. Every evening would not be so funny. Frannie and Max, the embodiment of sparkle and silliness, were not now dealing with leprechauns and fantasy. I didn't know what to expect from them.

During the previous two years, it had often seemed as if Frannie and Max were the twins, so close were they in temperament and personality. Even though Max, at age eight, was more than three years younger than Frannie, both were struggling to separate from me. He and Frannie shared an interest in popular culture. Their contests in the car to guess the names of songs being played on the radio and the artists performing them forced Nadia, who preferred *Rugrats* to MTV, to be the outsider. Among the three children, only Nadia still believed in the tooth fairy.

While Frannie would come home from school with her friends and close the door on Nadia and me, exceptions were made for Max, with whom the girls could safely practice their flirting skills.

Max and Nadia are fraternal twins. They do not share the common genetic structure of identical twins. They have never had a secret language; they have no ESP-like intuition about each other. Technically, they are simply a brother and a sister born at the same time. But from age zero to five, they shared a room, a double stroller, a bathtub, a nursery school classroom. They had the same friends, went to gymnastics together, and learned to roll over, crawl, walk, and talk within days of each other. Even the differences in their personalities reinforced their bond. Nadia, the worrier and protector, was the perfect complement to Max, who was more easily frustrated and prone to sickness.

At age five, Max and Nadia moved into separate bedrooms and to single-sex schools. Still, at the end of each day, the two of them had to check to make sure one wasn't experiencing anything too different from the other. They kept score of the number of books they read, the amount of homework they had, how many days they got off from school for vacation or parent/teacher conferences, who got away with practicing his or her instrument for the least amount of time, who spent an extra minute with me before bed. They were so accustomed to leading the same life that they would insist on watching a movie together even though they could never agree on what they wanted to see.

Max thrived apart from his Little Miss Perfect, I-can-do-anything twin. His teachers praised his intelligence, the care with which he handled the baby ducks in the classroom, how eager he was to help his peers. His friends copied him, even following Max through his Spice Girls obsession. But at home Max's confidence morphed into bossiness. *He* would decide what to watch on TV, grabbing the remote from Nadia and choosing a station to suit himself. *He* would demand that Nadia get off the couch if he wanted to sit there. *He* would decide when Nadia could use the computer if he wanted to stay on. Max silenced Nadia in the car if she tried to sing, refused to sit across from her during meals, and hid her homework or stole her favorite blanket.

Nadia's response to Max was erratic. If she was seeing herself as Max's protector or as our household's peacemaker, she would not argue for what she wanted. But if she had accommodated her brother once too often, she would snap in frustration. "Mommy," she would whine, "Max took my blanket, and he won't give it back."

"Max, give Nadia her blanket back," I would say knowing my effort was futile.

Then I would hear running and a high-pitched "M-a-a-a-x," followed by a drawn-out, "M-o-m-m-y," as one, the other, or both landed a punch, a bite, or a kick.

"Go to your rooms, each of you," I'd yell.

"I hate you," Nadia would scream, I don't know whether at me or at Max, while she ran down the hallway to her room, where she would sob behind her slammed door. Max wouldn't move. Instead, wherever I turned, he would plant himself in front of me, trying to insist that somehow Nadia had been the instigator. I had to restrain myself from going into her room to tell her she didn't have to be so good, rebellion was an option. But I was grateful for her cooperation.

There were rare moments of genuine connection between them. One came shortly after Max and Nadia's eighth birthday. The Children's Museum of Manhattan was mounting an exhibit based on *Mr. Rogers' Neighborhood.* As the museum's board chairman, I was expected to attend the opening. Grudgingly, Max and Nadia agreed to come with me. Max, of course, complained that he was too old. But since Frannie, who had loved Mr. Rogers as child, was going, Max had no argument. Nadia just didn't want to leave the house that evening. Once at the museum, however, Max and Nadia forgot their objections. Among their discoveries was a five-foot-by-four-foot frame holding thousands of pins, which, when pressed, would leave an imprint. Max and Nadia called me over, saying, "Look, isn't this cool?"

They reached their hands toward each other, then pressed the back of their bodies into the pins. When they walked away, I saw a perfect image of two children with arms reaching toward each other, hands entwined.

Reaching toward each other, pushing each other away—Max and Nadia would stretch the emotional cord that bound them, sometimes as if they wanted it to break, but it never would. Their ambivalence, as well as my own confusion about which child's needs I should attend to, was at first heightened by Nadia's illness.

After I tell Max the result of Nadia's biopsy, I overhear him asking Margie, who has come to baby-sit, "Will I get cancer too?"

Max's question reaches me through the closing doors of our apartment elevator. I am leaving home to return to the hospital, where Nadia must spend the night because of a bad reaction to the anesthesia. I could have gone back, swooped him up in my arms, stroked his back, and murmured, "No, no, of course you won't get it too." But I have already made the separation from Max and feel Nadia's pull on me like a homesickness.

I don't think about how deep Max's fear might be, how lost he would become not just without me but without Nadia. It has been too long since I have thought about them as twins.

When Nadia returns home the next day, Max doesn't know how he is supposed to treat his sister. He is perhaps too attentive, too gentle for Nadia, who shouts at him, "Go away!" She has to acknowledge that something is terribly wrong with her for Max to be this kind.

I am suspicious of this Max as well. It would be too much to expect him to remain so doting. The night before Nadia is to begin her first round of chemo, John and I allow her to sleep in our bed. She hadn't asked but it seems the only gesture of understanding I can make, the same way I slept with Frannie when she was eight and trembling in fear the night before she was to go on her first school overnight trip.

When Max sees Nadia getting into our bed, he asks, "Can I sleep in your room too?"

"No, Max," I answer. "Go back to your bed."

"But there's nothing the matter with her."

True, Nadia is not trembling, crying, or in pain. Indeed, she is snuggled quite comfortably between me and John. "Max, please," I sigh. "Tomorrow is a big day."

"It's not fair," Max screams. "She should have to sleep in her own bed too."

He storms back to his room. "Max, honey ..." I follow, too late.

"Get out of here," he spits.

It would have been useless to remind Max of all the nights I slept with him (lay awake, would be more like it) listening to his wheezy breaths, delivering his asthma treatments without disturbing his sleep, or, after a trip to the emergency room for treatment of anaphylaxis, watching over him all night. I don't tell him about the time John and I had to rush him and his struggling airways to the hospital at 3 A.M., the betrayal I imagined I had inflicted on his sisters by leaving them with a babysitter while they slept. I didn't tell him because I didn't make the connection between what it meant to care for him and what Nadia required. Cancer has a way of trumping everything.

The next afternoon, though, and each day after, Max visits Nadia in the day hospital. On the third day of her chemo, he finds her lying in bed watching TV and climbs in next to her. He doesn't switch the station, even though it is *Rugrats,* and when they get bored they play cards. I look at the two of them and am disoriented for a moment. We could have been at the Children's Museum, but a set designer seems to have changed the scenery.

When Nadia starts to tire and get cranky, she turns off the TV and barks at Max to go away.

Max resists. "I want to stay and watch the TV."

I wish Nadia had asked more nicely. I wish Max could accept that the one with cancer gets dibs on the bed? "Max, out," I order.

The push/pull continued. After Max dragged his mattress into Nadia's bedroom, he ended up sleeping there every night through May, even when Nadia felt good. In my vision of the ideal, Max is devoted to his sister and Nadia lets her brother know she is happy he is there, that he gives her comfort. But Nadia showed nothing—neither pleasure nor displeasure.

Max had no role. His friendship with Nadia had been shaky; he couldn't be a caregiver; he wasn't the sick one anymore; he barely had the opportunity to be my son. Max's complaint about the chemo pump keeping him awake reminded me of how an artist uses the space around an object to give that object definition. Max made sure I saw him by butting up against what was going on around him.

I craved Max. On visits home, I drew him onto my lap and wrapped my arms around him. He didn't tense up as if he were too old for this as he would have a month ago.

One evening, Max took out his cello and started to play. Ten minutes, fifteen, twenty. For forty minutes I leaned into the sweet singing of the strings. He discovered in himself a power to soothe.

When Nadia came home two days later, she walked into her room and didn't know where to look first. Frannie and Max had decorated it with colored lights and angels and streamers and piles of balloons, each with a handwritten get well message. I caught Max's eye; we exchanged a secret wink.

But the times when Max helped the most were when he did what he has always done—sing, dance, entertain. On New Year's Eve, right before Nadia was to begin her third round of chemo, Max dressed himself up in Nadia's angel costume and danced a *pas de deux* with his sister *à la* Isadora Duncan meets Ballet Trocadero. He made us laugh every day with his imitations of celebrities—the strut of Mick Jagger, the melodrama of Leonardo DiCaprio in the final scene of *Titanic,* the brogue of Fat Bastard in *Austin Powers* (a movie Max managed to see without my permission). When a friend sent a magician to the hospital as a treat for Nadia, Max slipped naturally into the role of clown, amplifying each trick with his screams of fear when a wand began to burn or searching under the magician's table or examining his props to unearth the source of an illusion.

After Nadia's surgery to remove the tumor, three months into her treatment, I didn't know what to do about Max. Family and friends made pilgrimages to the hospital, but I held Max off for a few days on the technicality that hospital rules had deemed him too young to visit. The truth was, I was scared about how he would react. The longer I delayed, the more frightened and isolated he became. I certainly didn't help by telling him about the swelling, the tubes, Nadia's constant coughing to clear airways of mucus and blood.

"Do you really want to visit?" I asked him.

"Yes, Mom, I do. I want to see Nadia."

"Okay, then. Daddy will bring you over tomorrow." I couldn't expect him to continue to divert us from sadness with his charm and humor if I were to exclude him now.

The next morning, I meet John and Max at the hospital elevator. In my best conspiratorial tone, I whisper to Max, "Don't slouch. Stand tall. Stick out your chest. Look eleven."

The smirks are still on our faces when we get to Nadia's room. It is crowded with family and friends—Frannie, my father, Donna, my sister, John's sister, Margie—and several nurses. Our timing couldn't have been worse. Nadia is having one of her more violent coughing episodes caused by congestion in her trache. I rush to her side but keep an eye on Max. He comes closer and stands at the end of the bed. At that moment, Nadia sits straight up and with a powerful exhalation propels a clot of blood and phlegm smack into the middle of Max's chest.

I freeze. I expect Max to let out a big "eww" or scream that Nadia is bleeding through a hole in her throat, to make her feel gross and disgusting, to vent his sibling resentment.

What Max does is give a tentative laugh. Relieved,

the rest of us join in, even Nadia manages an exhausted smile. The moment is like turning the cap of a shaken soda bottle just enough to prevent the explosion.

I was proud of Max. Laughing couldn't have been easy.

There was no confusion in Frannie's response to Nadia's diagnosis. Her immediate question when I told her Nadia had cancer was "Is she going to die?" In her voice was the real question: "Am I going to lose my sister?"

I tried to answer Frannie's question with the words the doctors used with me. "There is a 90 percent cure rate," I said. "A little chemo and she'll be fine." I was convinced that I sounded firm and confident, the mother Frannie was used to. But an unspoken conversation was occurring beneath our words; Frannie was hearing my own doubts, which she, through her refusal to meet my eyes, was transmitting back to me.

"Would you like to talk to Dr. Murphy yourself?" I asked.

I was surprised when the normally reticent Frannie said yes. She called Dr. Murphy and asked him if Nadia was going to die. He told her no. He told her why he could say that. He told her to call anytime, which Frannie did until she was satisfied. In my fog I thought, How wonderful that Frannie, at age twelve, could call Dr. Murphy all on her own, that she knew how to find support from other people.

Once Frannie's fears were under control, she devoted herself to Nadia. I had seen Frannie care for a sick sibling before. Just a year earlier, she had insisted on remaining with Max during a six-hour stay in the emergency room. She put together an elaborate game using Max's favorite toy characters from home and made up more activities as the hours wore on—cleaning my pocketbook, sorting coins, playing hand games. The fact that Nadia's treatment would last six months instead of six hours made little difference to Frannie.

Becoming a sister at age three-and-a-half had made Frannie whole. She was confused by Dr. Murphy's "It's okay to be resentful of your brother and sister" lecture. She woke up each morning with only one purpose—to find Max and Nadia. When they saw Frannie, their eyes grew huge with the excitement of a child opening a present wrapped with lots of ribbons and sparkles. I came to depend on Frannie, becoming jumpy and impatient for her to emerge from her bedroom each morning, to come home from school, to finish with a play date, so she could transform two cranky babies into excited, laughing children. Only she had the patience to have endless nonsense conversations with them, to make countless flight passes with the spoon to get them to eat, to maintain the same level of surprise for every game of peek-a-boo.

At the time of Nadia's diagnosis, Frannie was a young adolescent separating from home. It had been a long time since she had embraced her big-sister identity. But it didn't take her very long to become indispensable.

The day Nadia realized her castle project was all wrong, Frannie had been listening to our conversation. "I'll help you, Nadia," she said, as cheerful as if she were inviting Nadia to a party.

"Thank you, Frannie," I whispered as if in prayer. But Frannie was already halfway down the hall, her focus only on Nadia.

I have no idea what happened behind the closed door of Nadia's room, but the two girls emerged an hour later with a petite fortress. Frannie brought it to school for Nadia, where it joined all the others on display; and

Nadia's best friends posed in front of it for a photograph, which Nadia kept by her hospital bed.

After every chemo, Nadia needed a daily shot of granulocyte colony-stimulating factor (GCSF, or G-shot) to encourage the production of white blood cells in order to minimize her chances of contracting a life-threatening infection. Despite the application of Emla, a numbing cream, the shots hurt and, after Nadia's platelet count fell, left black and blue marks all over her thighs since her blood had become slow to clot.

Each evening Nadia and I struggled as she tried to insist she didn't need GCSF. I reminded her that it wouldn't hurt for long. I offered to put ice on the spot first. I let her take as much control as she could. She decided what time she would get the shot. She picked the spot on her leg, applied the Emla, got the Band-Aid ready, counted to three. But each night we had tears and fights and false starts. In frustration I would say, "Nadia, we just have to do this *now*." Afterward, she would refuse any comfort I tried to give her.

Frannie watched us carry on until, one night, she sat next to Nadia on her bed and said, "Nadia, hold my hand."

Nadia took Frannie's hand. She counted to three. When I pushed the syringe's plunger, Frannie let out a scream that was so loud Nadia and I were stunned until we realized the joke and we slid down onto the floor laughing. Frannie continued to offer her hand even after Nadia decided it would be a great addition to the game if she caused Frannie real pain by squeezing her fingers hard enough to stop her circulation.

Chemo made Nadia crave salty food. During Nadia's second round, Frannie decided to plan a Japanese dinner. We ordered food from a local restaurant. The girls dressed in matching, slim-fitting, black velvet dresses. Frannie took Nadia's remaining hair and combed it back and up and fixed it in place with two lacquered sticks. She did the same with her own. She made up first Nadia's face, then her own, with lip gloss and eye shadow. Here was yet another twinship, sister-to-sister.

It didn't take long before I began to depend upon Frannie's humor and patience the way I had years earlier. Even better, Frannie was older now; I could confide in her, I thought. I could confess how stressful caring for Nadia was and how much Frannie's help meant to me. One day, I forgot to pick Frannie up after school for a promised shopping trip. It wasn't my first lapse. "Frannie, I'm sorry," I said. "I'm just not myself these days."

"Stop saying that," Frannie insisted. "You keep saying that and I don't want to hear it."

Frannie's devotion was never for my benefit, only for Nadia's. Over spring break, I allowed Frannie to go on a ski trip with close family friends. It was a trip we had been taking annually for the past seven years, and I didn't want to deprive her of the chance to go, but I was angry at her for abandoning us so easily. The day that she left, Nadia clung to her crying, "Don't go, Frannie, please don't go." Unable to throw herself after Frannie, Nadia's sobs followed her down the elevator.

There were times, though, when I would be jealous of Frannie—when I heard her and Nadia giggling, saw the big hugs Nadia had only for Frannie, witnessed how much better Frannie was at getting Nadia out of a foul mood. I was so busy with all my caretaking chores that I didn't have the chance to think of Japanese dinners or the time to decorate Nadia's room like a Christmas tree. If I had to choose between Bingo or Bake Night in the hospital, which Frannie always attended, and the opportunity to go home and shower, see Max, stare out my bedroom window, I chose the latter even though this meant missing out on what Nadia found most fun.

The week before Nadia's surgery to remove the tumor, there was a lull in my caretaking demands. It was my turn now to do something extra, to make a gesture not born of necessity but of love. Since Nadia would be in the hospital for at least two weeks, I decided to make a collage of photographs of her, her family, and her friends. I thought I could make her room feel more like home, keep her connected to the life she had lived for the past eight years.

I spent hours selecting the pictures. There was one of Nadia in midair executing a flip, one of her as a roly-poly clown in kindergarten, one of her learning Irish step dancing. In one corner I tucked a picture of John, in another of Max dressed in a tuxedo for Margie's wedding, and in another, my favorite, of Nadia and me, our arms around each other's waists, on a beach in Ireland one month before her diagnosis.

Frannie joined me as I pored over the pile of photographs I keep stashed in a drawer. At first, I welcomed her company. Then she declared, "I'm going to make a collage too," and she started her own arrangement on a spare bulletin board she found in my closet.

"No. You can't," I told her. "This is my project. You can't do the same thing as me."

Frannie was stunned. "Why can't I make one too?" she responded.

"Because this is *my* idea," I pouted.

Frannie backed off, but then she had another idea. She created Popsicle stick figures by cutting up magazine pictures. She used a head from one character, arms from another, a torso from a third picture and legs from a fourth. She showed them to me with great pride and, of course, I had to laugh. So did Nadia. My collage would become important to the people who had not known Nadia before the cancer; and when Nadia could speak again, she would refer to it often when she talked to doctors and nurses about her friends and interests. But the collage did not cause her eyes to light up; it did not distract her from her pain. It could not compete with Frannie.

Frannie performs her greatest magic after Nadia's third round of chemo. I suspected that Nadia had developed a tear in her bowel caused by the constipating effects of vincristine. Tests confirmed that my concerns were well founded. To know for sure would require exploratory surgery. The solution would be a colostomy to be reversed only after Nadia's recovery from chemotherapy.

I expect Nadia to be angry, the way she had been a couple of months before, when I saw her resistance to the doctors and procedures as a sign of a spirited fighter. So I am disappointed when this news is met with more resignation than spunk.

I begin by telling Nadia that the doctors will put her under anesthesia, determine if there is a problem, and, if so, perform a colostomy.

"What's that?"

"It's when they bring a piece of bowel to the outside of your body and attach a bag to collect waste."

"Waste?"

"Poop," I answer.

"It's like a little pucker in the skin," Margie explains. "You change the bag every day. It lies flat against your body. It's really easy but pretty noisy when you fart."

While Nadia is still giving an uncertain chuckle, Frannie delivers her punch line: "Yeah, Nadia, now you'll have a Broviac and a Brovi-ass!" Our laughs erupt now without hesitation.

Thankfully, my intuition failed me this time. No Brovi-ass was needed. But if things had been different, would Nadia have seen the humor? Farting Brovi-asses are funny; colostomies are not.

To trust humor, I had to stop the memory of my mother's sobriety from feeling like a reprimand. Was all of our laughter a whitewash, masking the sorrow and tragedy that none of us wanted to feel? For Nadia, the answer was no. It wasn't my sorrowful eyes or Dr. Wexler's compassionate earnestness that helped Nadia accept that she had cancer; it was the girl in the hospital on Nadia's first day of chemo whose eyes shone with merriment as she told the story of her own diagnosis. It wasn't the calm efficiency of nurses trying to clear Nadia's windpipe that soothed her; it was seeing Max grin at the sight of his bloody shirt that enabled Nadia to answer with a smile of her own. And it wasn't me trying to convince Nadia that she needed her G-shots with the logic of a mother convincing her six-year-old that she needed to drink her milk that ended our battles; it was the game that Frannie made out of it.

And what about me? Yes, my children's laughter was a room to which I could retreat. No pain or shadow of death could reach me there. The view from my magical chamber was one of every mother's dream—seeing her children coexist in harmony, expressing only their joy in being alive and with each other. Yet I always knew my vision was illusory. Only for a few moments could I believe that losing your hair wasn't so bad, shots didn't really hurt, a colostomy wouldn't be the worst thing so long as it was only temporary.

11

Hannah's mother gave us some wine from Rabbi Schneerson for Passover. I was taking it out of the backpack last night when Nadia asked to kiss the bottle. I wonder how much faith—her own personal faith—is playing a role in healing her.

—journal entry, April 6, 2001

Whenever Nadia asked me about death, I could never have given her the answer my mother gave me; "You cease to exist; you go in the ground, and that's it." It had been too scary to hear at seventeen, when I had asked her, never mind at five.

Nor could I reassure her with a belief in souls and angels and heaven and rebirth.

When Nadia asked why she got cancer, I could only answer, "Why not?" Nothing about "divine plans" or "everything happens for a reason" or "karma."

Faith. I couldn't give it to her, but because Nadia follows me in my going-through-the-motions approach to Judaism, she believes in belief. One month before her diagnosis, John and I took Frannie, Max, and Nadia to Rosh Hashanah services at the Martha's Vineyard Hebrew Center. I squirmed as we began to recite the *Unitaneh*

Tokef, the prayer in which Jews affirm God's omniscience, how we stand in God's judgment, and how our actions can affect God's ultimate decree on our fate.

> On Rosh Hashanah it is written, on Yom Kippur it is sealed: who shall live and who shall die, who shall perish by fire and who by water; who by sword and who by beast; who by hunger and who by thirst; who by earthquake and who by plague; who by strangling and who by stoning; who shall be secure and who shall be driven; who shall be tranquil and who shall be troubled; who shall be poor and who shall be rich; who shall be humbled and who exalted. But repentance, prayer and charity temper judgment's severe decree.

I looked over at Nadia, saw the top of her bowed head, heard her try to follow the words in her earnest congregant voice. Burning, drowning, murder, starvation, disease. The premonition I have had since Nadia's birth that her life will bring her great pain now breathed its icy air on my neck; I had to stifle the urge to ask her to stop reading, as if nothing bad would happen if she just didn't say those words.

Two months later, my fears have been confirmed. When we register Nadia at MSKCC, I choose to answer the optional question about our religion. This isn't because I seek support from Jewish chaplains or have special dietary requirements. Despite my lack of faith—my fear of the *Unitaneh Tokef*—I love saying, "I am a Jew." The hospital must pass religious affiliation information on to the appropriate support groups because we soon hear from Chai Lifeline, an organization that supports Jewish families with seriously ill children. In the initial packet of material I receive from them—among the list of synagogues, kosher restaurants, phone numbers of counselors and teachers, all of which I will never use—I find a book of prayers and psalms introduced with the words: "One should recognize that all human misfortune or illness is a direct result of man's evil ways. This awareness will lead him to repentance, which is an important factor in alleviating misfortune and illness."

Where is the "lifeline" in that? Did God look down on the eight-year-old in synagogue and decide it was time to get her? An eight-year-old has not yet become a *bat mitzvah* and is not yet responsible for her own observance of the laws of Torah. They are for her parents to assume. If I have failed, why would God do such a terrible thing to a child?

On a Friday night in December, a week after Nadia's second chemo, she is admitted to the hospital with a fever and a white-blood-cell count of zero. One half of the room we are to share is filled with members of a large Hasidic family from all over the world visiting their daughter/sister just diagnosed with leukemia. I see no signs of the panic I was thrown into just two months earlier. No one is whispering about blood counts; no one is placing frantic phone calls or playing Game Boy or making nervous chatter over the sound of a distracting video. There is only peace and prayer. The sole illumination comes from the *Shabbat* candles (in reality, an electric candelabra since no flame is allowed in the hospital). The sights and sounds of *davening* (praying), soft murmurs, and rituals soothe me, return me to the cadences of my grandfather's blessings at the Passover table.

"Good *Shabbos*," I say, trying to soften our entrance, to acknowledge the disruption as we weave around legs and chairs and swaying figures.

"Gut Shabbos," they answer, surprised, pleased, relieved to find themselves sharing the room with one of their own.

Then I feel the pressure of what I have said (or half-said, since my greeting, unlike theirs, is in partial Yiddish). I do not see myself as one of them, even though our Eastern European roots grew in the same soil, all four of my grandparents having arrived here from Poland, Russia, or Lithuania.

My maternal grandfather was supposed to be a rabbi but returned to his *shtetl* from a distant Yeshiva, too homesick to continue his studies. There are no pictures of him with the *payis* he must have worn (the result of not shaving the hair at the temples to distinguish Jews in ancient times from the Egyptians who worshiped many gods) or of his youthful beard; but even though my grandfather turned his back on what was to have been his vocation—allowed himself to become Americanized and secularized to a degree these Hasidim would have disapproved of—he would have had more in common with them than he did with me.

My Judaism got its start in 1950s suburban America, where belief could only skulk in the shadow of assimilation. My mother did send me and my sister to religious school—a congregation so Reform that when my grandfather came with us to High Holy Day services he would mutter, "More pages he's skipping?" Never mind that nearly all the prayers in our book were truncated, English-language renditions of what my grandfather knew. We did eat blintzes and borscht at my grandparents', where we gathered every Saturday, and both my maternal and paternal grandmothers spoke to me in Yiddish as if I could understand them as well as their own children.

But the home of my suburban nuclear family was wiped clean of such references. The Yiddish that I knew my parents could have spoken to me died. Belief was never allowed to compete with my mother's pragmatism or the logic and orderly thinking of my father, who spent his days in a research lab testing hypotheses against reality.

When I reached twelve, the age a girl would automatically become a *bat mitzvah* under Jewish law whether or not she underwent any form of ritual, I had no ceremony, but I wanted more. I began to look for the history behind my long nose, my olive complexion, my love of minor melodies. I became fascinated with the chants my immigrant grandfather sang on holidays, the stories of Shalom Aleichem, the Yiddish phrases I asked my mother to teach me.

Passover *seder* one year coincided with *Shabbat,* so I decided to light the candles the way I saw the women do it in *Fiddler on the Roof.* I draped a shawl over my head, lit the candles, and covered my eyes while I recited the blessing. When I finished, my grandfather said, "So religious," his intonation unclear as to whether this was a statement or a question, whether he approved or was amused. Lacking the confidence of a true believer, I felt like an impostor. Even though my grandfather could no longer be called observant and did little to counteract the Americanization of his children, my attempt at inserting a ritual from his past made the gap between us seem wider than ever. I burned with embarrassment far longer than the candles' flame.

In the Judaism that I was being taught, belief seemed less important than knowledge, culture, identification, and pride in being Jewish. It should have been no surprise to me that, when I took my hands away from my eyes, nothing about faith was illuminated.

Other facts about adolescent life in the suburbs were

made clear, however. For example, the blond, blue-eyed guy I had a crush on, who teased me about the dark hair on my arms, was as unattainable as a seat at the cool-kids' lunch table. This, more than any sense of mission, led me to my temple youth group.

One would have thought I had found religion at last, given the time I spent at synagogue. But what I discovered there were the songs and dances of my people, not the ones in Eastern Europe but the ones that reached back through the history of *Yisrael— debkas* and *horas* and Yemenite line dances; ancient prayers that I could finally feel in my bones because they spoke to me through music; wordless *nigguns* (melodies) that I could harmonize with on my flute. I went to youth conclaves, dance camp, and Israel, where I worked and sang and danced and wrote a prayer to tuck into a crevice of the Western Wall in Jerusalem. My Judaism gave me friends, confidence, joy, spirit, a place to belong—not faith, not a single answer to the question about why kids get cancer or what happens when you die.

I was certain that my life as a cultural Jew would continue in college, certain that I would date only Jews, convinced that I wasn't being stupid by going to a university in New York that was all wrong for me just because the boyfriend I had met in Israel lived in Brooklyn. By the time I got to college a year later Peter was bored with me. In less than a month, I met John, an Irish Catholic. Although John professed a more definitive faith in God than I did, we both had a need for ritual and a belief system. We didn't share dogma but held common values. Our cultures were different; but for both of us, our ethnic heritage was inseparable from religion. John would play the spoons to Irish music, and I would tell him about getting my teaching certificate in Israeli folk dance.

John also had two qualities I had associated strongly with Jews. First, he came from a family of immigrants. Second, I recognized his work ethic and commitment to education as similar to my father's. Indeed, John would duplicate and surpass my father's success at moving out of the poverty and beyond the rudimentary education of his parents.

What ultimately drew me to John was the fact that, from our first meeting, he saw me as exotic. I had never before been adored for what I saw as my foreignness. For Chanukah that first year of our relationship, John gave me a necklace—a Star of David strung on a delicate gold chain with a tiny pearl on each side.

"What did he give you that for?" my mother demanded when I showed it to her. You would have thought that John was the Jew and I some heretic he was trying to convert.

"Why shouldn't he? He knows what being Jewish means to me," I answered.

But when I put on that necklace, I stopped growing as a Jew. I didn't understand that a Catholic bearing gold stars is not the same as someone who shared my religion. John would never be my partner to dance *Dodi Li* (My Beloved Is Mine). Singing *Hatikva,* Israel's national anthem, would not conjure in him memories of the sights, sounds, and smells of Jerusalem. He could not help me when I found myself forgetting the meaning of the few Yiddish words I had learned. I ate bread on Passover, when no form of leavening is allowed, and anything I wanted on the fast day of Yom Kippur. I restocked my musical repertoire with Irish reels, ballads, and folk songs.

John, for his part, neglected Catholicism. For our first Christmas together, I bought a tiny tree and decorated it, thinking my support of John's religion would make him happy. But echoing my mother, all he said was "What did you do that for?" Work had become John's new religion; a Christmas tree had no meaning for him.

Four years after our wedding, performed by a Unitarian minister whose authority came not from God but from the state of Massachusetts, I started work at the 92nd Street Young Men's and Young Women's Hebrew Association. By this time, I was a Jew in maiden name only, interested not in the Y's Jewish roots, programming, or traditions but in its secular performing arts program.

Again, by default, because John's work absorbed all his time, a Jewish institution became the center of my life the way my synagogue had in high school. I did not return to my songs and dances but immersed myself in Jewish organizational life, raising money for outreach programs or activities for the adult Jewish mentally retarded. I became an intellectual Jew, arguing with my colleagues about whether the health club could remain competitive and still close on *Shabbat;* whether the music of Wagner—a known anti-Semite—should be banned in our concert hall; whether we should accept funds from German companies, particularly those that made money by supporting the Nazi war effort. Being closed not just on Rosh Hashanah and Yom Kippur but also on Sukkot, Shmeni Atzeret, Simcha Torah, and Shavuot meant I had to think about these holidays and, at a minimum, be able to tell John what they celebrated.

Going to my enclave every day, I thought I had found the perfect way to be a Jew without challenging my personal commitment or the status quo at home. But I still had not become a faithful Jew.

The one purely religious touch point that I took advantage of was the opportunity to attend the Y's High Holy Day services. The rabbi had a tradition on the first night of Rosh Hashanah of calling all the children to the front of the sanctuary to say *kiddush* over the wine and to receive a blessing. For the four years I tried to get pregnant with Frannie, the opportunity to bring my baby up with the other families seemed the most important goal I could have.

John and I never discussed what religion our children would be. I was too afraid to confront the issue; I couldn't imagine raising non-Jewish children any more than I could accept that my first child wouldn't be a girl whom I could name after my mother. It wasn't until I was pregnant with Frannie that my brother-in-law asked us if she would be Jewish or Catholic. "Jewish, of course," John answered. At the time, I didn't think this reflected any profound contemplation on John's part, no careful balancing of what our respective religions had to offer, no sentimental remembrance of life as an altar boy. I assumed, for John, this was just an old-fashioned belief that mothers do most of the child rearing and that it would make no sense for a Jew to raise a child Catholic. While all this was true, John was also at the beginning of his own search for spiritual grounding, which would begin with Jewish studies and continue through his immersion in yogic disciplines.

When Frannie was ten weeks old, I put aside the t-shirts and onesies that had been her wardrobe until then, clothed her in a pink dress with a matching headband, and set off for the Y. She fussed as we sat waiting for the Rosh Hashanah service to begin, but I felt as if we glowed. When the rabbi called all the children forward, the anticipation of whatever miracle I thought was going to happen propelled me from my chair and down the aisle with Frannie in my arms.

I don't remember if John was with Frannie and me that

evening. He would join me now and again for the rare service I attended, in lighting the Chanukah candles or going to a lecture on Jewish thought or law at the Y. He was particularly taken with a Jewish teaching which says that one of the questions God asks when you die is how you conducted yourself in business. While I was grateful for John's growing interest in Judaism, I didn't mind if he chose not to attend services. With him, I felt I had to demonstrate that I was a Jew, that I knew what was going on, what all the prayers meant, at what point to turn the page in the Hebrew text.

I was more interested in absorbing the music of the cantor, the chant of the prayers, the transformation of the rabbi. The rabbi was my colleague and friend at the Y; I raised money for his programs. Many of the Y's employees were in the union; my and the rabbi's status as non-union employees was being challenged. At one negotiating session, my friend had leaned back so far in his chair that he fell over, arms and legs flailing, face red with laughter. Now, through his faith and passion, he was before me as a man of wisdom and stature.

As soon as the rabbi began the blessing over the wine, Frannie started to cry; by the time he had finished, she had thrown up. Clearly, there would be no bolt of faith but a slow turning toward reclaiming my identity as Jew.

By the next year, the rabbi had moved away and his successor had brought his own traditions from which I found new meaning. This was the rabbi who said, "If you don't have belief, try action—just one gesture—and see where it takes you." My first step was to stop eating pork. Since I sent my children to nursery school at the Y, where *Shabbat* was celebrated every Friday, we began to light candles and say blessings at home. I began fasting on Yom Kippur and eating no leavening on Passover.

After nursery school, I launched Frannie, Max, and Nadia on their formal training; but rather than make a commitment to a synagogue, I found a teacher who came to our home. I took little baby steps but still found no faith. It was easier for me to become a vegetarian than to grapple with the rationale behind keeping kosher and its rules not to mix meat and dairy or eat only fish with scales.

The rituals, though, did restore my sense of pride. Since Frannie began her religious education at age seven, I had been fantasizing about her *bat mitzvah* the way some women daydream about their perfect wedding. I knew it would be on the Vineyard. I knew there would be music. I knew that for a few hours it would be *my* heritage and *my* culture that we would be celebrating. But what I loved imagining most was the point in the service when I would get to speak to Frannie directly, to tell her in front of the world how much I love her. I would tell her how important her laughter was, how she drew me out of my solitude. I would talk about the sea, how through her love of the ocean she had returned to me a piece of my mother—her namesake.

I never imagined that planning for this joyous event celebrating Frannie's emerging adulthood would coincide with Nadia's cancer treatment. Now it had become intertwined with the sounds of IV pumps, kids crying, doctors being paged, distraught families murmuring in hallways. Invitation lists, to-do lists, lists of phone numbers and menus filled the inside covers and lined the edges of the pages of the knitting instructions and crossword puzzle books that provided a rare release for me while at Nadia's bedside. But my fantasy, if not my faith, remained intact.

I tell the woman at MSKCC who registers Nadia, "I am a Jew," but after I exchange *Shabbat* greetings with our roommates, the Barovs, I wonder how I can possibly pretend to be a Jew like these Hasidim. I withdraw behind our curtained half of the room before they can discover I am a fraud. I try my best to be respectful, but Nadia doesn't understand why I hesitate to turn on a light, why I am not rushing around trying to secure a television, why I shush John when he mentions the car downstairs waiting to take him home—all actions that violate *Shabbat* rules about work and creation. I want to watch, to listen, to bask in their faith.

But this family wants us to come fully into their world. The mother, Frieda, is not as focused on me as she is on Nadia. Right away, Nadia is eager to show off her learning, singing the Hebrew alphabet, chanting the blessing over the Sabbath candles, discussing Frannie's upcoming *bat mitzvah*. I don't have the heart to tell her how pale her knowledge is in comparison to Frieda's and her family's. Only I seem to care. Only I feel the magnitude of my failure to teach my children "real" Judaism. Only I recognize the jealous flicker in my soul when I realize how ready Nadia is to fall into Judaism's embrace.

The central prayer of Judaism is the *Shema,* which proclaims the singleness of God. Every Jew is supposed to recite it after waking up in the morning and before going to bed at night. On the second night of this hospital stay, Frieda pokes her head around the curtain. "Nadia, do you know the *Shema*?" she asks.

"Yes."

"Will you recite it with me before you go to bed?"

Nadia looks at me for encouragement. After I nod, Frieda says, "Cover your eyes." Nadia does, and together they recite, "*Shema Yisrael Adonai Eloheynu, Adonai Echad*. Hear O Israel, the Lord our God, the Lord is one."

When Nadia removes her hands from her eyes, I bow my head, not in prayer but so she won't see my tears. Could it be possible for a single prayer to so easily transform, or is it my own desperate hope that there is a divine plan and Frieda can show us the way that arouses such emotion? Perhaps it is the desire not only for faith but for a maternal figure that causes me to be so open to this stranger in our lives.

I decide not to care, to play along, to encourage Nadia's growing connection to the daughter, Hannah, a gentle eighteen-year-old who welcomes Nadia's presence and beams like a proud older sister whenever Nadia displays her knowledge. Hannah and Frieda soon become a constant presence in our lives. I cease to be surprised that every time we are admitted, so is Hannah. We meet as roommates or in urgent care. "Ah, it's you," we say.

Nadia embraces this relationship, sending me and John to buy Glatt Kosher cookies as a gift, dropping coins into Frieda's *tzedakah* (loosely translated as charity) box; covering her eyes during Sabbath candle lighting; treasuring the miniature bottle of Passover wine supposed to have come from the founder of the Lubavitch movement, Rabbi Schneerson himself; caressing Frieda's prayer book on the way down to her exploratory surgery; making herself more comfortable than I ever became at the hastily put together *seder* our new friends will host in the hospital playroom. I am with Nadia, but Frieda guides her.

As the surgery to remove Nadia's tumor approaches, however, I begin to resent Frieda and what I now see as her intrusions. She recites prayers for Nadia so God can answer them. She seems so certain that this is as important in healing as the chemo and the surgery. Without faith, I cannot share her certainty; Judaism cannot give me the strength I need for Nadia.

For the four days Nadia is in the pediatric observation unit (POU) following surgery, I get a reprieve. I see Frieda down the hall, know Hannah has been admitted for fever, while I am protected by the doors that separate the POU from the rest of the pediatric floor. When it is time for Nadia to be moved to a regular room, I learn that Hannah is still in the hospital and that she has no roommate. I'm sure we are destined to be together yet again, but now I want a stranger, someone who isn't constantly poking her head around our drawn curtain to do something Jewish.

"Do you think we can room with someone different this time?" I ask a hospital staff member I have come to know. I pretend it's not a big deal one way or the other; I don't want to cause trouble. "I don't have anything against them; I'm just not in the mood for being with anyone I know right now."

"Is all that proselytizing getting to you?" she answers. "They're on a mission, you know."

At first, I am defensive. There has to be more behind Frieda's attention than the fact that Nadia is just a Jew in the bed next to Hannah—a Jew who, according to the Lubavitch movement, must join all other Jews in strict observance of all Jewish law and the commandments as set forth in the Torah if we are ever to arrive at the Messianic age. One of those commandments is against committing *lashon hara,* gossiping or spreading slander. Now I regret having said anything; by opening the door to criticism of the Barovs, I have tainted our relationship.

But I've done the right thing, I tell myself. We even gain an extra night in our large and private room in the POU since no one else needs it. Then I learn that Hannah is in isolation because she has a virus that could threaten her life, and I feel the full burden of my sin of talking behind the Barovs' backs.

We visit Hannah, who is draped in yellow sterile covering. Nadia brings her a teddy bear with a Star of David on it. Frieda is happy to have company. "This is ridiculous," she says, pointing to her mask and gown. "Every time I go in or out, I have to put this on. Why do I have to do that, to be in here?"

Blood counts, fevers, sterile fields—it is all confusing for Frieda. The month before, Hannah had an emergency and had to be admitted on a Friday night. Frieda argued with the doctor, "Can't it wait until after *Shabbos?*" she begged.

"No, she must come in now," he insisted.

Frieda listened because the doctor himself is Orthodox, but she told me, "To ride in a car on a Friday night? I've never done such a thing. I thought I would be sick."

Frieda questioned the validity of science the way I questioned the existence of God. I tried to interpret the medical community for her while she tried to comfort me with belief. Who cared if Nadia and I were part of her mission? Isn't passion for my faith what I have been trying to create since I was a teenager?

Nadia ends up being moved to a room that is hers alone for now. It is Friday evening. Frannie is with us. I am glad when Frieda finds us to make sure we have our candelabra but don't regret when she leaves to join Hannah. Together, we, the three women in our family, turn the light bulbs and say the *B'racha,* the blessing thanking God for light. Nadia sleeps. Frannie and I sit in the quiet, talking softly in the warm shadows, eating our dinner, just being. I am at rest, can almost see the Sabbath queen. I can see how, if this moment were extended long enough, faith could enter. But this is not the place for such an experiment. The evening's visitors are soon to arrive. John is bringing Max; he and Nadia have been waiting all day for the next episode of *Survivor*. The lights go on; the TV reawakens; the voices get loud. The rustle of the Sabbath queen's robes becomes fainter, and I wonder if I ever felt her presence at all. My moment of peace becomes no more than a mini-vacation offering rest, not religion and revelation.

Three months later, in the pre-dawn hours before the first Passover *seder*, Nadia develops a fever. We enter urgent care at sunrise. "Ah, it's you," we say to Hannah and her family. Hannah is already in the bed next to the one they have assigned to Nadia.

"Our table was all set," the son says. "It looked so beautiful."

"What did you expect? I want to say. Cancer grows over everything. What does it care about *seder*? What is God caring about? Is it faith in medicine or faith in prayer that will cure our children?

Or maybe what's important is what God has faith in. The God of the *Unitaneh Tokef* is not asking us to beg for mercy: Don't kill me; don't stone me; don't make me suffer. This God wants us to believe in ourselves.

Halfway through treatment, a nurse wants to reassure Nadia that cancer is not a punishment for being bad. This idea had never occurred to Nadia, despite her diligent reading of the *Unitaneh Tokef*. "I think God gave me cancer because he knew I was strong," she will tell me when her treatment is over.

Nadia was strong—rebirthing herself over and over—generating blood cells, platelets, and hair follicles after every chemo at a pace that awed the doctors. I never thanked God for healing my daughter, just as I never prayed to God to cure her. But I was grateful for the doctors, for chemotherapy, for Nadia's strength and my own, all of which might never have existed if humanity had never felt called upon to examine, judge, and reform itself. Perhaps it is through this prayer—the one that seems the most punishing—that I will someday find faith.

II

Rebirth

She's been here before, so wise, so knowing, working so hard to become what she's already been. What is the gift I am to bring her?

She's a star, they all say, and I hear the static of her burning, biting my tongue since the day she was born. "Don't burn so bright, I do not warn," fearful she will be gone too soon.

—summer 1994

12

The doctors are very pleased with the operation, but to a medical novice like me, Nadia seems far removed from the girl she was this morning. If I look beyond all that was done to her, though, I can still see my beautiful baby.

—journal entry, January 31, 2001

Seven-year-old Nadia was the perfect age to be the flower girl at Margie's wedding in the summer of 1999. I didn't see her fully adorned until she walked down the aisle, but it wasn't hard for me to imagine what my dress-up queen would look like. She was competition for the bride, all in white, with full skirt and a big bow at her back, a sheer touch at the neck and shoulders, in white slippers with delicate pearl beading. She took her job seriously, with measured steps; her eyes, radiating pride and innocence, focused on her task, holding her basket as if it contained the actual wedding vows.

After the ceremony, Nadia did what I imagine all flower girls do. She tossed away her slippers and joined the other kids on the lawn in games of tag, hide-and-seek, and that age-old boys-chase-the-girls romp. Grass stains, a ripped lining, her dirty face—none of this could mar the picture of the perfect flower girl. I didn't recognize the intensity with which I was watching Nadia until my premonition, that something terrible would befall her, stirred, as it often does when I become engrossed in Nadia's force: I lost sight of the line separating us and had to turn my eyes away.

Halloween, eighteen months later. From flower girl to angel. White and silver—wings, wand, and wispy gown. Nadia posed and pirouetted joyously before me while I sneaked peeks at her face. I had always associated its perfection with vulnerability. Just one year earlier, she had been dressed as an M&M when she was bitten in the face by a dog. Now I searched for the barely visible scars. I had hoped that these tiny imperfections would give her a less defenseless beauty. If she were marred, somehow, I was sure she would be safe, that there would be no reason for her to be hurt anymore. But that October 31st was only a tease.

The incision to remove the tumor in her left jaw, the trick that my angel brought home with her treats on the following Halloween, would begin at Nadia's lower lip, proceed down, under the center of her chin, then across her throat to her ear. The doctors would remove however much bone they needed and reconstruct a new mandible from the fibula they would remove from Nadia's leg. Then her mouth would be wired shut. A tracheostomy would keep her airways open as her head swelled up like a balloon. A feeding tube would be snaked through her nose down to her stomach. Drains would extend from her neck and leg, a peripheral IV in her hand would supplement the central line implanted in her chest. She would be catheterized. The release the hospital required us to sign told us everything that could go wrong during the ten-hour operation—from nerve damage to death.

The decision to choose surgery over radiation had been made two weeks earlier and would depend on how the tumor responded to the first three rounds of chemo. Following the initial round, the nurse practitioner looked at Nadia's jaw and declared with great cheer, "Look! It's already started to shrink."

No similar declaration followed the next two cycles. I thought maybe I had just become accustomed to Nadia's face. I no longer had perspective or an accurate memory of how large the tumor had looked at the start. Any lump would have been too big. But Nadia's presurgical scans confirmed that there had been little additional reduction in the size of the tumor. Now it was time to choose between surgery and radiation.

Dr. Wexler called John and me to a meeting with Dr. Kraus, the head and neck surgeon; a radiologist; a general pediatric surgeon; a nurse practitioner; and, at the suggestion of Dr. Wexler, who said we should have a less emotionally invested person with us, my sister-in-law Maureen. Absent was Dr. Cordeiro, the reconstructive surgeon who would remove Nadia's fibula, attach it to Nadia's remaining jawbone, and connect the minuscule veins and arteries to ensure that this bone would throb with life. We gathered in an exam room in the Pediatric Day Hospital (PDH). The radiologist, a young woman only days away from maternity leave, sat casually on the examination table. The rest of us were clustered toe to toe in a haphazard circle of chairs. The doctors sat with their bodies forward, seeking eye contact. I slumped, like a truant called to the principal's office, and examined pictures of smiling patients pinned up on the bulletin board. In my memory, the room was dim, but there would have been no reason for the lights to be low.

Months earlier, we had felt fortunate to learn that Ewing's responded well to radiation, that we had an additional treatment option. For some hospitals, it is the treatment of choice but not at Memorial and not for Nadia.

Dr. Wexler began. "Nadia's scans have shown us that the size of her tumor has shrunk by only 30 percent."

I tried to dismiss the echoing of the word "only" like a schizophrenic desperate to banish the voices from his head. "What does that mean?" I asked, expecting grim news about a revised prognosis.

"It's about what I expected," he continued. "Nadia's tumor is deep within her bone. With less blood circulating there, it's harder for the chemo to reach it. It tells us that there is little reason to think radiation would be any more effective."

I had entertained fantasies about radiation. I had put aside its side effects—burns, fatigue, pain, and, most importantly, the fact that jaw reconstruction would not be a fallback option if the cancer returned once the bone had been irradiated. I thought instead that radiation wouldn't require tracheostomies and feeding tubes and removing leg bones and reconstruction or even a hospital stay. But all three surgeons who had had a hand in Nadia's recovery had children themselves and they all agreed: "If it was my child, I'd choose surgery."

The radiologist nodded her assent. At this point, her unborn baby seemed more real than my Nadia, whose absence filled the room. She had no chance to defend herself against this horrible betrayal we were plotting against her.

John's questions went in a different direction from mine. "Will she be disfigured?" he asked.

We had already talked about this at home. Despite years of living with John's fastidiousness, his obsession with hair, his impatience with anything that marred his appearance or the perfection of his home, I couldn't believe he was now worried about something as superficial as looks. When my mother was diagnosed with breast cancer and word spread through our neighborhood, she received a call from a woman who lived a few houses away who had had a mastectomy several years earlier. "Don't worry," she said. "You'll still look good in a sweater."

"Foolish woman," my mother said. "Does she think that's what I care about?"

Was John being foolish? I certainly thought so at the time.

Dr. Kraus answered by saying, "A lot will depend on how big the tumor is. If we have to remove soft tissue, that could affect the shape of Nadia's face, but we can be pretty sure bone growth will be the same on both sides of her face. Dr. Cordeiro does a beautiful job."

"You wouldn't hold back from doing what you need to do, would you?" I asked, making it clear that I, at least, knew what was important.

"No, we'll do everything we have to do," Dr. Kraus answered.

I had forgotten that my mother did want to wear sweaters again.

I prepared Nadia as best as I could. In our meeting, I had asked Dr. Kraus what most kids worried about. He said it was the inability to speak after surgery. So I took Nadia on a shopping spree at the local stationery store, buying pens, pencils, and papers in different colors and sizes so she could still "talk" to us.

Nadia, however, seemed consumed with fear that she would wake up in the middle of surgery. "But how can you promise?" she cried. Just as her fear of being buried alone prompted me to imagine that very thing, so her hysteria made it easy for me to picture her waking up on the operating table. The images I conjured were filled with blood and scalpels and primal howls of pain. Only when I tried to imagine Nadia's half-operated upon face did I force myself to stop. I needed help to ease her anxieties.

A few weeks prior to the surgery, I took Nadia to see a therapist, a middle-aged woman who specialized in these kinds of crisis moments in children's lives.

I don't remember the exact conversation. The therapist's voice was gentle but impersonal as she introduced herself to Nadia. "Why don't you tell me why you're here," she began. Or maybe she said, "Your mother tells me you're having an operation," or "I understand you've been in the hospital." Or maybe she just said, "How are you, Nadia?"

What I do remember is that Nadia was silent. Not just silent but closed, her fears hidden behind her barricade of defenses. It was up to me to read the story written in Nadia's body language to the therapist. She went into some of the science behind anesthesia, how and why it works, to draw a difference between sleep and being under. After this session, Nadia didn't speak of her fear of waking up again, either because she felt more reassured or because she was worried I would take her back to the therapist for another session.

Nadia and I talked about how morphine, which she had already received on several occasions, would help to ease her pain, although her ability to imagine that pain was limited, just as it is for any of us when we are feeling well. She knew John and I would be there when she woke.

John, Nadia, and I arrive at the hospital at 6 A.M. on the morning of January 31, 2001. The only sign of the three rounds of chemotherapy Nadia has received is her bald head. She has had only two other operations; but as she is putting on her surgical gown, she asks the nurse, "Why do I always go into the operating room in one gown but come out in another?"

"The first one gets messy sometimes" is the tactful response.

Nadia has chosen Snowball, a white puff of a stuffed animal, to be her comfort while getting ready. Pinned to its ears are notes from Frannie and Max and a picture of me in a little silver frame. I wear a matching pin with a picture of her. The pins are a gift from a friend. We play catch with Snowball—John, Nadia, and I—until the anesthesiologist comes to give her some medicine to relax her before we have to separate. Only Snowball is allowed to cross the threshold into the operating room; but it, too, will be taken from Nadia's side when she can no longer comprehend how alone she truly is.

It never occurs to me to say goodbye to Nadia's face—to its symmetry, its full smile, its complete set of teeth. How unusual for me, who looked with melancholy at the sight of my children's first tooth, knowing I would never see that gummy grin again; whose tears moistened the tops of their heads when I knew I was nursing them for the last time; and who still sits at the foot of their beds as they sleep because only then can I see in their relaxed faces glimpses of their babyhood.

At 8 A.M., Nadia enters her man-made sleep in the operating room, one floor above me. I leave hosting duties to John (although I have no idea if he was any more sociable than I was) as Frannie, Max, family, friends, and nurses all swirl around us. The best kind of company, they know to talk to each other, that all I need is their physical presence, not their conversation. I exist only for Nadia, as her spiritual respirator. Twelve hours later, at around 8 P.M., John and I are called to the recovery room.

When Frannie, Max, and Nadia were born, it was hours after their birth before I had an opportunity to study them closely. I was unable to see Frannie until I was transferred to my room which took most of the day. After Max and Nadia, I was unconscious from medication that was keeping me from hemorrhaging. Now, in the MSKCC recovery room, I have too much time to look at Nadia. It is absurd that my baby is here under the harsh lights, amid the moans and groans of the adults around us, the beeps and whooshes and gurgles of the machines keeping her alive. I fix my eyes on my daughter, who is wrapped in the sterile whiteness of hospital blankets. She is projecting power and purity, letting me know she will live.

Nadia sleeps as I watch. My eyes, as if adjusting to a dark room after being in the bright sun, react slowly. First, I find all the parts that are unchanged—the untouched side of her face, her same-as-before fingers, her right foot. In time, I notice the tape over her eyes; then the trache, the respirator, the feeding tube come into view. Only now do I look at the incision drawn across Nadia's throat and dare myself to look at the receptacles filling with blood and fluid. I circle my daughter carefully so as not to trip over the IV lines hooked up to the Broviac and the second IV in her arm.

They will not let me talk to her yet. It is too soon for her to wake. My voice would cause her eyes to flicker and start breathing tears. But I know the angel is still there.

13

She did it. She got out of bed in about two seconds flat. Not only that, she did it on her own. I don't know where she gets it from, but she's coming back to me.

—journal entry, February 5, 2001

The morning after her surgery, Nadia is still recognizable, her delicate features not yet swallowed by angry, engorged tissue. Small, swaddled, and bald; eyes shut, multiple umbilical cords connecting her to oxygen, fluid, and drugs, ridding her of waste, blood and toxins—Nadia is to be reborn. Her challenge is to grow from zero to nine in two weeks. She is not so far out of the first womb that she doesn't remember how.

Seeing …

For her second birth, she has a short trip through the canal separating unconsciousness from awareness. There is only one sign; her eyes open.

Eyes do not tear during surgery because anesthesia paralyzes the body. If the eyes weep, the patient is feeling too much and must be sent deeper. The lids are taped shut; a greasy ointment prevents corneal abrasions.

When Nadia's eyes open, they are not infant eyes. These eyes see; and when they see me, they weep. I have no numbing medicine to combat her tears. I have no power to help at all.

"You don't have to do anything but be there," my friend Maureen, a pediatric anesthesiologist, tells me. "Nadia will always remember that you were there for her." But I am not interested in memories; the present leaves no room for reflection.

Nadia's eyes move beyond me to the nurses who talk to her in nonstop cheery chatter, to the doctors who have come to alleviate pain, to others who cause it. I struggle to interpret what she might be feeling. I don't know where I can touch her because I don't know where it hurts. I can't slap away the hand of the doctor, a clumsy subordinate member of the surgical team, who presses Nadia's jaw too firmly with the probe that checks for a pulse in her newly connected bone. I can't turn the lights low or soothe her with my mother's milk. This is not my labor. This is not my delivery.

For almost two weeks, Nadia's eyes will be my only clue to her moods. With her entire face swollen, her jaw wired shut, her veins infused with morphine, her face expresses nothing. I will have to become a much better reader of irises.

Seeing ... breathing ...

Tracheostomies allow a person to breathe through a hole in her throat. I am petrified of that aperture. How can I care for a child who doesn't breathe the way I do?

Nadia is kept on a ventilator for twenty-four hours. Weaning can be difficult. Fortunately, the instinct that helps babies make the transition from gills to lungs when they are first born takes over again when Nadia must breathe on her own. No slap on the bottom is required.

Instinct, however, also works against her. When she becomes aware enough to realize that air is not entering through her nose or mouth, her eyes widen and her chest pumps faster.

"What is it, Nadia?" I ask.

Her hand reaches for her throat, points at her nose and mouth. She can't recognize that she is breathing.

"Nadia, it's okay. Remember? We told you about the trache. You're breathing."

She tries to thrash her immobilized head, *No.*

"Yes, I can see the monitor. You have 100 percent of the oxygen you need. You have more than enough."

She won't or can't believe me. Her eyes pull me into her fear.

"Nadia, look at me," I command, daring her to disobey me. Softer now: "Let's breathe together." I force myself to take slow, steady breaths. Her eyes relax and close.

But that night, Nadia doesn't get enough oxygen. While she sleeps, her breaths grow more and more shallow, setting off alarms and mobilizing nurses who rouse her to get her to inhale more deeply. Nadia becomes agitated, furious at the interruptions to her sleep. I station myself beside her head. I keep a constant eye on the monitor. As her saturation level dips below 92 percent I whisper, "Breathe, my love, breathe."

A nurse suggests, "Perhaps she's always had sleep apnea."

"She's never shown signs of it before," I respond.

"How would you have known?" she tosses back.

Why is she raising this concern now? Do I need any

more reason to hover over Nadia's bed for the rest of her childhood?

The time between alarms lengthens. Nadia breathes but doesn't wake. After a few hours, I can leave her side.

Breathe, my love, breathe. Twelve years of motherhood—of responding to nightmares, hurts, separation anxiety, monsters in the closet—and I finally find my mantra.

Traches may keep you from suffocating, but they also bypass many of the body's own defenses against choking. Nadia is unable to clear her throat or cough effectively. Phlegm and postsurgical blood and mucus have to be cleared routinely.

The first time her chest starts to spasm because of congestion, a sympathetic nurse shows her a suction tube that looks just like one you might see in a dentist's office. "I want you to let me know when you are ready to cough. I can help you with this tube."

Nadia nods. As the nurse inserts the piping into her windpipe, Nadia's back lifts off the bed. Gurgles and strangled breaths rise from her chest. Suction, rest. Suction, rest. Nadia's brown eyes turn on me, blaze with the hot red of anger and betrayal, pain and exhaustion. She pushes the nurse's hand away.

It is not hard to read her disgust and disappointment at my fumblings to help. The thought that she knows that I, alone, can't keep her alive right now sends chills through my soul. I remember what it's like to have a mother who can't take care of you. It made me meek and wary, the way I feel now. I prefer Nadia's anger, her knowledge that none of this is her fault. It will free her to fight.

The nurse places a mask, like the ones I used for Max during his asthma attacks, over the trache. "Nadia, this is just salt water, like the ocean," she tells her. "It will keep your windpipe moist and make it easier for you to cough."

"It's a little bit of Martha's Vineyard," I say, expecting Nadia to find some semblance of the island we love here at MSKCC.

After a few more rounds of suctioning, Nadia rebels so violently that the nurse shows us another method for clearing her windpipe and lungs. At the count of three, I drip saline into her trache while she takes a deep breath. No longer an embryo able to breathe water, she coughs, deep hacks that propel bloody phlegm to the plastic edge of her trache, which I mop up with a gauze pad. As much as I know Nadia hates suctioning, I think that what she likes most about the saline method is that I can replace the nurse. Once she figures this out, she lets no one else help.

Although less painful, the saline system is more exhausting.

"Don't you want a suction, Nadia? Just to get up the last bit?" I ask, thinking I can't tolerate seeing this struggle anymore—the thick liquid bubbling almost to the surface, just out of my reach, and then receding down that unnatural orifice.

She slaps at the sheets searching for her pen and paper. *Sea*, she writes.

"Sea?"

Nadia digs for her last bit of energy to make me understand. She points to her trache and gropes the pillow.

Finally, I get it. Sea—the ocean mist, her trip to the beach. I place it over the trache. For an hour, she has peace.

Seeing … breathing … eating

The stomach does not immediately awaken after a lengthy time under anesthesia. Sixty hours after the operation, Nadia still has not eaten. A nurse's stethoscope registers that her tummy is rumbling and ready for food. So, the feeding tube stitched into Nadia's nose is hooked up to a pump, and formula begins to snake its way down the narrow hose directly into her stomach. I hear no gurgle deep within Nadia's belly, no lustily drunk milk, only the whirr of the mechanism doling out the food.

I also have no worries now about putting the tomato sauce on the pasta instead of on the side, about letting the peas touch the chicken, about hearing her groan, "We already had hamburger for lunch." But without the aroma, the lip smacking, the colors, the crunching, the conversation, I can hardly equate being filled up with food like a gas tank with what I call *eating.*

The pump pours food into Nadia all day. The constant work of ingesting, digesting, and eliminating makes Nadia's stomach ache and churn. The volume of formula is equal to what a grown man would receive, not a sixty-five-pound eight-year-old girl. I suspect the doctors are trying to fatten her up. This isn't working, though. Now that I have become less reticent about speaking up, I question the amount of food she is being given and ask that they give her less. Her discomfort eases, but real dining is still a long way off.

After a week, the bands that have kept Nadia's mouth forced shut are removed. Her jaws are stiff and can open only wide enough to fit a straw, through which she can now take clear liquids. The few ounces she swallows per day are not enough to sustain her. The feedings continue.

It will be months before Nadia's new bone is knitted firmly enough onto the remaining section of mandible for her to take her first bite of solid food. In March, we travel to Disney World with a battery-operated hand-held blender, proudly displayed in our family photos. We laugh as we stop our tour through the park to puree pickles and pulverize potato chips. It is a struggle to maintain Nadia's weight; and when she resumes her chemo the problem is compounded by nausea, lethargy, and the reappearance of mouth sores.

Seeing ... breathing ... eating ... talking ...

I loved long car rides as a kid because I could curl myself into a corner, press my nose to the window, and enjoy the company of my own thoughts. I was lucky that my parents and sister either didn't talk much or knew not to expect much from me.

Making conversation in the car, at the dinner table, on walks home from school has been one of my greatest challenges as a mother. Once the thrill of hearing my children's first words and sentences wore off, I had to face the fact that they expected me to talk to them. I depended a lot on books. Other people's stories made it easier for me to tell my own. When I wished for my own company, I could recite someone else's words while maintaining a steady inner dialogue with myself.

Since her first words, "I do," Nadia has voiced her thoughts as they arise. Her flow of ideas runs underground only to surface in a pool of conversation that, to those of us on land, might appear to have no source or destination. The subject can be school, something silly Gaby did, or her latest accomplishment in gymnastics. Nadia will finish, be silent, and then resurface with "Mama. ..." Only now the subject might be my first-grade teacher and why she was so mean, a story from the summer camp Nadia went to five years ago, or the four girls who dressed up as Dorothy for the Halloween parade back in kindergarten.

With each "Mama," I answer, "Yes, Nadia." Never "later" or "not now." Nadia should grow up to believe that her mother is always ready to listen and to talk, even as I become irritated by her constant and disconnected interruption of my own inner ramblings. Asking Nadia not to talk would be like asking the wind not to sing.

The quiet after surgery is deeper than deafness. From the day Nadia was diagnosed, I found I had no moods of my own anymore; I was like water that takes the shape of the glass. Now I have no thoughts beyond what Nadia scribbles: sea, suction, itchy, pain, video.

It isn't just the wired jaw or the trache that prevents her from speaking. For the first time ever, she is at a loss for words. Her stream has dried up. She has no vocabulary, while I flounder to describe the vacuum in my own brain left by her silence.

Her mind is far from empty, though. She is processing information faster than a computer does. If the bands holding her jaw shut hadn't been cut a week after surgery, the force of so many pent-up emotions would have ruptured them, spewing forth an incoherent babble of frustration, confusion, terror, and sorrow.

Her first words, though, come slowly. They are the same ones she uttered as a baby. "Mama" squeezes out of the barely parted lips, bypassing the trache. "I do," she says, a little more forceful now as I try to dress her in a shirt that she grabs from my hands.

Then the dam bursts. "What's the nurse putting in my IV?" "When's Frannie coming?" "When can I chew?" "Is Paulette [Nadia's favorite nurse] working tonight?"

Paulette has a bright face and the kind of energy you expect from the best comedic actresses. She enters Nadia's room as if this is the only place she wants to be.

"How's my girl today?" she says, as if the only possible answer is "Wonderful!" Or maybe she only says that when she knows Nadia is doing well, because there are days when her entrance is softer, when the voice she directs at Nadia contains overtones of concern.

"I hear you had a lot of pain today," she says as she holds Nadia's hand.

"Yeah," Nadia answers. She always answers Paulette because Paulette's compassion is never laced with sympathy, never compassion-for-hire.

When the flow of Nadia's words returns, she directs it to anyone who will listen. Her subjects are broad—a family friend's new baby, the flip she did when she fell off a ski trail, the time she walked into a tree because she was too busy telling a story and eating an ice-cream cone at the same time. Paulette comes to be her most appreciative audience; and when she is promoted to supervisor, she returns often just to visit.

The demands, though, Nadia addresses solely to me—more Benadryl, go to the playroom and get a video, turn the light on, turn the light off, another blanket, don't leave, tell your friends to go away. Her words are an electric current, shocking my own mind into action.

Seeing ... breathing ... eating ... talking ... walking ...

Nadia was ten months old when, after weeks of tantalizing false starts, she took her first steps. "Look, look, look!" we all cried. We clapped and cheered and laughed at her perfect drunken-sailor-at-sea imitation. It's what we did for Frannie and for Max as well and what I see every family do for their children.

Anticipating getting Nadia out of bed two days after surgery brings only dread. I look at her swollen head and think of Sisyphus struggling with his boulder; I think of all those lifelines that I will have to avoid tangling or pulling.

It's our bad luck that our least favorite nurse is on duty that morning. This is the same woman who, while Nadia's breaths grew shallow the night after surgery, gave me something else to worry about by telling me Nadia might have always had sleep apnea. She is a sharp-featured woman, her face unsoftened by smiles, her hands efficient at IV machines and feeding tubes but not at touching. She enters a room like a mechanic might, checking on what needs fixing, oiling, fine tuning. If she were a mechanic I, would not take my car to her.

This morning, the nurse's eyes sweep over Nadia in the bed. Then she turns to me to accuse, "You mean, she hasn't gotten up yet?" as if our only problem is that we are lazy.

"We're getting ready; just waiting for some *help*," I say, trying to hide my ire.

She can't possibly know the real Nadia. I had shown every nurse and doctor who came in the collage I had made for Nadia: "This is the girl buried underneath what you see here."

They would all say, "She's beautiful." Not this nurse. And no one could see what I wanted them to notice—Nadia's strength, the fierceness of her love, the energy pulsing through every muscle, her determination to execute a flawless front flip.

It's true that Nadia doesn't want to get out of bed. I didn't want to go through all that pushing to give birth to my children. But neither step could be avoided so Nadia prepares.

We are given instructions: Go slowly. Move to the side of the bed. Rest. Sit up. Rest. Slide legs over side. Rest. Put weight on good leg, rotate clockwise, ease down into chair. Rest. Rest. Rest.

We assemble: me, Margie, and two nurses. We arrange tubes and drains, prepare a chair with blankets and pillows and a support for Nadia's leg. We wait for Nadia.

There is no resting. It takes forty-five seconds for Nadia to travel down her short aisle. She presses her morphine button only once because a surprise counterclockwise rotation pulls on various lines. I clap and praise, but my applause is not met by any mirrored joy. Nadia's eyes say, I'll sit here as long as you want me to but you should know that all I really want is to get back into bed.

Over the next few days, her cords are cut: first the catheter, then the peripheral IV. Next the drain in her leg comes out, then the one in her neck. Nadia is ready to learn how to walk.

Sometimes I look at my dogs watching me exercise and I imagine them saying, "This is so stupid. Get out there and fetch a ball, chase a rabbit, dig a hole." For Nadia, too, physical exertion has always been for fun and sport. Now she refuses to admit that she has to work at something as basic as walking. No longer a drunken sailor, she is a stubborn and mean old woman. She refuses to look at the physical therapist, speaks to her only through me.

In the past, I gave in often to Nadia's assumption that she knew best. If becoming an elite gymnast was her goal but she blew off practices in favor of birthday parties, I thought that was a decision she could learn from and either reevaluate or reaffirm her objectives. If she claimed she would have plenty of time to get her homework done after she finished painting, playing a game, and watching a video, no matter how many dire warnings I gave, then perhaps going to school unprepared was a lesson she needed. In moments of frustration I have let her convince me that a bowl of potato chips before dinner would not ruin her appetite, that she wouldn't spill a too-full glass of chocolate milk on her new shirt, that staying up late with her friends on a sleepover would not leave her irritable the next day. I tell myself I am not giving in to Nadia's stubbornness but helping her learn her limits, even as I know she will never admit that she was wrong.

But in the present, I become dictatorial. I do not forgive her rudeness. I won't let her go back to bed unless she walks. I won't let her use me as a crutch; I stay out of reach.

"Nadia, your P.T. is here," I begin gently, knowing what is next.

"Tell her to go away."

"You know I can't do that. Come on. Let's get you up."

"I'm only getting up because you're making me. I'm not going to walk."

Once Nadia is up, the P.T. comes over with the walker.

"Go away," Nadia says.

"Nadia, just take the walker and stand for a few minutes. Maybe a few steps."

"I'm only walking to the door"

"As long as you're at the door, why don't you go down the hallway?"

"I'll go halfway."

"Okay, Nadia, halfway."

The P.T. hovers around Nadia, hands at her waist but not touching, as if a touch would remind Nadia that the P.T. had won most of this battle. She is not done fighting, though. The process repeats itself when it's time to switch to crutches or learn to go up and down stairs.

When she finishes, I congratulate and grovel, hoping to get back into her good graces. I am not forgiven, nor do I derive any satisfaction from what I have gotten her to do. But it works. The therapist Nadia sees once she is released from the hospital writes out a list of exercises. "She should do all of these at least twice a day, but at her age don't expect much cooperation."

"Don't worry," Nadia tells her, "my mom will make me do them."

I *do* make her, but nothing can take the place of her own internal motivation. Only months later, when Nadia realizes she can't beat her brother in a footrace, do a split, or make a smooth run to the vault do I catch glimpses of her stretching and bending and mending on her own.

Seeing ... breathing ... eating ... talking ... walking ... self-awareness

There is a baby in the hospital whom Nadia loves to watch. He fills great portions of the day playing with his toes, and I know it is only a matter of time before he realizes they are part of him, attached to his feet. Soon he will discover his face—learn that it isn't his mother's or his father's face but his own. He will learn that certain actions result in the sound of a rattle, the sway of a mobile, the appearance of a parent, and that those actions come from him. Thankfully, he will probably never realize that he has cancer, that there is a part of his body that he can't control but is still his.

Nadia asks me, "Do you think having cancer is easier for a baby or an older child?"

"I'm not sure. What do you think?"

"I think for a baby because he doesn't really know what's going on and he won't remember."

Awareness. Nadia is aware that something bad is happening, and awareness means memories, and memories mean her experience will be present in her life always.

I, of course, do have an opinion about which I would prefer. There is solace for me in caring for a child with whom I can communicate, who can tell me where and why she is hurting; there is respite, when Nadia is well, in her conversation and her ability to be independent, to go to school, to play with her friends.

Surgery, of course, did not erase Nadia's awareness of her fingers or toes or the fact that she had cancer. Rather, it triggered often untouched levels of emotion, as sports or physical labor activates tiny muscles we forget we have.

First to fire is frustration. The more aware Nadia becomes of her dependency, the greater grows her resentment. Her third day after surgery is a day of chaos—scrawling orders, flinging markers and paper she then orders me to pick up, collapsing in tears but refusing any comfort I can provide.

Nadia writes a poem: "Roses are red, violets are blue . . . ," The rest makes no sense; morphine and misery have made her incoherent.

"It's a joke," she scribbles when I don't laugh. "Don't you get it?"

"Maybe you can explain it later" is my pathetic offering.

There will be no later because Nadia stabs at the paper with her pen, destroying what she has written, giving me no chance to understand her first effort at communicating something other than a want or a need.

At first, her behavior shocks me because I have never seen her so baffled and defeated. One of the most popular preschool toys in my house was a Sesame Street Pop-Up Pals game. Turn a dial, pull a lever, push a button, and you're rewarded with the appearance of Elmo, Ernie, Bert, or another favorite friend. Frannie would play this game with me at her side, asking for help when she got frustrated. Max would try; but when he couldn't get the solution right away, he would hurl the toy across the room. Nadia would take the toy into a corner by herself and work away. Periodically, I'd hear the satisfying "ker-ching" of a pal popping. If the silence grew too long, I'd wander over. "I do," she'd insist, so I would leave.

Nadia could do almost everything she set her mind to. As she drove herself to master one skill after another, I worried that she would burn herself up too quickly. I found myself wishing for small failures, little pinpricks in her invincibility. Few came. Nadia's uncharacteristic rage after surgery was her way of saying, "I do," but being faced for the first time with "I can't."

Isolation follows frustration. Parents of premature babies surely know the emptiness of not being able to hug their newborn or slobber juicy kisses on their cheeks. I imagine they sense their babies' longing for a touch, a stroke, the feel of flesh on flesh. When Nadia was a baby and I brought her into bed, she was not content to lie next to me. Imperceptibly, she would wiggle her little body until she was stretched out on top of my chest. Nearly nine years later, I hear no lonelier plea than Nadia's appeals to have someone near her, keep a hand on her good leg, stroke her fingers, place a palm on top of her head.

I tell Margie how sad it is for me not to be able to hug Nadia, how it makes me miss her even though we are apart barely an hour a day. I think Nadia is sleeping; but when I look at her next, her eyes are locked on mine, and she has her arms held out for a hug. It is a gingerly embrace and one of those upside-down moments I have so often with Nadia when I wonder who is loving whom, which one of us is being comforted, who is the child and who is the mommy?

Alone in her web of tubes, Nadia looks out on the rest of us—unencumbered, scarless, full heads of hair—through the scrim of self-consciousness, formed prematurely, years before the awkwardness and embarrassments of adolescence. While the visual blow of Nadia's appearance never softens for me, I am so consumed by caring for her and looking for signs of improvement that I never wonder what she thinks she looks like after her operation or whether it matters to her.

Now it is eight days after the surgery. Nadia is starting to leave her room for longer periods of time. Getting to the bathroom is cumbersome, so she has been using a bedside commode. On this particular day, we are in the playroom when Nadia tells me she needs to use the bathroom. I help move her into her wheelchair, and, without a thought, take her to the toilet. While I am preoccupied arranging the IV pole and tubes, I hear her gasp.

"Why didn't you tell me?" she screams.

I look up. Nadia is staring into the mirror. "Oh, Nadia, I'm so sorry. How stupid of me."

"I look like a monster!"

"Of course you don't, honey. The swelling has already gone down so much," as if the moment were no different from the time when my mother tried to reassure me that I would be the most beautiful girl at the seventh-grade dance despite my big nose, too full figure, and lopsided Sassoon haircut.

"How would I know what I looked like? Who cares anyway? Take me back to my room." The friends whom Nadia was so happy to have seen just the day before—those who came free of entanglements, on strong legs, and in their crisp school uniforms; those who had seen Nadia in her pajamas try to guide melted ice cream into her numb mouth around the feeding tube, who saw it dribble unnoticed down her chin, who weren't quite old enough to disguise their glances at the thinning tangle of hair on Nadia's uncovered head—were not allowed to come back.

When I look back on pictures taken shortly after this day, the images slap my memory. I see the asymmetry of Nadia's face, the amount of swelling, the rawness of the scars, the crookedness of her smile, the feeding tube like an insult in her nose, her lips puffy and bleeding from dryness. She still had stitches and the trache; the red scar at her throat still looked like a rope that was strangling her. At the time, I thought her appearance was approaching normal.

Nadia is scheduled to leave the hospital on February 14. John meets me that morning, and we undergo a reenactment of the day we brought Nadia home from the hospital after she was born. We pack up two week's worth of presents, art projects, clothes, books, videos, and new additions to our already impressive cache of pharmaceuticals. All that remains to be done is to remove the braces that had helped to set her bite after the surgery. John and I take our usual places—him pacing outside in the waiting room, me inside with Nadia, bracing myself for whatever anger she is about to vent.

Never having had any direct experience with orthodontia, I have no idea that braces are essentially pried, cut, and sawed off. Within thirty seconds, Nadia is hysterical. I want only to get the hell out of here. I stand behind her, insisting that she focus only on my voice, and I talk nonstop of home, of her room, of all being together again, as if, at last, life will be normal. Finally finished, John and I race Nadia's wheelchair to the elevator, afraid someone will call out to us, saying there has been a mistake, we have to stay.

Nadia's homecoming is nothing like her arrival as a newborn. Then a small entourage of immediate and extended family accompanied Nadia and me the four blocks from hospital to home, where she was fussed over like a rare rose. Nor was it like Max's, who had to stay two extra days in the hospital nursery because of jaundice. Alone, I zipped him into his snowsuit, carried him home, unzipped the suit, and brought him into the kitchen where he was absorbed into the household as if he had always been there.

Nadia's second homecoming has all the excitement of her first but is not as smooth as her brother's. "What's the point of being home," she laments. "I can't do anything."

She can't run up and down the stairs or share the same meals as the rest of us. She looks different; she won't be going to school. She is returning to her room but not her life.

Two weeks after coming home—one week after resuming chemo—Nadia is invited by some friends to see the Arms and Armor exhibit at the Metropolitan Museum of Art because her class is studying the Middle Ages. She gets dressed and is ready to go, with fifteen minutes to spare, when she flops down on her bed and mumbles into her pillow, "I've changed my mind. I don't want to go anymore."

"I don't understand. You were so excited a few minutes ago to see Gaby and Emily."

"Well, I just don't want to go now, okay?" she challenges.

"I'm not sure it's okay. I know you're not too tired. Are you feeling uncomfortable about people seeing you?" Nadia has lost more hair from the chemo, including her eyebrows and eyelashes. Her face is still swollen. The scars are still red. She walks with a limp.

"I hate it when people stare at me."

"I know, sweetie. But it will be so good for you to see your friends. It's been a long time. They want to see you very badly and it's important that you stay in touch so when you go back to school, you won't feel so left out."

Nadia's face darkens. "Stop talking to me!"

Gaby's mother calls and tells Nadia how disappointed Gaby will be if Nadia doesn't go. With the attention now focused on Gaby's needs, it is easier for Nadia to say yes. We have reserved a wheelchair, but Nadia refuses to use it. People do stare, but Nadia seems oblivious. She spends the better part of the weekend with her friends, but she will not return to school.

Nadia, who turned nine on February 19, celebrates her birthday belatedly on March 10. Her party is the final contraction in her redelivery. Unlike the first time, I, her mother, have little to do. Nadia invites the five people she is comfortable with. She plans the games, including a treasure hunt with prizes that she shopped for. She chooses the menu, even though she can't eat the food, and she makes her own cake. It is a beautiful confection, decorated with layers and swirls of color. The highlight is the message she writes to herself in perfect script—HAPPY BIRTHDAY NADIA.

III

Recovery

Scars should have zippers. Any second now you will remember a dream, a death, a descent that will rip open old wounds, old sorrows, old griefs so that the blood of emotions starts to ooze again. How much neater a zipper would be when you want to rummage around in your grief and pain for only as long as you can stand it before putting it away.

Weeks go by when I do not stare at the marks of Nadia's trauma, when my eyes do not bore into her with enough heat to cause new scars of their own. Does her chest still bear the red knot of flesh where her Broviac was inserted? Does that tender membrane at the base of her throat still show the sign of the trache through which she breathed? The long scar on Nadia's leg is overshadowed by the muscles of an athlete. And when Nadia lifts her chin in a gymnastics pose, I don't always notice the line that runs from lip down to throat and across to ear, now faded to a pale pink. But when I do look, the scars on my heart rip open.

One of Nadia's pleas still echoes. "I wish you could have the chemo but I would get better," she says.

I know she just wanted me to take away the pain. But I am stuck with the knowledge that I couldn't then, and will never be able to, protect Nadia from suffering.

Remission is a scar I cannot revel in. I need many zippers. I need suspenders for my spirit; pockets for the grief in my heart; heavy shoes for Nadia's soul to keep her weighted here on earth.

14

We have so many things to do—pills, dressings, the Broviac,
mouth care, Nystatin, physical therapy, G-shots, and now,
Epogen shots and iron because Nadia is anemic.
It seems to consume the day.

—journal entry, February 23, 2001

The day before Nadia is to begin her post-surgery chemo regimen, she tells me, "I don't really need chemo. I don't have cancer anymore."

"What do you mean?" I ask, startled by her certainty.

"In surgery, they took the tumor out. Now it's gone," she answers.

Nadia knows that cancer can spread. Perhaps she is aware that her MRI, bone scan, and CAT scan, taken just before the operation, showed no obvious signs of new growth. But I don't imagine her thinking is that sophisticated. What she knows is that what had been in her body is now gone. It makes sense for her to assume she is free of malignant cells.

But I want Nadia's words to reflect an inner wisdom, not childish thinking. "How do you know?" I resist asking. "Did you see it leave?" But all I can say without arousing her suspicion is "You're right. You don't have a tumor anymore." After three months of treatment and surgery, it is the only claim I can make.

I spent many hours trying to picture Nadia's tumor. I drew images of its ragged, creeping edges. I dug into its core, which I imagined as a squirming mass of poisonous bugs searching for escape. I wanted that tumor and its contents physically excised from my daughter's body so that, like her, I could say it was gone. But unlike her, I couldn't be certain some of those bugs hadn't gotten away.

Surgery not only removed the tumor but determined if or how much it had invaded surrounding tissue and whether any of the cells were still active after the three rounds of chemo. Two hours into the operation, Dr. Kraus completed the first phase of the operation, removing the tumor. He greeted us in the waiting room.

"Nadia's doing great," he reassured us. "I had to remove less than half the jawbone. We won't know for sure until the pathology report is completed, but all the margins look clean, no sign of malignant cells in the surrounding tissue."

"Will she need a skin graft?" I asked. If enough soft tissue around the bone had to be removed, skin would have to be taken from Nadia's thigh and grafted onto the inside of her cheek. This would prolong the healing period significantly and further limit Nadia's use of her leg.

"No. No skin graft was needed. I couldn't have hoped for anything better."

I could have—that this was all a big mistake, that the chemo had been unnecessary, that the doctor was terribly sorry for putting us through such anxiety. The doctor wasn't terribly sorry. He was smiling his pleasure, so eager to save my daughter that, for a moment, I ignored the fact that what made him happy was that he had expected worse—a bigger section of bone to be removed, margins that weren't clean. I, who had never asked how big the tumor was to begin with, tried to imagine the size of half a jaw on a petite, porcelain, eight-year-old girl.

Twelve days later, we got the official finding from pathology, including a necrosis report that would tell us what percentage, if any, of the tumor was still alive. So many days had passed in my total absorption in Nadia's recovery that I had forgotten about this crucial piece of information. Dr. Meyers took me by surprise when he arrived at the door to Nadia's hospital room. "We have the results of the necrosis report. I don't have the information with me and I don't remember what the precise number is, but it's not exactly what we were hoping for."

I don't think he said "exactly." I think I inserted that word in self-defense. I don't want to be mad at this straight-talking doctor who made Nadia laugh with his jokes about how long Abraham Lincoln's legs were (long enough to reach the ground), who spoke to her without condescension about politics and American history, whose eyes twinkled under arched eyebrows when she dared to challenge him that, yes, she will recover from a round of chemo in time to go to Disney World or a friend's birthday party. Dr. Meyers only wanted to return a healthy daughter to me, but he left me suspended in the realm of my worst imaginings.

He returned a few hours later with the number. "50 percent of the tumor was still alive," he said crisply.

"What does that mean?" I asked.

"Well, statistics show that there is a correlation between recurrence and tumors with little necrosis, but that is not the same thing as cause."

I reword this information in my head. Children who

have recurrences often have primary tumors with a higher rate of active cancer cells, but those with active cancer cells in their removed tumors don't necessarily suffer recurrences.

I have almost convinced myself that nothing has changed in Nadia's prognosis when Dr. Meyers, trying to reassure me, said, "Relax. It's not time to panic yet."

Yet. Only. Exactly. How can such small words change the impact of a sentence so dramatically? Now, I thought, is a perfect time to panic.

John was home with Max and Frannie while I was getting the news from Dr. Meyers. I had to tell him. I no longer had the right, if I ever did, to withhold important information about the kids.

I told him when he came to visit Nadia, a miscalculation on my part because we had to speak over and around her. "Dr. Meyers was here earlier. He had the report from pathology," I said.

"And?" John asked.

"Well, he said that 50 percent of the tumor was still alive."

"Is that good or bad?"

"He said it wasn't exactly what they would have wanted."

"What does that mean?"

"I don't know. He said not to panic." I didn't add the word *yet*.

"How could I not panic, Judi. He's obviously disappointed."

"Shh. Keep your voice down."

"Oh no, this is awful."

I didn't know if it was awful or not, but I didn't want to hear any more from John. One part fear plus one part frustration created a toxic smog that was engulfing the two of us.

When Dr. Wexler arrived later on his rounds, I sought his interpretation, as if Dr. Meyers and I had never spoken. I didn't ask for direct reassurance. Soothing words offered without prompting have to be truer than those that must be asked for.

"We got Nadia's necrosis report," I ventured.

"I wasn't surprised by the results," Dr. Wexler said. "You'll remember that the reason the tumor had shrunk by only 30 percent was because it was deep within the bone. For the same reason, the 50 percent necrosis isn't unexpected."

"What about her prognosis? Does this change anything?" I needed reassuring words now, even if I had to weasel them out of the doctor.

"I still have full confidence in Nadia's complete recovery. We're still talking cure here, not palliative care."

I had counted on Dr. Wexler, whose compassion always seemed as important to me as his medical skills, but again my ears went to the wrong word. *Palliative:* to provide care that alleviates the symptoms of a disease without effecting a cure. I had never been talking about palliative care, but now the possibility sat in front of me like an ogre begging me to acknowledge its presence so that it had an excuse to swallow me.

Dr. Wexler was not finished: "There's some research going on in Europe now that shows a transplant of one's own stem cells may be effective in treating recurrences of Ewing's. I want to stress that I still don't think that Nadia will ever need them, but it would be foolish not to bank them."

My mind took a detour. I became stuck on the idea of research being done in a foreign country. When we learned that Nadia had Ewing's, John and I had accepted the diagnosis, but neither of us had ever thought about seeking a second opinion regarding treatment options. We assumed we had all the expertise we needed right here in America, at MSKCC. Had we made a mistake? Maybe there was some better protocol out there, one that would have had a more lethal impact on the tumor.

Now Nadia is telling me the cancer is gone. The rest—the ifosfamide and etoposide—is just sweeping up, particularly in the lungs, the first place where Ewing's spreads. Blood flows freely there and I picture Nadia's chest as some kind of washing machine where chemo is the detergent and blood the rinsing agent that is taking all the dirty cells away.

Until Nadia's surgery, all I had wished for was a return to our normal life, to get her dressed every morning in her navy-blue tunic, her white puffy sleeved blouse with the Peter Pan collar, and to send her off to school. During her recovery, though, all I wanted was to be back on the familiar ground of chemo. I had some notion that, after surgery, all the hard stuff was behind us. The new chemo regimen had fewer side effects; at the hospital they even called it "chemo lite." I had become enough of a veteran by then not to be offended by this glib reference; I was just counting on it to be true. There was a good possibility that Nadia would avoid neutropenic fevers, that she could return to school. But imperceptibly—the way you never notice the days getter shorter in autumn until you wake up one morning at 6:30 and it's still dark out—our world narrowed, as if the cancer had moved from devouring Nadia's body to destroying the major elements of our previous life. Since leaving the hospital post-surgery, I was busier than ever. In addition to the routine care of the Broviac, dispensing pills to make Nadia more comfortable, and administering the G-shots to help stimulate white-blood-cell production, I had to change the dressing on her leg, give her iron supplements and shots of Epogen to increase her red-blood-cell count, wean her off pain killers, and make sure she did her jaw and neck exercises.

Nadia resumes chemo five days after her discharge from the hospital, twenty days after her operation, on February 19. Cancer has swallowed her birthday. We celebrate in the hospital playroom. A cake is miraculously produced from the freezer, one that Nadia can't eat because she still can't chew; and Max, who is off from school for Presidents' Day, can't have because it contains soy protein, one of the foods he is allergic to.

The new chemo regimen takes a full five days instead of the three and a half days of the former one. The rhythm of the PDH returns to us. Arrive at 8:30 A.M. Check in, check weight, check temperature. See the doctor. Go to the bed area. Get hooked up to IV fluids. Take steroid and Kytril to ward off nausea. Go to playroom. Begin daylong discussion of what to eat, now made harder by the fact that Nadia can't chew. (Hot dogs with carcinogenic nitrates, pureed in the inpatient playroom two floors up, are a favorite.) Start chemo. Watch it drip. Return to bed when tired. Watch TV—*Angela Anaconda, S Club Seven, Rugrats, Bob the Builder,* shows that have been permanently stained by their association with cancer. Syndicated *ER* reruns are a favorite, and not just for me and Nadia. The theme song can be heard from bedside televisions all over the PDH. At 6:00 P.M. gather homework, discarded layers of clothing, knitting, books, cards, playroom artwork, crutches. Pile all into wheelchair with Nadia and her chemo pump for the trip down the elevator and out to the street, transfer all to car, go home for a night of anxiously waiting for something to go wrong.

At the end of the week, on Saturday, I disconnect

the pump. I begin to entertain fantasies of what could be a two-week run at school for Nadia, despite the fact that she hasn't managed more than four consecutive days since she began treatment.

Because of damage to her salivary glands, Nadia's face is swollen with trapped fluid. The doctor has already drained it twice, a procedure similar to amniocentesis involving a long needle that draws as much as two ounces of liquid at a time. Within hours, however, the fluid returns. While she sleeps, blood and saliva ooze from her mouth, staining her pillow and sheets.

On Saturday night, Nadia and Max have a sleepover at Margie's house. I assume this will be a respite for me. Out of sight, I won't have to worry about the swelling that I imagine will cause Nadia's face to explode at any moment. But Sunday night when she gets home, Nadia's skin is stretched so tight that it shines like a nine-month's pregnant belly. I make the dreaded call to urgent care.

The trip to the hospital is a family outing, the first time all five of us have gone anywhere together in weeks. While we wait for the doctor, Max entertains us with a blown-up surgical glove; Nadia reaches out toward Frannie who comes to sit on the bed with her.

Our cubicle is tiny. Once the doctor enters, John takes Max outside, not just making more space but relieving the two of them from having to watch the needle be inserted, the plunger lifted, and the fluid snake through the plastic tubing. Frannie stays; she always stays. When Nadia is asked to lie on her side, she curls toward her sister. The doctor, a soft-spoken, sympathetic young woman, stands behind her. I position myself so that Nadia can't escape my eyes. If she focuses on them, she'll be okay. When the doctor finishes, she shows us the nearly quarter-cup of fluid she has drained.

On our trip home we engage in our usual evaluation of the doctors and nurses—the first nurse was nice, the second one didn't smile, this doctor was gentler than the last one. It is the kind of conversation most families have after seeing a movie or going to a restaurant; it unites us. I go to bed praying that no more fluid will collect, but on Monday morning, Nadia's face is already beginning to swell.

I am desperate for her to return to school. But when she sees her face in the mirror, she refuses to go.

"Are you sure you don't want to give it a try?" I ask. "You can always come home." Let her be somewhere else, I beg silently. Wouldn't it be better for her to suffer a few moments of self-consciousness than to live in the shadow of my anxiety?

But Nadia will not go. I know the issue isn't just the swelling. It is the crutches, the worry about what to eat, the acknowledgment of being even more different than she had been when her only problem was being bald.

I call the teacher and ask if she can see Nadia at home. Ms. Cinquegrana is young. She exudes a quiet serenity, which is a soothing contrast to the bubbly smiles and cheerleading attitude of hospital personnel. As necessary as this enthusiasm is, it grates on me and makes my cheeks ache from so much false smiling. Ms. Cinquegrana is always unflustered by Nadia's appearance or latest medical crises. On the three or four occasions that she has come to our home to work with Nadia in the past few months, I would sneak peeks of her sitting with Nadia on the floor. Their bodies are always leaning toward one another; their quiet talk is punctuated occasionally by giggles. It is a vision I cherish; their time together is a true oasis for Nadia.

Ms. Cinquegrana assures me Nadia is keeping up

with her work, so I relax a bit thinking that Nadia is actually well enough for us to enjoy a leisurely run of carefree days together.

On Monday, the day after our trip to urgent care, John has to leave on a business trip. I imagine the telephone lines sagging with the weight of his sadness and loneliness each time he calls. Meanwhile, the three kids and I enjoy a slumber party. I lug mattresses into my room, where the four of us eat junk food and watch TV before going to bed, conjuring memories of my father's business trips when my mother would serve my sister and me Swanson frozen dinners on TV trays in the den in front of our new black-and-white television.

I should have known, though, after four months in the cancer world, that there is no such thing as a run of anything that resembles the life you had before. Wednesday morning, four days after Nadia has finished her week of chemo lite, I need only a quick glance at her to know our party is over. The fever is in her eyes, her mood, her breathing. Her counts had dropped.

I feel betrayed, lied to. It is too soon to be going back. Leaving home this time feels like an amputation.

Nadia's only concern is the peripheral IV she knows will be placed in her arm. If the fever has been caused by an infection in the Broviac, this second line will be her lifesaver.

I have a friend whose daughter is needle phobic, who has to be dragged out from under examining tables and pinned down for the smallest procedures. But after learning what Nadia had to tolerate, she said, "Knowing what Nadia's been going through, I can do this."

Thank goodness Elizabeth never saw Nadia get an IV.

When we arrive at the PDH, Nadia is assessed and

prepared for admission to the hospital. She is weighed, her temperature taken and her blood pressure checked. Then the IV must be placed. I know we are in trouble when I see three nurses approach us. Two are Nadia's regular nurses; one is newer, less familiar. I know what they are up to and can't believe they are going to use her for practice. Do they think that, because Nadia has done this so many times before, she finds it easy? If so, they are wrong.

Nervous but unsuspecting, Nadia says her usual, "Don't do it until I count to three."

The new nurse readies her needle and vials and taps to find a vein. "Okay, Nadia, whenever you're ready," she says.

"1 . . . 2 . . . 3," Nadia counts.

The needle goes in. There is no rush of blood up the tube. Nadia's mouth opens, then the scream comes: "Is it in yet? Is it in?"

"Almost, Nadia, almost," I say, as much an appeal to the nurse as a response to her question.

The poking continues. Sometimes the needle is taken out and reinserted; other times it wiggles around like a blind worm seeking to tunnel its way back into the earth. I can already imagine the black-and-blue mark that will appear the next day. I'm a good twenty years older than this nurse. Is that excuse enough to tell her to go away?

I don't have to. Nadia's regular nurse takes over.

"1 . . . 2 . . . 3," Nadia whimpers. The needle goes in again, and finally the blood flows.

By the time Nadia goes to Bake Night in the playroom that evening, she no longer holds her arm as if it can't bend. Her fever is gone. She spends four days playing with a new friend, Marie, as she waits for her counts to go back up. On the fourth day, Nadia and Marie make

French toast in the playroom kitchen. They talk, giggle, and make a mess; I feel sick to my stomach seeing Nadia feel so at home here, even though I know that I, alone, could not make her life such fun. I am the one who feels displaced; my longing to leave settles in like an ache. That afternoon, we receive the results of Nadia's latest blood test. Her white count has gone up and she is discharged in time to welcome John back home for dinner.

While Nadia was in the hospital, Dr. Wexler decided that she would begin stem cell harvesting the next week. In preparation, Nadia began receiving two G-shots per day to boost her cell production. So even though we return home on Sunday, we head back to the hospital on Monday.

Other than the shots, the worst thing about harvesting is the fact that it is boring. Nadia arrives on Monday and is hooked up to a contraption that reminds me of a giant sewing machine, whose thread takes a circuitous route through holes and hooks to the needle. The needle, in this case, is in Nadia. Her blood is drawn out, sifted of stem cells, and returned with the addition of donated blood. The process takes about three hours. Nadia lies in bed, watches videos, chats with the nurses and sends John or me on the usual quest for food. This doesn't seem so bad for one day, maybe two—the time I thought it would take to gather the 4 million cells needed. If necessary, 2 million would be used for a transplant; the remainder would be stored as backup in case the procedure failed.

On the first day, only 600,000 stem cells are collected. On the second, 500,000. The doctor orders three G-shots per day. It is hard to find a spot on Nadia's leg that isn't already bruised from previous punctures, but she refuses to let me give her the shot anywhere else on her body.

Her arms are so thin that she tells me she is afraid the needle will hit her bone.

On day three, we reach 2 million. The doctor says this is enough. "The extra 2 million were needed in the early days of transplantation. They are rarely needed anymore."

I confirm this with Dr. Wexler. "I would agree," he answers. "Besides, I don't expect that Nadia will need any of them anyway." Free reassurance when I'm not even looking for it.

Nadia's face continues to swell, despite being drained for the fourth time. This constant filling-up of fluid prevents the skin of her cheek, which had been lifted up during surgery in a procedure called a flap, from readhering. Dr. Cordeiro suggests putting in a temporary drain. An IV-like needle will be inserted into her cheek and connected to tubing, which will lead to a vacuum bulb to be pinned to her shirt. We go to see him after Nadia's first morning of stem cell harvesting.

Dr. Cordeiro is a small, neat man with the long capable fingers of a surgeon. During our gathering to determine whether Nadia would undergo surgery or radiation, Dr. Cordeiro had not been present and I had given little thought to his significance. Nadia had, however. When we finally met him in the days before the operation, she asked him, "Are you any good at what you do?"

I was pleased when Dr. Cordeiro looked directly at her and answered her question without condescension. He told her that he had performed more than two hundred jaw reconstructions using the fibula on adults, more than anyone else in the country. He had also performed the highest number of these procedures on children—eight. Nadia would be number nine.

She continued to confront Dr. Cordeiro after surgery

when his various proddings and procedures hurt her. To Nadia, he appeared to shrug off her concerns, but I recognized the underlying discomfort of someone who hates the fact that he causes pain to a child and thinks, perhaps, he can minimize it by claiming it's not so bad. Nadia, however, was angered by his seeming lack of sympathy.

John has yet to see Nadia's cheek drained, so he is less skeptical when the doctor assures us that the procedure won't hurt since so many of Nadia's nerves had been cut during the surgery. The doctor inserts the needle but, after so many previous drainings, has trouble getting past pockets of dried or old blood. With each attempt, Nadia screams, "Stop it. Get off me. It hurts."

"It doesn't really hurt," the doctor says to me. "She's just scared."

I ignore him. "I know it hurts, honey. Just hang in there a little longer."

"No. Make it stop, now!"

John, sitting against the wall across the room, asks, "Does it hurt, Nadia?" I know he feels helpless, wants to do something to participate, but I wonder how he can be so foolish not to at least pretend to believe her. But he has not been the one to reassure the kids over the years by searching for monsters under the bed, sweeping corners to root out spiders, or explaining how hard it is for murderers to get past doormen and double-locked doors or to defy gravity to crash their way into their fifteenth-floor bedroom window.

Nadia won't answer him, not even with her anger.

I don't know where to look. In Nadia's eyes I see pain and accusation. If I look at the doctor, she will think that I chose to side with him over her. If I look at John, my own fury and frustration will have a focal point. *You come stand here if you want to know if it hurts.* But I'm not so certain that my way is any better than theirs at fending off monsters, murderers, spiders, pain, and fear. Isn't it the combination of John's success and his desire to protect his family that allows me to tell Nadia her bedroom is safe? John needs me now as a buffer between him and Nadia. If I leave Nadia's side, I will be abandoning John as well. If I stay, I know John can be comforted too.

Did it hurt? I don't know. The needle was scary and the doctor had to poke around for a while. If a person can experience pain from an amputated limb, why can't Nadia, who retained the vast majority of the left side of her face, still feel pain?

Then again, maybe the pain she felt was just the power of suggestion, an eruption of disgust over everything that was happening to her—another procedure, another needle, another glitch, another moment when she couldn't communicate her feelings to the people around her. It was all out of Nadia's control. Why not cry?

In a follow-up telephone call, Dr. Cordeiro's nurse practitioner told me, "It didn't really hurt her, you know."

Because Nadia was already over her anger, I felt no need to argue the point.

On the next day, after stem cell harvesting, Nadia declared that she wanted to go to school for a few hours. The urge came on suddenly: if she didn't put on her uniform and enter the halls of Nightingale-Bamford that day it, she might never be able to again—or so she seemed to claim. The thin tube draining her cheek was red with blood. Nadia said she didn't care. She came home happy but exhausted by the pretense that she was like everyone else and that no one was staring at her. She chose not to go to school again.

By this time, it was only in school that Nadia felt much self-consciousness. She had no trouble parading down

Madison Avenue with her head bared and her chemo pump on her back. During intermission of the Broadway show *Annie Get Your Gun,* Nadia took her bandana off to retie it. When a friend commented on how fast she did it, she answered, "It's easier when you don't have any hair." And she thought nothing of attending the annual Bunny Hop, a fundraiser held by the Society of MSKCC at FAO Schwarz to support the hospital's pediatric cancer program.

FAO Schwarz is a massive multilevel toy store taking up nearly a full city block. It is to toys what Willy Wonka's imaginary chocolate factory is to candy. The Bunny Hop is a high-society affair. When we arrived, I saw girls with blond curls, velvet headbands and flowered dresses with big satin bows. The boys were in navy-blue blazers with ties and perfectly parted, slicked-back hair.

Nadia had just started her fifth round of chemo and was connected to her pump, which she carried in a pack on her back. She wore a white jersey and black pants. She still had the drain in her cheek and had no hat to cover her head. She limped along, oblivious to the stares, especially of other parents. But I wasn't oblivious. One coiffed and powdered socialite passed us and whispered to her friend, "Oh, that poor boy."

Nadia had told me she didn't have cancer anymore, but how could I believe her? The pump, the drain, the limp, the scars, the bones poking through bruised skin, the Broviac, and the eyes that looked so exposed without the brows and lashes to shelter them, turning Nadia's face into a mask far removed from the angel she was just four months earlier. At no time had she ever looked more like a person overtaken by disease.

15

On the terrace outside the hospital playroom I hear cars, sirens, construction, and, once in a while, a bird singing. But the sun is on my face, and the air doesn't smell like hospital. Nadia is inside, excited to be doing syringe art—spattering paint with the same supplies I had used to drop saline into her trache.

—journal entry, April 9, 2001

When Nadia became a patient at MSKCC, she received a video called *Why, Charlie Brown, Why?* The story begins in the fall when a little girl, Janice, learns she has leukemia. As the trees grow bare, the days get cold, and snow puts the world to sleep, we see Janice undergo chemo, lose her long blond hair and become isolated from friends. Finally, as the snow melts and the first flower pushes its way up through a crack in the sidewalk, Janice's treatment comes to an end. By the time spring arrives, Janice is back on her favorite swing, her tresses once again long and swaying in glorious fullness.

The tale is a cliché, of course, but an apt one. Our natural world dies in winter to be reborn every spring, and what else is the treatment of cancer but a killing so that life can continue? The nurses had told me that October is a particularly busy time at MSKCC.

Nadia fit the timetable perfectly (although hair long enough to blow in the wind would take at least a year to grow). I thought that I would be rushing toward springtime as I always did—searching for the swans' return to Central Park or my first butterfly, wondering if I would again see a newly fledged hawk perched on my windowsill as I had the year before. Now the natural world, which had captivated me from a young age, had vanished.

Lexington, Massachusetts, in the 1950s of my early childhood still retained pockets of its rural roots. My house sat on the edge of conservation land, woven with long-unused horse and carriage trails, old stone walls, swamps and cliffs. Not far from my house, but out of sight from anyone inside, was a small brook beside which grew my favorite tree, a beech, whose branches hung low to make a tent where I could retreat. This is where I would run after a fight with my sister, the loss of a pet or during a bout of the nobody-understands-me blues. What I loved most in spring was watching the swelling at the tips of the branches grow from bud to leaf. I observed the slowly unfurling foliage with the same intensity I would later apply to imagining the daily in utero growth of my babies. It was a visual mantra: while I was watching, I had no room for anger or sadness.

The sky is what I sought when, at age sixteen, I returned from eight weeks in Israel and the exotic beauty of the desert. Restless back under my parents' control and feeling smothered by the closeness of the woods surrounding my house, I got out of bed at two o'clock in the morning of my first day at home and ran to the top of our long driveway where the trees cleared. There, the sky was revealed as vast as the desert I had just left. I stayed for an hour, looking so hard into the sky that I was no longer looking up but seeing through the layers of the spheres, where I was certain I could see stars being born, others dying, moons in their orbit around distant planets. My breaths grew deeper; my muscles relaxed. I returned to my room, now cozy instead of clutching, ready for sleep.

My escapes were never calculated. I only knew there were times I had to bolt and that outside my door were trees and swamps and frogs and sky ready to receive me.

It is harder to run outside in New York City. There is no expanse of sky or starlight. I walked concrete sidewalks from an apartment with windows we never opened because of noise and dirt to an office with no windows at all. But there was one September in the mid-1980s when a rare hurricane swept through the city, its advance winds beckoning me. I walked the mile to work, feeling heroic. On my way home, I went to the East River and lost myself in the sight of the swirling water and the wallop of the wind, which merged with the rush of blood and saltwater roaring through my own body.

I learned to use the weather to awaken my senses. During one particularly frigid winter, on clear nights with the air crackling with cold, I would walk down silent streets, daring myself to shiver, gulping arctic air into my lungs, feeling the iciness refresh my skin as if I were dousing myself with cold water on a sultry summer day.

My most enduring memory from what had, until Nadia's cancer, been the saddest day of my life—the day my mother died—is of tulips. I noticed them in the meridian of Park Avenue while driving home from the restaurant where my father had reached me with the news. When I recall them now, they are taller, denser, richer than they had any chance of being early in April, as if all my years of turning to nature had made its magnificence so ingrained that I could create, from a patch of budding flowers, a field of brilliant reds and yellows to remind me of my own vitality.

John and I share a love—no, a need—for the ocean. We began going to Martha's Vineyard before we had children. The island is my ultimate refuge. Every visit is an opportunity for meditation. I sit on my lawn, on the beach, in my kayak and watch. Sometimes my vision is panoramic—gathering ocean, pond, meadow, and sea birds in one visual grasp. But mostly I am captivated by small scenes—the aerial gymnastics of swallows catching insects or of a monarch butterfly tagging along behind a flock of finches. As low tide gives way to high, I'll see how long it takes the barnacles on the rocks to be covered by life-giving saltwater, or I'll take my kayak only a few yards from shore and drift silently, scanning the brackish water of the pond for the glitter of minnows or the shiny cap of a river otter's head.

I rarely seek companionship on my explorations. John and I have kayaked together; we had heard a theory that the teamwork required is good for relationships and decided to test it. We laughed a lot as we tried to coordinate our steering and strokes; but when we returned to shore, I had to go back out on my own because I had failed to notice what wildlife was in the water or along the shore. I have never doubted nature's ability to soothe and heal.

On a late September visit two years before Nadia's diagnosis, when Frannie was eleven, I found myself in one of those pointless, circular arguments you can only have with a preteen daughter who insists she doesn't need your rules anymore. Outside my window was a field of wildflowers teeming with butterflies absorbing what were the last warm rays of summer. I felt trapped by the escalating anger that Frannie and I were generating.

"Let's take a walk," I commanded suddenly.

"But. ..."

"No," I interrupted. "We have to go outside. Now."

As we walked through the swirl of butterflies, whatever point I was trying to make didn't matter anymore.

But from the moment of Nadia's diagnosis, all I wanted from nature was that it not get in my way. Rain slowed traffic, making the ride back from the hospital after chemo feel like a trip through a tunnel with no end. Snow meant that Margie wouldn't be able to get to the hospital to relieve me. Extreme cold brought on a respiratory infection that could spread to Nadia.

We had gone to Martha's Vineyard only once during Nadia's illness, over the long Martin Luther King, Jr., weekend. This was after Nadia's third round of chemo and before her surgery. There was a lull in her treatment as we waited for her body to regain its strength. I noticed, though, that on arrival, my pulse didn't quicken as it usually does; I didn't have my seatbelt off and my hand on the car door handle as soon as we turned into the driveway. No land- or seascape diverted my eyes from Nadia. She alone had been in my line of vision since November. Nadia in an MRI tube. Nadia in a hospital bed. Nadia inside the house, the hospital, her narrowed universe.

On the Vineyard, I saw Nadia too far away from the manmade world that was keeping her alive. I went through the motions of rising just before the sun as I always do on the Vineyard, of going into town, of walking on the beach. But I felt like the weatherman standing in front of a blank screen rather than the map we see on the television. Nature's images were all around me, but I couldn't see them.

One afternoon, I forced myself to drive over to Squibnocket Beach, just up the coast from our Stonewall

Beach home. It's not a particularly dramatic stretch of shore but it retains a rocky ruggedness that reminds me of Ireland. During the winter, seals warm themselves on the massive boulders jutting from the water, and it was these animals that I sought. Seals will watch you from the water, following you as you walk down the beach. I needed the seals to see me, to embrace me with their soulful eyes.

For the first time that weekend, I felt engaged. The ocean was clear. The water was calm. It was low tide and sunny—perfect conditions for seals to haul themselves out onto the rocky coast. But none came, no loving eyes, no messages from nature that I would be cared for.

That night, Nadia came into my room crying. "Mama, I can't sleep. I keep having to go to the bathroom."

"Does it hurt or feel like it's burning?"

"A little," Nadia answered. "I'm so tired and I just want to go to sleep."

While Nadia stood there, waiting for me to make everything better, my stomach began to churn. As if in response to my own turmoil, Martha's Vineyard itself turned against me; the weather became ominous with heavy rain and strong winds. I didn't want to be stuck here if Nadia was getting a bladder infection. If she was in immediate danger, the local hospital wouldn't be able to medivac her to Boston in these conditions.

At 11:00 P.M. I called my friend Maureen, a physician, who was also on the Vineyard that weekend. She arrived at my house within minutes, examined Nadia, and found no distention, no fever. In fact, Nadia seemed ready for sleep.

Maureen told us that, driving over, she had startled an owl. "He seemed to come out of nowhere, this huge owl, and he swooped down low over my car as if he thought he could carry it away. It was amazing."

The story was meant to relax Nadia, but I was the one fixated on Maureen's animated face. For a moment, the outside world flickered back on. I wanted to grab Nadia and run outside to see the owl. Nadia's face, though, was blank.

I had expected too much from nature. Sickness is natural. Chemo is derived from plants. Bodily functions going awry: these are natural, too. Back in New York, I burrowed into Nadia's disease.

Once Nadia resumes chemo after her surgery, time doesn't pass. It is measured: the number of Broviac dressing changes I have left to do, how many more G-shots to deliver, the quantity of special spongy green toothbrushes that protect Nadia's fragile gums we still need. In this way, I count myself to the observance of Passover, a holiday intimately tied to freedom and rebirth.

As we had at Thanksgiving, we decide to begin our celebration of Passover in Pound Ridge. I am feeling relaxed. Nadia has just finished her sixth round of chemo, which included the more toxic drugs of the first three treatments. We have been warned that this time, when Nadia's counts fall, they will plummet and stay down longer than any previous cycle. Every single side effect will be worse—fever, sores, the need for transfusions, fatigue. This time, I am ready with my arsenal of palliative treatments. But Nadia should be fine for the holiday.

I have no memory of the weather as we head up to the house for the weekend. I no longer seek to escape from Nadia as I did on Thanksgiving. I have stopped searching the stars, the trees, the water for help. Nadia is my barometer; and if I can't see her, I don't know what to feel. She is in a festive mood when we arrive. There are no cries of "Owee" on the trip, no withdrawing to my room. She stays up late playing Scrabble and Cranium with Donna, Frannie, Max, and my sister.

It is 11:00 P.M. when Nadia feels an urgent need to go to bed. As soon as she gets under the covers, in the room she will share with Frannie for the weekend, she begins to shiver.

"Mama, I'm freezing."

I assume her chills are her response to the excitement of the family arriving for Passover, the lateness of the hour, the thinness of the blanket that cause her to shake."Let me get you something warmer," I murmur. I pull the fat down comforter off Frannie's bed. "Here, love." I cover and tuck and pat her.

"I'm still cold," Nadia chatters, looking very small under her mound of bedclothes.

I remember when I was breast-feeding Max and Nadia, how cold my chest would feel when no baby was nestled there. I'd sleep under a stack of pillows, but nothing could warm me like a baby. When I took the infant Nadia into bed with me, as if sensing my chill, she could never just lie next to me but would squirm herself onto my chest and belly. Now I crawl into bed beside Nadia to share my heat.

"M-m-mama, it's not helping."

Because Nadia's counts could not have dropped yet, it doesn't occur to me to take her temperature right away. Besides, in the four previous rounds, we had escaped these bone rattlers. Her fevers had crept up like cats—a wisp of tail, a tickle of whisker before the full rub along the leg.

When I finally take her temperature, the thermometer reads102.5 degrees. The doctor says she could have a virus. It's okay to give her Tylenol, but I need to bring her down to the hospital to urgent care to be examined.

Finding the Tylenol should be easy, but nothing is

simple anymore. I hear the dogs bark at the late-night arrival of my niece and her boyfriend. I have never met the young man before, and now my first words to him are "Do you have any Tylenol?"

Someone produces the elixir. John goes to warm up the car. I wrap Nadia in the down blanket and step outside, where I am assaulted by the high-pitched mating call of hundreds of tree frogs. The sound slaps me out of my stupor. I recognize the cacophony as a spring fanfare. I smile for a moment at this noise, a happy sound from my childhood, so unlike the melancholy music I typically conjure of a lone cricket in early fall. I can't stop and listen, though. I make Nadia a bed in the back of our minivan and wonder how long the next hour will take.

Time moves faster once Nadia's tremors stop. She has a smile for me. She sleeps. I exhale.

The fever is gone by the time we arrive at the hospital. Nadia's counts are fine. We are sent home. "Maybe we should just go to the apartment and head back up to Pound Ridge in the morning," I suggest to John. It isn't the ride I am worried about; it is being too far from the hospital in case of a real emergency.

"Why don't we just go up now?" John says. "Then we won't have to worry about getting up early. The doctor said Nadia was okay."

"Fine," I answer, wanting to get this night over with.

At 2:30 A.M., the house in Pound Ridge is silent. I tuck Nadia back into bed. I fall right to sleep. It's a new skill, one I never had as a child, a teenager, a new mother, a used mother. I do not understand Frannie when she comes in to wake me two hours later.

"Mom, Nadia says she's cold again."

"No, she's not," I mumble.

"Mom! Come on! She's calling for you."

The fever has spiked again. "Wake up," I say to John.

"What?" he complains.

"Nadia's fever is up again. We have to bring her back in."

John throws the covers back in a foul mood. He is always angry at being woken from a deep sleep, but this isn't the midnight ringing of the telephone, someone dialing the wrong number.

I bundle up Nadia once more. Frannie follows with a pillow. It is just before dawn. Outside, the frogs are quiet. It is the birds' turn now.

My burden grows too heavy. If I could put Nadia down for a moment, I know my spirit would rise on the sound of song and the light from the lifting sun. I do not know when I will hear nature call to me again.

"I'm c-c-cold," Nadia reminds me.

The birds have chosen the wrong audience. Who but a creature with foolish optimism would sing with such promise of new beginnings, trusting that the sun will rise for another day of perpetuating life?

I look back at Frannie, who won't go inside until our car disappears from view, expecting to find a six-year-old with a mop of Shirley Temple curls wearing her favorite soft cotton dress with the cherries on it, not a beautiful twelve-year-old. It's as if the illness that I couldn't prevent from attacking one child has exposed the vulnerability of the others.

But Frannie is not a fragile little girl, and the newly arrived robins and warblers and waxwings are not singing innocently. They are singing their life. As dawn breaks, they have no choice but to begin their melodies, staking out their territory or announcing their desire for courtship, just as I have no choice but to pick Nadia up, settle her into the car, and reclaim our place in the hospital.

During the nine days that Nadia is in the hospital with neutropenia, I sit as often as I can outside on the playroom terrace. Birds are hard to hear over the noise of traffic and sirens, the hum of air conditioners, the banging of construction at a nearby building site. But periodically, a house finch finds its way to the scrawny limbs of the potted trees of this rooftop. It sings furiously. I pretend it has come specifically to see me, trying to make up for the seals that never came. But my need for it is too strong. I feel abandoned when it flies away.

Six weeks later, Nadia will finish her treatment and return to school. For me, there will be no joy or relief. Without Nadia's presence filling every corner of my existence, I become homesick in my own house.

Instinct will take me to Central Park. At first, I will just sit on a bench in a patch of sun and stare in the direction of Nadia's school four blocks away with the solemnity of one facing Jerusalem. But the park is coming fully awake after the winter, and it will demand my attention: bird calls, cherry blossoms, turtles warming on the rocks around the reservoir. It will take only a couple of days before I begin bringing my books with me, a lunch, and my dogs with whom I pace the wide, gravelly horse trails. I will walk, listen, sniff the air, turn my face to the sun and the breeze, and for a minute at a time I won't think about Nadia.

When school ends, we will return to Martha's Vineyard where I will resume my contemplation of the sea, meadow, and pond. I will discover the nest of a pair of barn swallows under the eaves of my porch. The mother has already laid her eggs, and for weeks she and the father will take turns warming the nest, fattening themselves up, and protecting their home. Then four fledglings will emerge. The parents will work tirelessly to feed the hungry mouths. During a rare moment of rest, the father will look disheveled, his long shiny-black tail feathers lopsided as if he is a groom who has celebrated too long at his wedding. I will beg for the babies to fledge, to give their parents a rest. Finally, they will.

"Look," I'll call to John. "The babies are flying."

All except one—one who maybe didn't get as much food as the others or who was scared or weak. While the family flies off and its brothers and sisters practice a graceless form of flight, the baby will perch and watch.

I have no idea what the mother will do. In the animal world, isn't the story all about the survival of the fittest?

The next day, I will see the mother come back often, sometimes with her whole brood, sometimes alone, to feed her baby and make it strong. On the second day, she will fly up to the nest as if to feed her fledgling and then start chattering and singing and flitting around as if she is telling her baby, "It's time now: follow me." Eventually, the little bird will, plummeting more than flying down onto the porch railing. With all of her children together and strong, the mother will resume her normal repertoire of soft chirps and whistles.

Just a year earlier, I would have believed the natural world was trying to teach me a lesson. *Go on, you can return to singing your life by the old melody.* That woman has been lost to me. I admire the swallow, but the task ahead of me will be so much greater than getting a bird to fly. If I am able to sing anything at all, it will be in a minor key, in a slow tempo with many rests.

16

For six months, I have looked forward to the end, but now I don't know what it means. I have no job now. I miss Nadia like I would miss an arm.

—journal entry, May 3, 2001

Can you tell when cancer ends any more than you can know when a river entering the ocean is no longer a rushing force of fresh water but an indistinguishable part of the sea?

Nadia's last day of chemo is a day full of errors—an IV bag hung but the clamp never opened to begin the drip, the etoposide never delivered from the pharmacy, a broken pump. It is a metaphor for the past year: nothing is predictable; don't make plans to be home at 4:00 because chances are you won't arrive until 7:00.

Eventually we do arrive. We have left the flowers a friend brought for this day of celebration at the PDH. Our only take-away is the pump that still circulates protective fluids through Nadia's body. I listen to it cycling all night. *It's not chemo. It's not chemo. It's not chemo.* When the bag is drained, I disconnect the tubes and hang the backpack on Nadia's headboard so I won't forget to return it.

"Congratulations, Nadia," Max says as he goes to give his sister a hug. "You're done."

"Get that thing out of my sight," Nadia hisses from a vein of venom that, in all their poking, no nurse had ever tapped.

I stash the pump in the closet. There. Done. But the last day of chemo was not the last day of cancer. The past six months cannot be stowed away, removed to the attic with all those other artifacts of our history. We will not be collecting dust now anyway. G-shots, blood counts, transfusions, Broviac dressing changes, hand washing, not kissing on the lips or sharing a drink all continue.

And fever.

The two days following the final infusion of ifosfamide and etoposide hold two events Nadia has been looking forward to for months—a performance of Cirque du Soleil and the annual Children's Museum of Manhattan benefit, a huge indoor carnival that this year would include a climbing wall and live camels. I am relieved to get into the car on Saturday evening and be on our way to the circus. Our plans have been tentative for so long that I have stopped counting on being able to do anything even while we are in the process of doing it.

Nadia makes it through 90 percent of the performance. Not feeling well comes on suddenly. "Mama, I want to go home now," Nadia whispers to me.

The contortionists are on the stage, but Nadia can't wait for them to return to normal human configuration. "Now, Mama, please now."

I hesitate because, as in the first weeks in the hospital when I worried so much about not annoying the nurses, I don't want to disturb the audience around us. I hope people see Nadia's scarf-covered head and understand.

The usher doesn't. "You can't leave until the performance is over," he declares with arms crossed and his feet planted in a broad stance.

"My daughter is sick," I say. Even though what I say has never been truer, I feel like the kid who said he couldn't get his homework done because his very healthy, living-in-Miami grandmother is dead. I wish I could say that I brush on past this man, defending my daughter at all costs, but I wait like the good girl for permission to leave.

On Sunday at 4:00 A.M., Nadia wakes with feverish chills. "Don't make me go to the hospital. I want to ride the camels," she cries.

All the disappointments of the past year are released by that cry, a Pandora's box of sadnesses. No swimming, no fencing, no medieval feast, a Thanksgiving with no national anthems, a Passover in the hospital, no Vail, canceled sleepovers, a year lost in gymnastics, no dressing up in her perfect school uniform—blue tunic, Peter Pan–collared white shirt, blue knee socks, and tie shoes—to recite poetry and sing songs to all the dads at the father/daughter breakfast.

"I'm sorry, baby, but the doctor says we have to go."

Only one other patient is in urgent care. By the time we arrive Nadia's temperature has already dropped; her white count is fine. She won't have to be admitted, but her hemoglobin is low. Orders are put in for a transfusion and an antibiotic.

By now it is 6:00 A.M. Only six more hours until the Children's Museum party. Urgent care is filling up. When there were just two of us earlier, I had heard the nurses complain about being too busy to take on any extra tasks. How would they respond now if I told them to hurry, that a very important date with a camel was at stake? Also a climbing wall, art projects, exotic food, auctions and, of course, Gaby.

I take my chances. Nadia's nurse responds, not because we have some place to go but because she knows that any place would be better for a nine-year-old than the adult-filled urgent care unit of a cancer hospital.

With two hours' worth of sleep but an infusion of red-blood cells, Nadia arrives at the party an hour and a half late but with enough time for multiple camel rides and several trips up the climbing wall. While I watch Nadia, I think, Look at her, everyone. She's the girl with cancer who came straight from a night in the hospital and she's climbing that wall.

What I also want, though, is for people to look at me, the mother of the kid with cancer. I'm not sure what I want everyone to see, however: a woman who's strong or sad or different or a martyr? Am I anticipating the time when I will be just like every other mom in the room—no longer special or super? Or will I realize that I was never either of those; I was just a mom with a sick kid surrounded by people with their own stories disguised by smiling faces so similar to my own facade.

After mothering with such intensity, what do I do now? Soon Nadia's hair will grow back, and she will fill out, and the visible traces of what she has been through will fade, like the settling of a grave.

Already by Monday, when we return to the PDH for a blood test, I feel like an outsider, as if I am sucking up too much oxygen, taking it from people who really need it.Nadia's white-blood-cell count is .2, officially neutropenic. The next day, her temperature starts to creep up but then returns to normal, as if it has lost the will to fight. I can put my syringes away now, stash the spongy green toothbrushes, close the medicine-cabinet door on the Ativan and Vistaril and the Nystatin mouth rinse. Now are we done?

Only one symbol of Nadia's treatment remains—the Broviac, the representation of Nadia's cancer since the beginning. "Can I get it out now?" Nadia begs the nurse practitioner when we come back the next week for a blood test.

"When is your next set of scans?" she asks.

"In two weeks," I answer.

"We really can't take the Broviac out before then, just in case."

Nadia and I both know what "just in case" means. Nadia is angered by what she sees as a challenge to her newly acquired health. I am only frightened. After all, this is the same woman who thought John and I were so pathetic before Nadia's biopsy, when we allowed ourselves to believe there was a chance Nadia would not awaken with a Broviac.

On May 11, Nadia's scans—MRI, bone, and chest CAT scan—are all clean. On May 16, the Broviac comes out. It is a quick procedure done at the PDH. True to form, Nadia's only worry is that she will need an IV.

"No," the doctor says. "We put the anesthesia in through your Broviac before we take it out." The final act of compassion of Nadia's central IV line.

Once again, I despair at the sight of Nadia going under. It's too fast a transition. She's too vulnerable, too far away. While I wait outside in the hallway, I have daymares that they have given Nadia too much anesthesia and are in the room right now giving her emergency resuscitation. I create drama where there is none because I have no other way of rationalizing my tears, which I now shed with a fervor I haven't experienced since Nadia's diagnosis. My sorrow is a fine silt that needs only the mildest of disturbances to set it swirling.

Nadia is in no rush to leave the PDH when the procedure is over. She lingers in the playroom to do the art project of the day as if she, too, isn't certain of what is over, what part of this identification as citizen of MSKCC she is expected to take home with her and what to discard.

Nadia has a bandage where the Broviac was. I'm still afraid of hugging her for fear of pulling on her tubes. When she removes her shirt that night, I stare at the uncluttered surface of her chest. What I want to see is a tree whose limbs, suddenly unburdened by heavy snow, spring back to their full outstretched position. The reality is more like the slow unfurling of the roots of a repotted plant. Freedom is not easy to grasp because I am not free. The shadow of the Broviac keeps me tethered to Nadia.

Nadia returns to school for the last few weeks of the term, but I do not move forward easily. I have always clung to the past, gathering it around me in great folds of sentiment and melancholy that the present can never provide. Even when I'm away, every time I close the door to a room where I might have stayed for a night or a week, with family or by myself, I feel an ache. For whatever brief moment of time, those four walls contained my life, the cycle of my days, my possessions, and literally my dreams. Nadia's cancer defined my life in as exotic a way as the room I stayed in on a kibbutz in Israel when I was sixteen. It represented one of the most intensely lived periods of my life, when every moment was clear in purpose, rich in emotion, thick with love. But the door won't close behind me all the way; it stands ajar, inviting me back, drawing me into a cancer underworld.

I Broviac myself to my computer. Google: Ewing's sarcoma, National Institutes of Health, National Cancer Institute, Pediatric Cancer, MSKCC, bone cancer. I start with sites that confirm what I already know: a description of Ewing's, the standard treatment, survival statistics. I progress to clinical trials, digest prechewed information for families and patients. Still, I need more. I want the same information the doctors have. Morbidity, survivability, toxicity. Someone should do a study on the stupidity of curiosity. In the pages of jargon, I find these words: "Patients whose tumors did not respond as well to chemo had higher rates of relapse and death."

I finally OD. I swear I'll never go online again.

My efforts to stay clean are sabotaged by the mail. Our contribution to MSKCC's Bunny Hop has put us on the hospital's mailing list. Cancer news, delivered to my door.

Then there is Friends of Karen. Named in memory of a girl who had died of cancer, this organization supports families who are coping with the demands of caring for a child with a life-threatening illness. Frannie, Max, and Nadia had all participated in Friends of Karen swim-a-thons sponsored by their day camp four years before Nadia's diagnosis. The group's newsletter has a clever tactic—portray the worst, most helpless scenarios to generate the most sympathy and the most dollars. And every quarter there seems to be a child with Ewing's who didn't make it or one whose odds are low.

St. Jude's Hospital for Children had been sending us mail since we sponsored a friend in a walk-a-thon the year before. Now their fundraising appeal features a little girl with Ewing's in its deadliest form. How did they know? I wonder as I write out another check.

Ronald McDonald House of New York—which provided housing, socializing and support for so many of the out-of-town families we met at the hospital—added us to their mailing list two years earlier after Max and his classmates had participated in the charity's annual kids' run. I write out yet another check.

Despite my lifelong obsession with reading, I had read only one book since October 31. It was Steve Martin's

Shopgirl, not a book I would typically select but a friend had given it to me. It was short, and I was hoping for a few laughs that I don't remember getting. I began my return to serious reading with Lucy Greely's *Autobiography of a Face*. Months earlier, I had read about the author, who'd had Ewing's of the jaw when she was nine. I knew enough not to read the book in the throes of caring for Nadia but set it aside for my dessert. In the park, four blocks from the school where Nadia went about her day, I devoured Greely's words, not questioning how I could be hungry for something so horrible.

Nadia didn't join me at my warped feast. She slipped back into life not as one who had undergone an experience radically different from her classmates for six months but like a person who had been frozen in time and saw no reason, upon awakening, to expect anything to have changed.

My flute, which had lain in its case like a forgotten marionette for the past year, still held no seduction for me. I knew how hard it would be to get back in shape, to make music that sounded like silver rather than stone. Ultimately, tooth grinding and clenching would cause misalignment in my jaw and an injunction against playing for another year, if not longer. Returning to music would be a long way off.

Nadia returned to school just in time for Famous Women's Day, an annual presentation in which each third grader delivers a monologue in the character of a leading historical or contemporary female figure. The first step for the girls was to select four choices from a long list of names.

Nadia's first choice was Kerri Strug, the American gymnast who got attention for continuing her Olympic competition with an injured foot. Her fourth choice was the flamboyant track star and another Olympic champion, Florence Griffith Joyner, who'd died from an epileptic seizure in 1998 at age thirty-nine.

I was certain Nadia's teachers would assign her Kerri Strug. Before cancer, Nadia had been the only serious gymnast in her class. She couldn't wait to start training again, and the image of Strug competing with a serious handicap was an additional element of serendipity. When she came home from school on the day the girls got their assignments, I thought my question to Nadia would be a mere formality. "So, who'd you get?" I asked.

"Flo-Jo," Nadia said matter-of-factly.

"Flo-Jo?"

"Yup," Nadia answered before bouncing off to her room, eager to start the biography she had checked out of the library.

"But," I started to say. *But it's so unfair. You just had cancer. You have suffered. You lost so much. Would it have killed them to give you Kerri Strug?*

What were Nadia's teachers thinking? They knew Nadia would be happy with whomever she got. But who's to say that was the best thing for her? What kind of tension and pressure was she absorbing in the name of cooperation? Where were those forces settling in her body, still weakened and compromised? And why did they have to pick someone who had died so young?

But Nadia loved Flo-Jo. She loved wearing a wig of wild hair; she loved decorating her hands with long, fake fingernails; and I should have understood, after watching her ignore all the art project rules in the hospital playroom, that designing a costume in Flo-Jo's style would be much more interesting to her than donning yet another leotard.

On the day of the presentation, I couldn't "ooh" with

all the other parents when "Kerri Strug" made her entrance doing a back walkover. I tried to see Flo-Jo in my daughter, but I kept imagining the bald head under the wig, seeing the eyes with no lashes and wondering how such a skeletal figure could ever have the muscle and stamina to run a race.

This was not what Nadia was projecting; she was indistinguishable from any of the other third graders whose nervous energy and excitement propelled them through their presentations. It was what I chose to see, a reverse version of the mother who strains to hear perfect intonation and musical genius while her child warbles through a solo in the school play.

School ended a few weeks later. At the end-of-year picnic, Nadia tried to keep up with a few girls doing cartwheels and handstands but hurt her leg on a clumsy landing. She came to sit by me, not talking, observing her friends. She drifted among the other mothers, at ease in adult company. When a wheelbarrow race was organized, Nadia chose to join.

Nadia and her friend Marlena made up the fourth pair of girls at the starting line. Nadia supported herself on her arms, while Marlena took hold of Nadia's legs. At the word "Go," the other girls leaped ahead, as if their wheelbarrows were empty, while Marlena and Nadia struggled with their heavy load.

"Marlena keeps dropping my legs," Nadia complained in frustration after they had lost for the third or fourth time.

It's not Marlena, I wanted to say. You don't have the strength to help. What would have been the point, though? Nadia would not acknowledge that she has been weakened.

I could not see Nadia as strong. Two weeks later,

when we got to Martha's Vineyard for the summer, I made her wear sneakers for races on the lawn because the foot on the leg that had had the bone removed didn't flex and I was afraid she'd trip over her toes. In the pool, I decreed that no one could swim near Nadia. What if she got kicked in the face? When she went water skiing, she asked me to come. "I think you'll have more fun without me there worrying," I said and whispered to my friend who would be driving the boat not to go too fast when it was Nadia's turn.

It was hard for me to break the habit of fearing so much for Nadia's health, but she didn't want to be the sick one anymore. After a game of Monkey in the Middle, when she complained of a sore shoulder, I suggested she might have pulled a muscle.

"There's nothing wrong with my shoulder," Nadia said, annoyed with me and annoyed with illness. "There's nothing wrong with *me*."

I had one distraction that summer: Frannie's *bat mitzvah*. To the years' old thoughts I had always had about what I would say to her, I add one more observation. *Tikkun Olam,* repair of the world, is an obligation of every Jew. To Frannie I would say that through her *Tikkun Mishpochah,* repair of the family, she was already well on her way to fulfilling her role as a *bat mitzvah,* an adult Jew.

Beginning with the writing of these thoughts one week before the ceremony, to the family-only *Shabbat* dinner the night before, to the lifting of the dense mist that had shrouded the Vineyard for thirty-six hours at the precise moment Frannie assumed her place in front of the congregation, I hoped to enter a shelter built of such joy and celebration that none of those hospital sounds that accompanied so much of our preparation for this event would be able to penetrate. Not true. The shelter was there, but so were the sounds. The sounds had helped to build this sanctuary, gave us the spirit to celebrate where we were on this day. When I looked at Nadia, the sounds grew louder; when I turned to Frannie, they became fainter. Only when I finally had my chance to speak to Frannie did I take my first step back to being a mother of three.

As if she had been saving up a list of complaints for me, Frannie would be the next one I would be taking to the doctor. As part of the protocol for annual physicals, Dr. Murphy performs a routine check for any curvature of the spine. At Frannie's exam in May, Dr. Murphy found a lump alongside her lower vertebrae. "I think it's just some fatty tissue," he said. "They're never anything, but, given what you've been through, why don't you have one of Nadia's doctors look at it?"

There was no urgency in Dr. Murphy's tone this time, no calls to John, no need for special appointments, just a suggestion that I bring Frannie with me to Nadia's next follow-up. But given what I had been through I went numb. I willed my brain not to feel, but I couldn't control my body; my skin could barely contain the shaking inside of me.

Nadia's next appointment wasn't for two months. I couldn't just show up with Frannie, though, so I called the hospital.

"This is Nadia Hannan's mother. Nadia has an appointment with Dr. Wexler in July. I wanted to let you know that I was going to bring her sister Frannie, too. She has a lump her pediatrician wants you to check out."

"Is she a new patient?" the receptionist asked.

"Who?"

"Frannie."

"She's not exactly a patient. We just need someone to look at her back."

I heard the sound of computer keys. "Nadia's appointment is at three," the receptionist told me. "How about I put Frannie in at 3:15?"

This was becoming too official. Frannie was supposed to just tag along.

"But she should come in earlier so we can register her," the receptionist continued.

"Register?" I tried to figure out how to argue this. I couldn't. "Fine," I said and hung up. No way in hell am I going to fill out one piece of paper with Frannie's name on it or have them put one of those plastic hospital bracelets on her wrist.

We flew into New York from the Vineyard for the appointment. Without coordinating beforehand, Frannie, Nadia, and I all dress in the same colors—turquoise, blue, and white—the three Hannan girls in solidarity on a trip to the city. Only this would not be a shopping spree, a Broadway matinee, or tea at the Plaza.

When we got to the hospital, the person who would have registered Frannie was busy. When Nadia was called, I brought Frannie with us, pleased with my little act of rebellion in bypassing the authorities. Two doctors examined Frannie. The second, a surgeon, closed his eyes, felt, and probed. The silence in the room was total as he looked, felt again, and measured. Then he delivered his diagnosis: there's no lump or mass. Frannie's spine was curved, creating a small bulge. My relief left room for no other feeling; Nadia's clean bill of health almost seemed secondary.

Leaving, I asked, "Do I have to register Frannie?"

The doctor disliked this idea as much as I did. "Go,

get out of here," he said. I couldn't push the girls out the door fast enough, back to the airport and the Vineyard.

I declared a moratorium on cancer. No more research on the computer, no more defining myself as the mother of the daughter with cancer.

A month later, I met an acquaintance I hadn't seen in almost a year. We began to chat. "How are the boys?" I asked her.

"They're great."

"How old are they now?"

"Two and four and a half."

"Already? How come everyone else's children seem to grow so fast? I guess you must be preparing for kindergarten."

I kept the subject on her boys but eventually she asked how my kids were.

"They're doing well," I answered, "enjoying the summer."

"Where does Max go to school?" my friend asked.

She doesn't know about Nadia. She really doesn't know.

"Allen-Stevenson. He loves it there."

I could tell her. But I remembered my moratorium, not recognizing at the time that it is too soon to be so silent. I was still a mother who cared for a daughter with cancer so recently that we didn't even know yet if she would be a survivor. But I didn't know how to introduce the topic without feeling as if I were dropping my burden like garbage on her doorstep, as if such conversations can't be had at a garden party.

So instead I said, "Let me know if you want to know more about Max's school. I'd love to talk to you about it," as we continue our talk about kids, the summer, the upcoming election.

Back in New York in September, though, flashback triggers were everywhere. Walking Nadia home from school, I remembered her exhausting efforts to keep up with Emily and Gaby after her initial round of chemo. Smelling the residue of antibacterial soap on my hands, I pictured those same hands changing Nadia's Broviac dressing. Preparing for Halloween, I wanted permission to pretend the day never existed.

I tried to confine my cancer fixation to my close friends, but my ban on seeking fresh doses of sympathy ended when I received a card from a friend with whom I had lost contact. She had included a picture of her children and a note about how stressful it was to live with the anxiety caused by 9/11.

I wrote back, enclosing a picture of my children from Frannie's *bat mitzvah,* when Nadia's head was still bald. I told myself it was the best photograph I had, that it was a way of sharing the joy of Frannie's achievement, but I could have chosen from among other, more recent ones that showed Nadia with a pixie cut. I told my friend, "By seeing how much your children have grown, I realize how long it's been since we've seen each other. Here is my crew. Nadia's bald because she spent the last year being treated for cancer, but she's fine now and her prognosis is excellent." My friend didn't write back.

That fall, Nadia develops a parallel focus on her cancer experience. I feel there has to be a reason—the same triggers I am experiencing, losing the sense of elation she had in the spring, a sense similar to my own that an intensity of purpose is missing in her life, or maybe she is missing me as much as I am missing her. No doubt, all the above affect Nadia but I never consider the most basic reason. Her cancer experience is like a new person whom she has to get to know and understand and figure out how to place within her life.

"Mama, do you think Marie needed to have her leg amputated?" Nadia asks about the friend with whom she made French toast.

"Mama, remember when Yaakov and I made up that tonic for making hair grow and we put up signs all over the inpatient floor or when we got stuck in the electronic doorway because it was *Shabbat* and he wouldn't let me push the button to open it?"

"Mama, will you stand with me at services to say a *Mishabeyrach* [a healing prayer] for my friends?"

So I am not surprised one afternoon when Nadia says, "Mama, I want to make a scrapbook." She has just come home from school and has found me moving stuff around her room, not quite knowing how to give it a proper makeover to reflect the life of a healthy nine-year-old.

"A scrapbook?"

"Yeah, with all my stuff from last year," she answers.

In a basket in the corner are all of her hats and scarves. Her art projects adorn shelves, her bulletin board, and her desktop. In a corner of her bookcase are a couple of notebooks containing her scribbled postsurgery notes—suction, hot, itchy, Benadryl, pain, put on a video, and this note after an episode of *Survivor:* "It is not good to get a really close friend and no other friends because if he gets voted off you don't have any friends." At the time I loved this note because, while everyone else watching *Survivor* was concerned with alliances and strategy, Nadia was concerned with true friendship.

Hospital ID bracelets are as ubiquitous as sand in a beach house. I find them in drawers, my pocketbook, a basket of neglected hair ties, the plate on my dresser that holds my loose change, on the arms of stuffed dogs and teddy bears. The bathroom cabinet holds pill jars, medicine bottles, bandages, unused tooth swabs, syringes, the bag Nadia used for irrigating her mouth. In a wardrobe compartment are Broviac dressing kits. Nadia's crutches stand in a corner in the closet. On the wall is the photo collage I made to decorate her hospital room. In my file cabinet are printouts of blood counts and the huge pile of cards of concern and prayer I had received from family and friends and distant acquaintances. Among the videos in our playroom is *Why, Charlie Brown, Why?* which Nadia has begun watching again, always with me at her side. How can all of this fit into a scrapbook?

"Maybe you can take photographs of some of this stuff," I suggest.

Over the next few days, I see Nadia arranging hats and bandages and medical supplies and snapping away. But whether she grows uncomfortable with such face-to-face reminders or just bored, her enthusiasm wanes. We decide to store everything in a big box. This consumes days as Nadia insists on reading every card and letter, reviewing the ups and downs of her blood counts, recounting the circumstances behind each art project—whether she was inpatient or outpatient, in for fever or surgery, which friends were there with her.

I am happy to have an accomplice. What I don't recognize, though, is that, unlike me, Nadia has another life at school, a disease-free place she goes to without me for eight hours every day. Like the realization that Frannie's devotion to Nadia had nothing to do with supporting me, so does Nadia's abandonment rouse me to the fact that, as the mother, I cannot ask my children to soothe my emotional pain. Sometimes, though, the temptation is too great to resist.

It is an annual tradition at Nadia's school that, in March, the fourth graders put on a gymnastics show. This year the most coveted role, climbing the rope in the grand finale, will go to only one girl. The theme—heroes—is pure post-9/11.

Nadia comes home a few weeks before the show to tell me she has been chosen to be the rope climber. Finally, some justice, I think.

For the first twenty-five minutes of the show, we—the parents of the fourth graders as well as the students in grades K–3—watch the girls go through their rotations on the various equipment. The final sequence brings all forty-five girls together for a choreographed routine set to Mariah Carey's song "Hero." I don't see Nadia anywhere in the gym. The image of her being incapacitated is too fresh for me to assume she is okay. (Indeed, she has the flu and woke up with a 102-degree fever, but nothing was going to keep her home on this day.) My anxious voice can be heard on the videotape I made, murmuring, "Where's Nadia? I don't see her. Where is she?"

The song is nearing its final chorus. As Mariah sings about what it is to be a hero, Nadia makes her entrance. Nadia is the only one moving now as she walks the full length of the gym. Her eyes are fixed ahead of her. Her chin is held high. I recognize the sense of determination I have come to know so well. There is a gap in time when I don't make the connection between Nadia and the song, don't recognize when my tears start to flow or understand that every other mother in the gym is crying too and trying to catch my eye. The kindergartner sitting next to me stares at me, mouth agape. "Do you know Nadia?" I ask. "She's my daughter," as if that should be explanation enough for my blubbering.

By the time the song ends, reminding us that a hero

lies within each of us, Nadia has reached the top of the twenty-foot rope, where she pauses a moment before descending in silence and then applause.

Nadia has become the focus of everyone's attention, and I break into my own thoughts to wonder how this must feel to the other girls. Could she possibly be a hero to them since they, thank God, can have no understanding of what she has gone through? And how about the other mothers whose tears are so genuine? When they come up to me afterward, I feel I am stealing the attention their own daughters deserve.

After the show, I stop crying long enough to congratulate Nadia. "That was amazing. You had everyone in tears."

"I didn't see anyone crying," she answers.

"You didn't? Don't you understand why they picked you to climb the rope?"

"A bunch of us tried out and from the group that made it they pulled a name out of a hat."

"Nadia, they picked you because of what you went through last year."

I *need* Nadia to admit that she was a hero, that this opportunity I am getting through her to weep openly will not be taken away from me. But Nadia is furious.

"Stop it," she cries. "I hate it when you say things like that." She turns her back on me, setting off to be with her friends, people whom she is determined to blend in with once more.

Alone, however, Nadia clung to our cancer bond. She was thirsty for the stories of other kids with cancer. I quenched her desire with the profiles I found online. By now, I knew all the best places to look. But I could be an overbearing suitor, smothering my sweetheart with too many flowers and endearments. I missed the cues that told me when Nadia was sated, when she would wave me off with a dismissive, "Yeah, interesting," or "I just want to watch TV right now."

As the second cancer-free Halloween approached, I wondered how long I was going to be allowed to memorialize this day. One friend told me this was the last year; another said I should be free to wallow for the next twenty.

I should have listened more to my second friend. It was folly enough to assume I could even contain my sorrow to this one day. I was in emotional menopause, unable to regulate my temperature or my moods.

Eighteen months into Nadia's remission, I gave a tour to prospective parents at my daughters' school. On the science floor, I started talking about the opportunities for independent study. "In tenth-grade biology, students do a research project. Frannie is doing hers on chemo."

"That's a serious topic," the father said.

"In the fifth grade, they also do a long-term research project on any topic the student wants. One girl did hers on the intelligence of fish. Frannie did a really lame one on tree bark."

"What's Nadia's topic?" the couple asked, stepping into my trap.

"She's thinking something about cancer."

The husband stepped closer to his wife. "Cancer's a big topic in my house. Nadia had cancer a couple of years ago," I said, my voice rising as if I have done something dangerous, "but she's fine now."

I waited two or three beats, time enough for what I have said to register but not enough time to elicit any sympathy before moving on to the language program.

For a second, I felt great. *Look at me, see how to-*

gether I am after my ordeal, how I can slip these words so casually into a conversation. But after a few minutes, I felt dirty. If I had achieved acceptance, I wouldn't have felt the need to erupt in inappropriate places. I was acting as if the experience of Nadia's illness was itself a cancer, something to be excised and killed. The thought came to me that maybe this is how I have absorbed my mother's insistence that, when we were sick, we should be downstairs by lunchtime. Now, a year and a half after Nadia has finished treatment, I should be ready for lunch.

I began to feel more natural speaking about Nadia. In the winter of 2002, Frannie gave me another scare when she found a small lump between her jaw and right ear. Once more we were back at Dr. Murphy's office. I no longer joked with him but used all my concentration during the exam to keep from crying. He thought it might be TMJ since Frannie loved to chew ice or, perhaps, an infection. I took Frannie to a maxillo-facial specialist, specifically avoiding the doctor I took Nadia to, but I told this new doctor all about her.

After Frannie's X ray, the doctor disappeared for a long time. He returned with Frannie's films and a great deal of knowledge about Ewing's. I was impressed by what must have been some hastily done research. He saw no sign of a tumor and suspected a swollen lymph node.

This took us to an ear, nose, and throat specialist. At this point, I was so wrapped up in Nadia flashbacks that, when the doctor asked a question about whether Frannie had seen anyone before him, I answered as if he were asking about Nadia. "Yes, Dr. Meyers and Dr. Wexler."

After the appointment, I called Dr. Murphy to say that Frannie had been put on antibiotics for an infected lymph node. He asked, "Did you tell the doctor about Nadia?"

"You mean, miss an opportunity to talk about her? Of course I told him."

But suddenly the urge disappeared. At her two-year checkup, Nadia got a clean bill of health. A few weeks later, I was with a group of women I didn't know well when the conversation turned to someone's mother who had breast cancer. The mother had chosen to receive radiation at a hospital where the decor is pretty as opposed to the one with the better radiology department.

"I can understand that," another woman said. "Think how horrible it would be at MSKCC where everyone has cancer. It's so depressing there."

This woman's mother is a fool to choose aesthetics over quality, I thought. But I didn't speak. This wasn't the place.

Minutes, hours, sometimes most of the day can go by when I have no thoughts of cancer. I think I am finally beginning the process of moving on, a phrase that has entered our lexicon as a necessary component of healing after tragedy. I prefer the phrase *moving with*. Just as those molecules of fresh water will forever be a part of the ocean, so will the days of Nadia's illness always be a part of me.

17

Nadia says she misses me all day at school. She wouldn't sleep on the mattress I brought into our room last night. I had to be in the bed next to her. She says her thoughts about death are too much for someone her age.

—journal entry, October 20, 2002

During treatment and for nearly a year afterward, Nadia didn't speak of death except to insist that she knew she wouldn't die. She ran toward her life with such gusto that she had none of the morbid associations with Halloween that I had developed.

For her first post-cancer Halloween, Nadia was going to be a leprechaun. She found an old pair of green leggings and a vest in a matching shade in my closet. We covered a striped red-and-white Dr. Seuss hat with green felt and added green felt buckles to a pair of her old school shoes. A fluffy white beard completed the costume.

Nadia posed for me, her Irish grin twinkling her delight, and waited for my oohs and ahs. I tried to muster the appropriate Halloween spirit. "Wow, Nadia," I said. "You make a perfect leprechaun."

Perhaps it was the way I hesitated before speaking,

my averted eyes, or the tenderness in my voice, but before Nadia left with a friend to go trick-or-treating she said to me, "Mom, don't worry. Last year I was an angel. Angels live in the sky. This year I'm a leprechaun. Leprechauns live on earth."

I marveled at the vision of Halloween costumes as divine symbols assuring me that my daughter was fine. How brilliant of Nadia, I thought, to choose a character who not only resided firmly on earth but who also possessed magical powers and a hint of immortality. I was happy to play along with Nadia's fantastical thinking; it was what I sought from her as a child—if it would keep her fears away. But the power of the leprechaun would soon fade.

In the spring of 2002, as Nadia anticipates her first-year checkup, the awareness that her cancer could recur explodes in her consciousness. "I'm not going," she insists. "I hate Dr. Meyers. I hate Dr. Wexler."

"They saved your life, Nadia," I respond, surprised that she isn't grateful the way I am.

"They gave me chemo. They hurt me. I don't have cancer, and I don't ever have to go back there again."

I have seen so many flashes of Nadia's anger before that I don't yet see the larger meaning of this specific blowup. Like the cancer itself, the symptoms of Nadia's growing fear have emerged in stages.

Nadia had a friend from school, Sarah, who lived a block from our apartment on the Upper East Side. Our windows faced each other; and if we squinted, we could see into each other's living rooms and wave back and forth.

In the fourth grade, Nadia and Sarah were on the same gymnastics team, and they had started a tradition of sleeping at Sarah's the night before a meet. Nadia loved these sleepovers, particularly their tradition of waking up early so she and Sarah could fix their hair with festive ties and glitter just like the Olympians. One night in early May 2002, however, Nadia calls me from Sarah's, her voice thick with sadness, whispering, "Mama, I want you."

"I'm just a block away, honey," I soothe her. "Do you want to wave to me?"

"No. I want to come home."

"Okay, love, I'll be right there." I walk to Sarah's in tears. My sense of loss since the earliest days of Nadia's diagnosis and treatment is a chronic insomniac, awakening at the slightest disruption to Nadia's happiness.

Nadia's relief at seeing me when I pick her up is short-lived. Once home, she throws her overnight bag on the floor and spins toward me, saying, "I hate my feelings. They keep me from doing the things I want to do."

I know it would be a mistake to say what I am thinking, that feelings like these are what you can expect after what you've been through. Nadia still will not admit that having been treated for cancer is a reason to be physically weaker or more emotionally fragile.

"Why don't you go to bed, and in the morning I'll take you back to Sarah's so you can still get ready for the meet together?" I suggest.

"Will you lie with me?" she asks.

"Of course," I say, not wanting to disappoint her about one more thing.

Two months later, Nadia begins talking about death again. She no longer assumes the wise voice of the practical little girl who has told her brother that he could see no one but himself when he died. Nor does she express the childlike fear that she will be bored or lonely all by herself, forever.

"What's it like?" she asks, the pleading in her eyes magnified through the prism of her tears. "Is it like blacking out but you never wake up or like the universe just ends?"

Nadia keeps hammering away at my fears, which go beyond whether or not we will survive death, all the way back to the day when the sun will explode and the universe itself will die.

"I don't know, Nadia," I begin. "It's scary because there is no certainty."

If Nadia had a different mother, she might be taught to believe in heaven or reincarnation or spirits, but these were not beliefs my own mother passed down to me. Nor can I buy my mother-in-law's vision that she will join friends and family she pictures enjoying themselves on an eternal beach. The Jewish version—which says that, once the Messianic age arrives, all who lived, who live now, and who are still to be born will exist together forever in a perfect world—is equally unbelievable to me.

Instead, I repeat some form of the view my father has expressed. "Grandpa says that, as he grows older, he doesn't feel scared to die. I've heard other older people say the same thing."

Nadia's blank eyes tell me that ten-year-olds can't be expected to think like their grandpas. But then again, ten-year-olds aren't supposed to have thoughts like Nadia's in the first place.

Nadia asks John as well. Two years earlier, she wouldn't have turned to him with such questions. Now she tells me she feels closer to him. He had been with her nearly every day for six months. While I was reacting to his anxiety and helplessness, Nadia was finding comfort in his presence. While I felt his grief, she absorbed his benevolence. While I hurt Nadia and fought with her,

John became her playmate. He had watched so many episodes of the television show *Gilmore Girls* with Nadia that we still occasionally find him watching the program by himself.

But John cannot tell her what death is. When he seeks my advice, I can only repeat what I have already told her.

At the start of fifth grade, in the fall of 2002, Nadia had several more failed sleepover attempts; soon, even falling asleep at home became a torment. Sudden flashbacks, unbidden visions of painful procedures or the Broviac or the feeding tube, became more numerous and vivid. "I can hear the chemo pump. I can smell the alcohol they used to clean it with," Nadia complained.

More disturbing and hallucinatory images followed. Nadia would see herself standing on the terrace of our fifteenth floor apartment and then falling to her death. Or she imagined jumping off the side of a boat and getting sucked under the hull and drawn into the propeller as if it were happening to her at that moment.

These visions terrified Nadia, not only because they were so horrific but because she couldn't understand why she was having them. I found it easy to identify with Nadia's visions. I have had the experience of driving on the highway and thinking that, with one turn of the wheel, I could smash the car into the guardrail and into the path of oncoming traffic. It's as if I have to tell myself how thin the line is between life and death; self-control is a powerful weapon against destructive actions but also a threat since the act of killing yourself is also a form of control of self. Nadia was afraid because she couldn't see the barrier between her thoughts and the actions she might take.

I tried to reassure Nadia that she was not going to throw herself off of the roof. But the only way she could fall asleep now was if I sat with her and reassured her as her mind alternated between memories of her own pain and sadness and the even worse scenarios generated by her own imagination.

Always, Nadia tries to imagine the black void of lifelessness. "I'm thinking of death." She says the phrase so often that it loses its potency. I no longer struggle for answers or soothing words but insist that, if her mind can think about death, it can also think about something happy or pretty or safe.

Each night, I try to steer the conversation toward something positive—an upcoming party or a visit with a friend's baby. We try lavender oil, sound machines, and different lighting. But as soon as I am quiet or try to leave Nadia's room, her thoughts return.

"Mama, I'm falling again," she calls.

"Nadia, you're not trying to think of other things," I say in frustration.

"I am," she cries. "I can't help it.

"You must be able to. You seem so happy during the day." Nadia is now in fifth grade. "You're fine at school, aren't you?" I ask.

"I'm happy sometimes, but I miss you," she answers. "In between classes, when I'm in the halls and don't have anything to distract me, I'm always thinking about death."

I feel a piece of my soul wither. I try to picture Nadia carrying her nightmares from class to class, and I wonder how she makes it through each day. Her anxieties have gone beyond what I can handle. Our pediatrician, Dr. Murphy, puts me in touch with a therapist who specializes in diagnosing and treating post-traumatic stress disorder.

John is not a believer in therapy. "I can handle my own problems," he says. "Talking about my childhood isn't going to help. That's the past. Never look back."

Stubborn Irishman. I'm not sure if John even believes in psychological disorders. When the topic of my experience with phobias and anxieties comes up, or when I refer to the disordered eating that caused me to drop from 125 to 95 pounds during my freshman year, John will say, "C'mon, it wasn't that bad."

"It was," I always respond. Because my pain was bloodless, because there were no broken bones and no scars etched into my flesh, John will never believe me. So I do not ask him whether he thinks Nadia needs counseling. I tell him. He doesn't resist.

Predictably, though, Nadia balks at going to this new doctor. She does not want to talk to a stranger, especially one who will be more probing than the eye of a camera. I experience an eerie déjà vu as John and I pick up a hostile Nadia at school to return her, through words, to the realm of cancer.

At first, I am relieved to talk to someone, to unburden myself of her fears. I relished talking to a social worker during my mother's treatment for depression so that *my* concerns could be the focus of someone's attention. My views are helpful, but the psychiatrist will listen to my own anxieties only to see how they might be affecting Nadia. What she says counts the most.

Nadia sees the therapist several times and answers pages of questions rating her feelings and moods in a wide range of circumstances related to her cancer and life in general. They ask about how she is eating and sleeping, feelings of dread or helplessness, whether she has trouble paying attention in school, if she has friends. To all of these questions, she says she has little if any concern, telling the doctor that she thinks her dependence on me is just a habit. I wonder if she says this to mislead him into thinking she doesn't need help.

I have to complete a set of forms, too. One asks about how I perceive Nadia's mental state. The other addresses my own. At the final evaluation, the doctor begins by observing that my responses showed enough anxiety and depressive thoughts to indicate that *I* might need therapy. I don't dispute this. It has been on my mind, but I feel defensive anyway. There is no more discussion about me, though, and we move on to Nadia.

The doctor isn't fooled by Nadia's desire to downplay her terrors. He continually refers to Nadia's nighttime terrors as suicidal thoughts and is concerned that her reliance on me is too disruptive to the household. He says that Nadia doesn't seem to want to confront her fears right now. Therapy could certainly help, but the choice is mostly hers.

As we leave the building, before saying anything about Nadia, John turns to me and says, "I guess the first thing we need to do is send you to a psychiatrist."

Fix me, fix Nadia—is that what he is thinking? John shows no reaction to anything else the doctor has said. He is only happy his daughter won't have to be the one in therapy.

Nadia is determined to walk away from the whole process. I just want to be freed from her bedside at night. So we make a deal. No therapy if she can find a way to go to sleep on her own. That night, Nadia doesn't dare call me.

Stubbornness was not an effective means of coping for very long. When Nadia was once again calling me to her side and stuck in her visions of death, I was certain I'd be dragging her back to the therapist. This was a science

I believed in, was reared on by a mother who both went through her own intensive analysis and also became a psychiatric social worker. And wasn't Nadia at heart a practical little girl, unknowingly channeling the pragmatism of her grandmother, whom she refused to see dancing out on the ocean waves. I was surprised, then, when Nadia called back the spirit of Halloween to become a believer in magic and superstition. If I had not been so quick to classify her as a realist—indeed, to stand in awe of her all-knowing insights—I would have seen that she had turned to the fantastical from the start of her illness.

A month before Nadia was diagnosed, our family went to Ireland. In a jewelry store in the southern town of Kinsale, I was drawn to a necklace on which hung a three-faced head. In ancient Celtic tradition, I was told, both the number three and the head were considered lucky, so this amulet was considered a symbol of protection. I've never believed in such charms. But like my desire for faith in God, I've always wished that I could put my trust in crystals under my bed, four-leaf clovers, or the *hamsa,* a protective image in the shape of a hand common to both Arabs and Jews. So I bought the necklace and put it on right in the store. I wore it until Nadia, after her diagnosis, asked me to hang it on her bedpost at night before she went to sleep.

This was the first of several talismans Nadia came to depend on. In a pink box by her bed, she kept a tiny gold angel pin given to her by one of the first nurses she met at MSKCC, an Irish woman whose brogue evoked the warmth of Nadia's own Nana. After one of my dogs chewed a wing off the angel, I was afraid Nadia would be angry. But I was the one who was becoming superstitious, worried that, if an angel could be broken so easily, so could Nadia. I decided, instead, to take the accident as an omen that physically imperfect beings, like the one Nadia would eventually become, can still thrive.

When Nadia was seven, I had bought her a ceramic angel. Neither she nor I had a belief in angels at that time. I bought this one only because it was mounted on a piece of wood with the name *Nadia* written at the top. This angel, too, watched over her; she took it with her for every hospital stay, where we hung it over her bed.

Perhaps Nadia's most treasured keepsake was a little white hat, like an infant's cap, that she adopted as her favorite head cover when she lost her hair. It was comfortable and represented the security that a well-worn baby blanket gives to an anxious child. I became attached to the hat as well. Its resemblance to the cap Nadia wore in the hospital nursery after she was born softened the effect for me of her bald head—unlike the bandanas she wore at other times, which only seemed to broadcast her cancer. Often during her recovery year, Nadia would put her hat on and come stand in front of me with a shy smile. It became shorthand for "Remember the year we had together?"

While my attachment to the hat was sentimental—like the meaning with which I imbued Max's first eighth-size cello or Frannie's favorite jacket, which she wore for so many years that it went from reaching her knees to just skimming her waist—for Nadia the hat became yet another amulet. It gave her confidence and strength, she told me, the way an imaginary thinking cap is supposed to make us smarter or a dunce cap really can make us feel stupid. She was convinced her hat was going to make her healthy.

When Nadia was in the fourth grade and her anxieties began to surface, she started to sleep with a small

Torah—a gift from a rabbi—under her pillow. I was reminded of the way she had clutched at Frieda's prayer book before one of her surgeries the year before. I wondered then, and did again, whether Nadia found solace because she had true belief in the sacred words of these documents or whether they were just some elevated form of a good-luck charm.

I believe it was the former. In the winter of fourth grade, a club at Nadia's school—Students for a Free Tibet—hosted a group of exiled monks for a week-long residency. Over a period of four days, they created a vibrantly colored sand mandala. The mandala's design represents the universe and is used in meditation. Intricate and beautiful, the mandala is nonetheless disassembled to express nonattachment to the physical world and to release the healing forces it contains. In this case, the sand was dispersed in the waters of the East River. Some of the sand was reserved for anyone present for the ceremony to take home. Nadia accepted hers with purpose and reverence; with great solemnity she handed it to John to be put in a safe place. For weeks after, she was like an overprotective mother watching her child at the park, always checking to make sure no one had thrown out her sand.

Amulets, angels, Torahs, sand. Nadia had always presented such a rational approach to life, but there must have always been a more mystical side to her nature, one that was overshadowed by the overt fancifulness of Frannie and Max. One morning, when Nadia was six, I was brushing my teeth when I heard a loud cry from her bedroom. Racing to her door I asked, "What's the matter, Nadia?"

"She forgot," Nadia sobbed, prostrate on her bed.

"Who forgot what?"

"The tooth fairy."

"The tooth fairy?"

Nadia sat up, holding a piece of wadded-up tissue in which I now realized, with a sinking heart, resided a tiny baby tooth. Shaking the little package in frustration, she wailed, "The tooth fairy didn't come last night. She forgot me."

"That can't be," I said as if I hadn't yet recognized my role in this drama. "Just a minute. I'll be right back."

I ran to my room where I saw the dollar bill, the glittery picture frame, and the letter from Fairy Samantha just where I'd left them before I fell asleep. Then I had an idea. Nadia had come in to sleep in my room during the night. I could put everything under my pillow instead of hers. But I would also have to explain why Samantha hadn't taken the tooth. I grabbed a piece of paper and hurriedly wrote a new note.

"Dear Nadia," I began. I tore through the usual part about how beautiful Nadia looked, how I'd heard she was having a great time in school, and that, no, in response to her last letter, I didn't know Frannie's or Max's tooth fairies. Then I apologized:

I am so confused tonight. I went into your room and you weren't there and I didn't want to just take the tooth and leave without seeing you, so I went into your parents' room and there you were, so I slipped your presents under the pillow there. Then your father let out a big snort, and I got so scared. Now I'm scribbling this note really fast and don't think I'll have time to get your tooth. I'll be back tomorrow night to get it. I'm so sorry.

I still heard Nadia crying as I put the letter, the money, and picture frame under my pillow. Then I called, "Nadia, look what I just found while I was making my bed."

"What?" Nadia shuddered, looking suspicious as she shuffled into my room.

"Here. Under my pillow. Look."

Nadia picked up the pillow with the enthusiasm of someone expecting coal for Christmas and spread her treats on the sheet. With a sigh, she picked up the letter and read it. She didn't buy my made-up story, I could tell, but her need to believe in Samantha was too strong.

In time, Nadia's eyes brightened. "I'm going to get a picture for the frame," she said, not exactly bouncing off my bed with glee but at least smiling now. On the surface, it appeared her faith had been restored.

I dismissed any idea that Nadia's faith was in an actual fairy. I was more worried that she had lost her trust in me. One of my jobs, I thought, was to be the keeper of the bubble of childhood. I thought I had found a clever way to make that bubble bigger. My children weren't to be visited by any old generic tooth fairy. They each had their own personal fairy—Priscilla for Frannie, Samantha for Nadia, and Geraldo for Max—who wrote long letters and to whom my children wrote back. But I had threatened Nadia with the truth by nearly exposing the fiction I had created.

Two years and many more successful visits from Samantha later, Nadia recovered from the surgery to remove the tumor and asked, "What did they do with my teeth, Mama?" referring to the four bottom teeth that had to be pulled along with the bone.

"Your teeth? I . . . I . . . guess the doctors threw them out."

I recognized my mistake right away. Nadia was disgusted at the thought of a part of herself in the trash. "Why didn't you get them back? Now I can't give them to Samantha," she accused.

In my exhaustion, I was tempted to give her the adult answer: I'm under a lot of stress, I'm doing the best I can, and, oh, by the way, there is no tooth fairy—no Priscilla or Samantha or Geraldo. I made the whole thing up because I thought it was fun.

But my anger faded when I saw Nadia's face—always so delicate and exposed, like a paper boat on a rough sea. "Oh, sweetie, I'm so sorry. I never thought to save your teeth, but why don't you write a note to Samantha and tell her what's been happening and leave it under your pillow? I'm sure she'll understand."

Nadia wrote her note, and I wrote back. "It isn't the teeth that are important to us fairies," Samantha said. "It's watching you grow. You have been so brave, so strong. I am very proud of you. You can write to me anytime."

Nadia emerged from cancer treatment with an unshakeable belief in fairies. She collected fairy figurines, read fairy books, dreamed she could fly like the fairies. Despite her passion, which bordered on obsession, I assumed her fairies were just another example of her magical thinking. After all, when you are having visions of falling from buildings, being able to stay afloat in the air is the only way to be sure you are safe. To a child, who would seem more capable of performing miracles: enchanted beings who come to your rescue with kind words and fairy dust, or doctors and drugs that hurt and make you sick? I was grateful that Nadia didn't ask me if I believed in fairies. I didn't want to confess to her that I had never meant for her to take Samantha seriously.

Max, who until age seven believed in leprechauns and said he didn't mind dying because he would visit me as a ghost, loved teasing Nadia about her fairies. At her two-year anniversary, he gets particularly nasty.

"You're so stupid, Nadia. There is no such thing as fairies." We are on a plane returning from a visit to my father in New Hampshire.

"Yes, there is," Nadia insists.

"No, Nadia, there isn't," Max sneers. "Mom doesn't believe in fairies, do you, Mom?"

I am trapped. Several weeks earlier, in a private moment with Max when he was feeling so neglected that I thought it was more important to be candid with him rather than to back up his sister's beliefs, I had admitted that, no, I didn't believe in fairies.

"Max, it doesn't matter what you or I believe. Nadia believes in fairies. Why can't you just let her? You wouldn't tease someone because they were a different religion or because they have faith in a man they call the son of God?"

I look out the window at the clouds. "You know, Max, after my mother's funeral, on my flight back to New York, I thought of Einstein and his theory that energy can never be destroyed, only changed. And if there is a force within us then, in this whole wide world, there might just be a place where my mother's energy exists."

Max pauses in reverence, as he always thinks he has to when I speak about my mother. My respite, however, is short-lived. "But fairies, Mom? I mean, come on."

"Max," Nadia declares, "it was the fairies that helped me get through my cancer. They were there with me during my surgery. I saw them."

I don't know if I am more taken aback about the fairies or by the fact that there is something about Nadia that I actually didn't see during her illness, an inner life that she has kept only for herself.

How I respond to Nadia's declaration is important. We are far beyond the realm of tooth fairies. Only one response seems available to me. "I didn't know you saw fairies," I say quietly, matching the expression in my eyes to hers to let her know how seriously I have taken her admission.

Max is revving up to say more when the plane hits a huge air pocket and drops rapidly. Nadia screams. She needs me now, not fairies, and Max, who is sitting next to me, agrees to switch with his sister.

"Thank you, Max," I say, relieved to have a reason to reward him for a change. But soon the plane levels out and Max demands his old seat back. The fairy wars continue. My mind drifts. I am disappointed that Max has become so jaded. He's just following the natural progression of childhood, I tell myself, when reason takes over and you realize that Tinkerbell could never hear you clapping through the television set. His fantasies were never rooted in anything beyond his imagination, a formerly fertile field that has been eroded by age. But someone who thinks so deeply about death as Nadia has does not entertain frivolous thoughts about fairies. I allow myself to be drawn into her enchanted circle.

In support of Nadia's belief, I begin to buy her fairy pins and pictures and sculptures. I borrow her fairy oracle cards whenever I have a question about my future. I discuss with her the design of fairy wings versus angel wings the way two old *yentas* might compare the relative merits of their daughters-in-law. I encourage her attachment to fairies in the hope that she can prove to me that they exist, that it is not magical thinking but actual magical beings that are protecting her.

Abruptly, though, Nadia tells me that she doesn't want to talk about fairies anymore. She knows I do not have true faith. To draw the strength she needs from fairies, she must enter her inner sanctuary alone.

The fairies have not resolved Nadia's questions about death. The "fear of death," as she writes in a poem at school, is one of the qualities that defines her. But she writes that line without a shiver, her terror, for that moment, replaced by acceptance. The flashbacks and suicidal images exist mainly in the dimension of dreams—usually forgotten at sunup. Only I have any memory of the deep-souled moans and thrashing they induced.

18

I cannot give in to my longing for Nadia. I must ration my hugs to help loosen our bond, and that makes me so sad. How did my mother ever let us leave her when she knew she had so little time to live?

—journal entry, December 18, 2002

Stonewall Beach on Martha's Vineyard got its name from the banks of stone that have been formed over many decades by the powerful tides and waves that, fall and winter, batter this rock-strewn stretch of coastline. The stones, round and smooth from the relentless force of the sea, make for treacherous walking as they shift under your feet and trap toes in crevices.

In the warmer months, calmer waters deposit a thick blanket of sand on top of the stones, creating a pristine beach friendly to tender feet. Yet there are summers when the ocean does not follow its predictable pattern. In early July, water temperatures may rise to levels more common for the end of August. Riptides become more frequent and powerful. Huge rollers bear down on the shore even though there are no wave-generating storms out at sea. And on Stonewall Beach, only a thin layer of sand forms over the rocks before it is stripped away.

Since Nadia's cancer, I have become like that beach. I have days of fair weather when an inner calm buries unhappy memories and coats my anxieties. And I have days when flashbacks, fights with Nadia, or health scares make it impossible for me to hide from my confrontation with her mortality.

Every trip to the hospital—a minimum of once a month for checkups in the first year, every other month in the second, and twice a year for scans plus visits to various surgeons in the third—reactivates my emotional muscle memory. The hospital clings to me, Nadia, and John. It hitches a ride home in the car, tucks itself in beside each of us at night, lingers for days, never completely fades. I confess I don't always mind this presence; it brings Nadia back to my side for mother love even as she veers away from me toward adolescence. Not every parent gets to hold their nearly teenage daughter the way I get to hold mine.

This consolation, though, proves to be a vapor when Nadia's MRI at her nine-month checkup shows an enlarged lymph node. Dr. Wexler's attempts to reassure me fail to keep me from tumbling into my darkest thoughts. I remain in this pit for four days until Nadia undergoes a follow-up PET scan. These scans work on the theory that cancer cells like sugar, so Nadia is injected with radioactive glucose. While the solution circulates, she has to stay completely still (which also means no talking) for half an hour since muscles absorb sugar, too. Then her body is scanned for concentrations of the radioactive solution.

The first few minutes of the test involve an X ray, so I have to wait outside in the hall. I stand alone and cry as if this were all new to me. Whatever kind of veteran status I thought I had achieved will be useless if this test proves positive. Yes, I know I could once again take care of Nadia if I had to, but receiving one cancer diagnosis has not toughened me for a second. If anything, anticipating the anguish I had felt before makes me wish for my former naïveté.

When the scan is over, John makes it his job to wait outside Dr. Wexler's office until the results come back. While he sits stone-faced and immovable, I rush Nadia to school. When I return an hour later, he is in the same position, his expression hardly changing to acknowledge my presence. I imagine his brainwaves pulsing in synchronicity to a mantra of *there's nothing there; there's nothing there.* It is late afternoon before Dr. Wexler arrives with news. There is nothing there. The swollen node was the result of a cold; and as a bonus, we learn there are no signs of cancer anywhere else in her body.

I am surprised to find myself giving John credit for this happy ending, as if he were rewarded for keeping guard rather than going home to wait for a phone call. And it's true that John, while never being the one to change bandages or stay up all night, was a constant overseeing presence that I neglected to value. For the past few hours, though, I have engaged in my own magical thinking that John's diligence could actually create the perfect life for us. I collapse my body into his, relishing this moment of dependence that feels like stepping out into the heat of sunshine to warm bones made cold by air conditioning. Slowly, I crawl back up to the lip of my dark pit, but to this day, I have yet to make it all the way out.

In September 2002 Nadia needs surgery to remove the metal plates that had allowed the new bone in her jaw to knit to the old one. Each step is a reenactment of the whole cancer experience, the mini-golf version of the eighteen-hole tournament she had already been through. Two nights before the surgery I wake at 1:00 A.M. in a panic. I can't remember where Nadia is. I know she isn't in her room, and I can see she isn't in mine. I have a terrifying glimpse of what her death will feel like until I recall that she is spending the night at Margie's. When I fall back to sleep, I dream that Nadia is in a beautiful place with open, emerald-green fields, rolling hills, and a perfect blue sky. What is she doing in this utopian place, a heaven no mortal could enter? It is too scary for me to imagine.

As with previous surgeries, Nadia is to receive her sedative with me at her side before going into the operating room. The nurse inserts the needle into the IV in her arm. When the line clogs, Nadia becomes hysterical.

"What's going on?" she cries.

"Your IV line isn't working, honey," I say as gently as I can.

"Try again," she insists.

The nurse makes one more attempt with a saline flush; but rather than entering a vein, the fluid swells up beneath Nadia's skin.

"Nadia," I say, "they're going to have to give you another IV."

As the nurse approaches, Nadia's voice becomes more frantic. "Get away from me," she screams. "Don't touch me."

"Nadia, please, ..." I begin, but she cuts me off.

"Get off me."

"I know you don't like this, but you have to do it."

"Don't tell me you understand. You don't." Nadia won't look at me.

The nurse and the anesthesiologist try to reason with her, too. Maybe she would prefer going into the operating room awake, they suggest. Once there, she could inhale the anesthesia. Then, when she is asleep, they can change the IV.

"Do you want to do that, Nadia?" I ask.

The medical personnel look at her expectantly, but now she is confused. She is trying to speak, to say no, but everyone starts talking to her at once. *"... won't hurt," "... just a second," "... sure you don't want.," "... got to get going," "... a decision now."* Finally, I say to the nurse, "Just put the new IV in." Nadia will never calm down, and I can sense the staff's growing impatience.

Nadia screams as the new needle is inserted and weeps as the sedative goes in. My heart does not break for her right away; I am too conscious of the nurses and doctors in the room, all of whom, even those attending to other patients, have turned to stare at her. I offer them a sheepish smile of apology.

Only when Nadia has fallen asleep, when I can focus on her face, still wet and blotchy from tears, do I allow myself to cry for her. I am ashamed of how I treated her, as if experience had taught me nothing. As she did during that very first MRI, Nadia needed a chance to breathe. Maybe she still would have cried; maybe the fear would still have followed her into sleep. But maybe she would also have felt like a human being who, if she couldn't control her medical treatment, could control the noise around her.

Nadia wakes from the surgery in a fury, as if she is still fighting me, the doctors, and the nurses. John keeps asking me what's wrong as Nadia pulls at her IVs and tries to get out of bed to leave. I have no trouble reading her eyes this time; they are angry. I tell John it's a reaction to the anesthesia. As Nadia herself will tell us later, after she has had a chance to sleep, "I think I tried to wake up too soon."

I dread our return to the inpatient floor, but Nadia only wants to know what is scheduled in the playroom that night.

The staff member who greets us timidly whispers to me, "You're back."

"Just for one night," I answer, and I can't help feeling like someone who has been moved to the front of the line for no discernible reason.

The playroom is quiet; only the five-year-old girl who is Nadia's roommate and her family are there. Today's project is making butterflies. Nadia gets to work, but the other girl suddenly slumps and asks to go back to her room. Her father looks concerned. "Don't worry," I say. "It happens. There's just so much going through their little bodies. They have to sleep so much."

I don't know if I've been helpful to him, but what I do realize is that I am finally speaking as if Nadia's cancer is in the past.

The past, however, does not always stay put. I do not need to be in the hospital to be plagued by sudden visions of Nadia as a cancer patient. Many have no obvious trigger. Two years after her final treatment, I was walking on the beach, completely focused on a group of terns scanning the water for fish. I was anticipating their sudden dive and successful catch, wondering if I would be happy for the birds or sad for the fish. I didn't know I was thinking about cancer until the terns gave way to the remembered sight of Nadia hooked up to an IV pole as the two of us maneuvered our way into the tiny patient bathroom in the day hospital. Surprising a huge water bug scurrying down the floor drain, we screamed, as if the giant insect were the true threat we faced, and then ran as fast as we could with Nadia's tangle of lines to another bathroom down the hall. I have no explanation for why that memory surfaced at that time, but other flashbacks have more obvious causes.

While in the hospital, either in-patient or for the day, Nadia accepted few legitimate reasons for me to leave her side. The easiest to exploit was the bathroom, a retreat I used often just to get away from the boredom or the visitors, the whining or the pain. During a post-cancer ski trip, a visit to the rest room at the top of the mountain triggered a mental journey back to the day hospital. In preparation for a diagnostic test, Nadia had to drink a horrible-tasting liquid that she kept threatening to throw in my face every time I encouraged her to take a sip. In frustration, I ran around the corner to the bathroom, hoping a few minutes away from her would help me calm down. But once behind the closed door I found myself asking the question that follows me everywhere, even to the top of a 12,000-foot mountain top on a pristine winter day: will I ever be able to understand what happened? My grief follows me everywhere. But a year later, two years later, I am still stunned.

Some memories I stumble upon by accident. Nadia had allowed me to take many photographs and videos of her when she had cancer. We looked often at the pictures but more than two years went by without my seeing any of the videos. Digging out my camera before one of Max's cello recitals, I checked the tape that was already inserted to see if there was any room left on it. I was greeted by the sight of Nadia nearing her last round of chemotherapy. She was wearing a pink leotard, black tights, and a bald head, and she was dancing and tumbling with so much joy and energy that I was filled with the simple, hopeful thought that people with cancer *can* dance.

As jarring as the flashbacks and unexpected images

are, so are the sudden declarations by Nadia that something hurts. The complaints are as varied as a stomach ache that she cannot describe to a sharp pain under her breastbone that keeps her up all night. She can move from being tired to becoming breathless after running a few steps, from having a headache to feeling that her jaw is about to crack.

The night of the chest pain we were in Martha's Vineyard at the start of the summer. Nadia had been in remission for more than a year. Yet sitting with her at 2:00 A.M., my stomach churning with anxiety, it might as well have been January eighteen months before, when fears of a bladder infection had me imagining an emergency medical evacuation. A single firefly kept us company that night, twinkling outside the living room window, never straying far. I imagined it was one of Nadia's fairies come to make everything all right.

Shortly before her two-year checkup, Nadia got hit in the head with a soccer ball hard enough to knock her flat. She didn't lose consciousness but got up after a few minutes and seemed perfectly fine for the rest of the day. But she woke in the middle of the night saying she was dizzy and nauseous. Nadia often had trouble sleeping; dizziness, nausea, and stomach aches in the middle of the night were nothing new and usually reflected anxiety or exhaustion. I sat with her for a few minutes to comfort her before going back to my room, but soon she was standing over my bed crying, "Mama, I'm still dizzy. I can't go to sleep."

"Nadia," I answered, "you've hardly tried. You have to lie still for more than a minute."

"Will you walk me back to my bed?" she asked.

"Sure," I answered.

Back in her room, I decided to give her a Tylenol (no

ibuprofen, I thought in my midnight paranoia, in case there was some kind of bleeding in her brain) more as a placebo than as a painkiller since Nadia had become accustomed to taking a pill for so many of her discomforts. But her cries grew worse, and I was on the verge of taking her to the emergency room when she finally fell asleep. I lay awake the rest of the night, fighting the urge to wake her up to make sure she was okay. The earth's rotation seemed to slow, delaying the arrival of morning when Nadia arose bright and happy.

Dr. Meyers had what I assumed was a standard line that he used with parents to warn them about becoming so focused on the medical trauma their children were undergoing that they forgot to look beyond a life of hospitals and drugs and painful procedures. "Our hope is that we return to you the same child you brought to us," he told me at the start of treatment, meaning, "We will do our part to make your child healthy, but you must keep raising her, teaching her, and disciplining her."

It wasn't hard for me to heed Dr. Meyer's advice while Nadia was in treatment. My mother's insistence, when my sister and I were sick, that we be "out of bed and down to the kitchen by lunchtime," was all too easy for me to follow. In the midst of cancer, I pushed Nadia about everything—keeping up with school, turning off the TV to read a book, going to Max's cello recital or to Frannie's dance performance, getting out of the house to see her friends. Except when she was in great pain, I could not excuse her rudeness to me, her nurses or doctors because she was angry at what was out of our control. There were stretches of time when I felt as if we fought every day.

With the crisis of her cancer in the past, however—

once her hair began to grow, her bones to recede under muscle and flesh, her breath to come slowly and deeply instead of in quick gasps and gulps—my vision began to blur. How could I ever be expected to define a new normal for me, Nadia, and my family? I could only dimly recall what was considered routine before cancer—days when I could neglect her, go on dates with John, get mad at the kids because I was tired of their mess, know what to do in the emptiness of my home when everyone was off at school or work.

Time has only heightened my sense of disbelief at what I thought passed for standard during Nadia's treatment. I think, in particular, of the hospital playroom, of watching Nadia dancing with the Easter Bunny in her big fluffy purple slippers, with the dome of her bald head painted in shades of pastel, her soft pink robe slightly parted to reveal the IV lines hooked up to her Broviac. And I am beaming, as if this is what kids everywhere are doing at that moment.

I knew how to care for a child with a life-threatening illness but was helpless when confronted with coughs and colds. To handle my flying phobia, I would be certain to get an aisle seat so I could keep my eyes on the flight attendant, watching for the tiniest indication that something was unusual. Now, when Nadia sneezed or sniffled or if she got a fever, I studied the mothers at school whose children were also sick and tried to mimic their calm while on alert for any sign that there was reason for panic. When I wasn't battling the urge to protect Nadia, I became harsh, as if to convince myself that she was no different from the rest of us now.

Our first post-cancer fight occurs barely two months after the Broviac has been removed. It is a weekend morning, and Max has woken up early so that he can bring Frannie breakfast in bed. There is no special occasion; it is just an opportunity for Max to test his newly acquired ability to prepare a perfectly fried egg. With the skill of a short-order cook Max flips the egg, puts two slices of toast on a plate, and pours a glass of orange juice. As he is setting the tray with silverware, a napkin, and some flowers he has just cut, Nadia comes into the kitchen and says she wants to help.

"No, Nadia. I want to do this myself," Max answers.

"Why can't I do it, too?" Nadia asks, a whine creeping into her voice.

"Because it was my idea, and I've practically done the whole thing already."

"Can't I just carry it up with you?"

"No, Nadia," Max insists.

"Fine," she says. "I'll make my own tray."

"No, you won't," Max yells as he pushes her away.

I can't side with Nadia, despite the pushing and her still obvious fragility. "This was Max's idea, Nadia. Let him do it himself," I say as gently as I can.

"But *I* want to bring Frannie breakfast," she pouts.

"That's very nice of you. You can do it tomorrow," I answer.

"I just wanted to walk upstairs with Max. Is that so bad? I hate both of you," Nadia yells as she runs up to her room, the sound of her uneven gait adding to the sorrow I feel for her.

I want to chase after her, to tell her she can do whatever she wants, to just stay calm and I'll make it all up to her. But I am not the one who stole a year from her, so there is nothing I can give back. I have no gift to offer her as a second prize—no medicine to dispense or temperature to take or amusement to fetch—nothing to show her how much I love her except a hug or a stroke of her hair which her closed body is ready to repel.

Once Max catches on that Nadia no longer warrants special treatment, he actively provokes similar scenes as if both to punish me for neglecting him and to convince himself that his sister is strong enough now to be punished as well. He tells on Nadia for drinking too much soda. Even though I know Max routinely drinks more than the one soda on Saturday and one on Sunday he is allowed, I still discipline Nadia for her rare infraction.

Max sabotages every game he plays with her. In one, they each have to set up an obstacle course to see who can go through it fastest. Max is quick to find a flaw in Nadia's; he has to climb a rope ladder that hurts his bare feet. I suggest that she revise her course even though all three of us know that Max's real issue is the fact that he is not as nimble a climber as Nadia is. When she tries a similar gambit, asking for a second chance because she isn't ready to start when I say "Go," she is so obviously retaliating that I won't give her a second chance. Nadia glares at me as if she has been wrong all this time to put so much faith in me and, as expected, encloses herself within an emotional stonewall where she seems to me so much more tragic than she ever did during her treatment.

Max was not the source of all of our conflicts. At the school picnic at the end of fourth grade, Nadia had a misunderstanding with one of her friends who had said she would sleep at our house that night but ended up making plans with another child. Nadia claimed it was my fault for not confirming the plans quickly enough with the girl's mother. Leaving the picnic, Nadia walked briskly, trying to get as far away from me as she could. I knew that it was easier for her to be mad at me than to feel the hurt of her friend's rejection, but I was in no mood to be the scapegoat. I chased after her shouting, "I don't feel sorry for you."

But of course, I did. Her strength seemed so fragile. The smallest incident over the next few years would cause her to crumble. Once, returning from a shopping trip without the bathing suit she had just bought, Nadia dissolved into tears. I called the store owner, who said she would hold it for us, but Nadia could not stop crying. She had no tolerance for even minor disappointments. On another occasion, she spent all day preparing a chocolate Pavlova only to have it burned by our temperamental oven. Thinking that Nadia would not want to decorate it the way the recipe called for, I started picking around the edges of the crusty cake.

"What are you doing?" she yelled. "You've ruined it. The whole thing is ruined."

"I'm sorry, Nadia. I didn't think you were going to continue."

"Go away. Let me finish," she said as she pushed me aside. Grimly, she spread the frosting as shown in the cookbook and served the Pavlova for dessert. I attacked the hard, charred meringue base and ate until Nadia finally admitted it wasn't very good. By then, she was no longer sad or angry; she seemed numb, as if she had stopped expecting anything to be good.

I began to feel as if there was no such thing as an innocent action or conversation. If I wasn't trying to convince myself that Nadia was as strong as the rest of us now, I was worried that a wrong word or reference would threaten her precarious emotional balance.

More than a year after treatment, Max, Nadia, and I are watching a television commercial showing kids floating in air.

"Max," Nadia asks, "do you think you'd want to live in space? It would be so cool. You could do flips all the time."

"I bet you can't wait to get to heaven then," Max answers, knowing how much she loves those moments in gymnastics when she leaves the ground, how she dreams about flying.

"I think she can wait a little while," I say. I hope my tone is light, that Max knows I understand the sweetness behind what he has just said, but I am not ready to hear references to Nadia in heaven.

I have become a too-conscious mother. On a Saturday night a few weeks after this conversation, Max and Nadia make a spur-of-the-moment plan to sleep at Margie's house. When it is time for them to go, Max gives me a big hug, which I return freely. He tells me he'll miss me. "I'll miss you, too," I say as I hug and kiss him back.

When Nadia comes to me for an embrace, her ambivalence about leaving comes between us. Her tears are just waiting for permission to flow. "I'm going to miss you so much," she says.

She is wearing the same puffy North Face jacket I had buried my face in at the hospital during the biopsy, and I want to lean my head into it now, to give and get a hug, to stroke her face and look into her eyes and say, "I will miss you, too."

But I can't. I can't reflect back to Nadia what she is feeling, or else she won't be able to go. I must measure the hugs I give her so that she will learn how to be free from me.

Protecting Nadia's feelings is not what Dr. Meyers meant by returning the "same" child to me. It is a lesson I learn only when I let my guard down. In the fall of 2002, John, the kids, and I go to New Hampshire to visit my father. His house, in the village of Hill, is as close as I can come to a family homestead. My father bought the house as a weekend retreat when I was nine and established residency there when he retired.

When I go to New Hampshire, my thoughts are usually trapped in the past. It is a portal to my memories. It is a place where I lived with my mother—she had stood at the kitchen sink, the pots and dishes are ones that she used, a set of sheets in the linen closet is one that she bought me for college. I can see her reading a book by the fire and in the hospital bed that had been set up in the living room when she became too weak to walk up the stairs to her bedroom.

At night, I put Max and Nadia to sleep in the room I had shared with my sister, Joanny. It was the room that held my adolescent loneliness, exaggerated by the two hundred acres of forest that surround the house and by the early darkness that descended in the winter when my father dragged us up there every weekend to ski.

Through this house, I talk to Frannie, Max, and Nadia about my childhood. I tell them about the Thanksgiving dinners we had there, about my aunt Jenny who would come every year to this rustic outpost in a black cashmere skirt, silk stockings, and high heels and pose like a 1940s movie star under an ancient pine tree. In that same tree, I tell them, I had placed the baby blue jay I had rescued, only to see the poor fledgling defenseless against the attacks of other birds that wanted to oust this predator. I showed them the bright orange hats and jackets we had to wear during hunting season while walking the trails left by loggers years before. I promised I wouldn't make them sing the same stupid songs my father would intone to announce our presence—"Oats, Peas, Beans, and Barley Grows" or "John Brown's Body." Nadia's cancer does not exist for me in this dimension. The house makes room only for tradition—walks to the beaver pond, hot chocolate, driving my father's tractor, tending the fire, making a mad dash to get under heavy blankets on beds in drafty rooms.

The weekend we go is cold and rainy. An early snow squall covers enough of the ground so that Max and Nadia can go sledding before it turns to slush. By the second day, they are restless, so I have my little time capsule to drive them to a nearby outlet mall. Signs promoting one political candidate or another are ubiquitous, particularly those of conservative Republican John Sununu. New Hampshire politics is enough to get me started on a liberal rant; and this day, surrounded by all those *Live Free or Die* license plates, I swoop down on the topic of the death penalty. "It's barbaric," I say. "We don't have the right to take someone else's life."

Nadia interrupts, "Please stop talking about killing people. It's too scary."

Max, though, wants to know why President Bush supports the death penalty.

"It's this idea of an eye for an eye. But justice shouldn't be about equal punishment but about equivalent consequences." I'm sure Max and Nadia have no idea what I am talking about. I continue anyway. "The death penalty doesn't even keep anyone from committing a crime, and it ends up costing more than keeping someone in prison for life. Besides that, it's arbitrary."

"What does *arbitrary* mean?" Max asks.

"It means some people get the death penalty and some don't, depending on their race or how much money they have or what state they live in or who they get as their judge."

Nadia, despite herself, is interested and says, "It's horrible that we shoot people."

Max says, "Don't we chop off their heads?"

"This isn't the French Revolution," I answer. "We use lethal injection."

"Stop," Nadia pleads. "I'm only ten. I don't want to know all this stuff."

I come down from my lectern and can see how gruesome all of this must sound. Is Nadia picturing being executed the way she can picture herself falling from our terrace?

I don't think Nadia reacted the way she did because she had had cancer. Pain, death, crime, suffering, injustice—these are subjects that have always reached deeply into her soul. Now I have to choose between trying to safeguard her innocence or helping her to explore those realities that I know intrigue her even as they cause her great unease. I choose the latter. My approach to talking about the death penalty may have been dramatic, but in fact Nadia will return to her fifth-grade history class where, the teacher will tell me, she will have a great deal to say about the meting out of justice, including death, in ancient South American civilizations.

What ultimately becomes the norm for Nadia and me—the means, beyond caregiving and discipline and supervising homework, through which I will raise her—is conversation. I no longer want to run, yawn, or fidget in response to the flow of her words.

When Frannie was a preteen, I was eager for her to read *The Diary of Anne Frank*. It was one of my favorite books at that age, because it told me about something I couldn't experience—the Holocaust, and something I was going through just like Anne—adolescence. Because I was trying so hard to get Frannie to read the book, she wasn't interested, so I was thrilled when Nadia asked me to read it to her when she was ten. It seemed that every page gave us something to talk about—what made the Franks Jewish if they never observed, how odd it would be for a girl to have to share a room with a grown man, how it felt to get your period, how come Anne didn't get along with her mother.

Nadia challenged me to think in new ways. When in fifth grade she studied different theories about how the world was formed, she asked me before bed, "Do you believe in creationism or evolution?"

"Evolution," I said as if this is the only possible answer.

"Me, too," Nadia said.

But after confronting mortality during Nadia's illness and the years that have followed, of searching for faith, of acknowledging the possibility that fairies exist, I found this answer too easy. "Nadia, you know, you may not have to choose between creationism and evolution."

"What do you mean?" she asked.

"Well, if you took the Genesis story and got rid of the idea that a day means twenty-four hours—that it could be hundreds or thousands or even millions of years—then you would have a description of evolution. And maybe we are now in the seventh day and God is resting, leaving us on our own to care for the world. Maybe that's why bad things happen."

I was proud of my theory, but Nadia only nodded, then kissed me goodnight. I knew, though, that somewhere inside of her, my words were being stored, examined, and measured against her own thoughts and could reappear at any moment in a future conversation.

What used to scare me about Nadia, the very qualities that made me feel as if I were incompetent to raise her—her wisdom, her old soul, her exploration of the mysteries of the universe—are now the linchpin in our relationship. If she were to tell me again that when she was my mommy she gave me my pacifier, my answer would be, "You were a very good mommy, but it's my turn to take care of you now. I will protect you when I can, but, more importantly, you can trust me to walk on the beach with you every day, whether it is rocky or smooth."

19

I love the continuity of memories. But everything, for me, is always tinged or even darkly colored with melancholy. The memories are reminders of what will never be again. Tradition becomes a minefield when you realize that no two years are exactly the same, that you can never be certain or in control.

—journal entry, November 29, 2003

Carl was one of Nadia's friends in the hospital. He was also being treated for Ewing's sarcoma; his tumor was in his arm. Although Nadia and Carl were on similar chemotherapy schedules, they didn't meet until the day of their surgeries. At 6:00 A.M. that morning, there were only our two families in the waiting room of the PDH. Nadia and Carl were both hooked up to IV drips of fluids and dressed in their hospital gowns, ready for transport to the operating room. It would have taken more discipline than I had not to overhear Carl's surgeon comment on how little of the tumor remained after the three initial rounds of chemo. How lucky, I thought. It shrunk to near nonexistence. Besides, it's in his arm. Carl won't be facing feeding tubes or traches or disfigurement.

As Nadia and Carl were being operated on in adjacent

rooms, our two families remained in our separate, invisible, protective bubbles. I pretended I was respecting their privacy, but I watched to see their reaction every time a doctor or a nurse came over to give them a report. Would good news about Carl reduce Nadia's odds because only a finite number of people could be saved that day, or would bad news for Carl mean the worst for both? By late afternoon, I finally approached his mother and father. Carl's surgery was nearly finished, they told me, but it appeared he would need a skin graft because the doctors had to remove more soft tissue than expected. No one could proceed, though, until Dr. Cordeiro, the reconstructive surgeon, was finished with Nadia.

Carl was only six at the time, and in the recovery room his bandaged arm looked as big as his tiny body. There was only one bed available in the hospital's post-surgical pediatric observation unit (POU). Either Nadia or Carl would have to be transferred to New York Hospital across the street. Because Nadia's head and neck had to be completely stabilized, Carl was moved.

We didn't see him for about a week. By that point he had come back to MSKCC to continue his recovery. Fibulas might be perfect for replacing mandibles but not elbows. Carl's new bone had come from a cadaver, and he was spiking fevers as his body tried to defend itself against this intruder.

Two weeks later, when Nadia returned to the hospital to resume chemo, we saw Carl and his father walking down the hallway. They were not going to the PDH as we were to begin the last leg of treatment. Carl was there for radiation; the margins around his tumor weren't clear.

It was a month later before we met at the PDH and I learned more about Carl's recovery. Because of the skin graft, he would never be able to straighten his arm fully, play a sport, or do a pull-up I was ashamed that I had ever thought Carl was lucky, that I had become so entombed in my own pain that I thought it was somehow unique from what others were experiencing. I was startled to realize that I still thought there was something predictable about cancer.

Nadia and Carl finished their treatment within a few weeks of each other. Without the hospital as our common ground, we lost touch with him and his parents. I knew, though, that Carl and his mother and father were living two lives—the one on the surface where everything passes for normal and you make plans for vacations and birthday parties and school plays, and the underground one where you wait for the cancer to return, for the latest stomach ache or chest pain to "be something."

Above ground, you tell yourself you are liberated. Below, you hold yourself hostage. Above ground, your chest opens for big gulps of air. Below, the air stagnates in your lungs because you are afraid that the act of exhaling will alert the cancer to your presence. Above ground, you skip and skim across smooth water. Below, violent riptides sweep you far from safety.

Eighteen months passed before Nadia and I saw Carl again. We were at the PDH for a checkup. Carl's father saw us first. "Hi," he said. He seemed truly happy about this reunion, and I couldn't wait to ask about Carl. But I froze when I saw that the father's eyes didn't match the rest of his face. He was speaking to us from underground.

"We're back," he continued.

"What?" I said, not because I hadn't heard but because I couldn't seem to translate the words "we're" and "back" into anything I could understand.

"Carl has a new tumor in his lung," the father continued.

"Oh, I'm so sorry." My voice emanated from the

world of light and air where I could still claim to live. But below the surface I sighed. At least now they know, I thought. Now they know what they are supposed to do, how they should feel, where they need to be.

How could this have been my first thought? Of course I didn't want to trade places, but at the moment the piece of me that wants certainty is stronger than the sorrow I feel.

I forced myself to go to the playroom to see Carl. He was playing a video game, an intensified regimen of ifosfamide and etoposide coursing its way through his bloodstream. "Hey, Carl," I said.

"Hi. I'm back," he answered.

"I see. That stinks, huh?" I couldn't think of anything else to say but the truth.

"Yeah," he responded.

I stayed with him long enough to stop him from morphing into Nadia every time I blinked or looked away. I refused to hide.

I couldn't, and will never be able to, escape the fact that Nadia's future is no more certain than Carl's, which is no more certain than Frannie's or Max's or anyone else's. This knowledge exists in the bellies of most parents, sequestered behind fortresses made of car seats, safety caps, helmets, multiple vitamins, self-defense classes, CPR training, curfews, and tracking devices planted in children's cell phones. The exaggerated mother will never be able to rebuild her fortress. I have no desire to. I want to feel the heartbreak, the sorrow, the pain, and the loss as well as the joy, the beauty, and the freedom of an undefended life. How else can I learn to live without knowing what is coming next?

Thanksgiving, 2003—our second extended family gathering on Martha's Vineyard since Nadia finished treatment. We are mostly all here—my father and Donna; Joanny, her husband David, their daughter Rachel, and her boyfriend Mike. Essie has come with my aunt Alice and my cousin Bobby. John's mother, his three sisters, their spouses, and our nephews and nieces are all present. Only my cousin Miriam can't come because her husband's grandmother has just died. I think of the Passover *Seder* plate—its symbols of tears, bitterness and sacrifice but also of sweetness and renewal. Miriam's absence is a reminder that life holds all these elements and that we cannot control when each comes to us.

Thursday is so beautiful and warm that, even though I stay outside all day, I am frightened because the weather feels so wrong. In the afternoon, I am sitting on the lawn talking to my father about his sister who is losing more and more control over her mind, when I see a spray of water offshore.

"Whales," I shout. Everyone pours from the house to see, even Frannie, Max, and Nadia, who tease me about my obsession with anything that can be found in the sea. I have never seen a whale from my house before, but now I see another blow and then the slow rolling backs of two more of the giant mammals as they lumber toward their winter destination.

It is warm enough to kayak. I am the only one on the water. I miss the seal that I later learn wandered into the pond I had paddled through. On Thursday night the air is so still that we build a bonfire and watch sparks shoot upward as if trying to join the stars before falling to the ground like flaming orange snowflakes.

The cousins, ranging in age from eleven to twenty-nine, move from home to town to dinner to the movies like a single-celled organism. They weave a constant stream of conversation, binding themselves together with invisible knots that I tell myself will never fray.

The older generation is feeling contemplative. My mother-in-law, who is eighty-five, asks Essie, Alice, and my father if they believe in an afterlife. Peggy has never doubted the existence of heaven, and I am disconcerted to see her so afraid now. I sense my father is about to say something profound, that I will finally hear the truth. But Essie speaks first. "Nothing happens after you die," she says with the same certainty as my mother.

I am still waiting for my father. "It's silly to worry," he says with a shrug, "because you'll never really know."

That's it? The secret?

I want to press further, but Peggy wants to close the subject. "I think there is a heaven," she says. "There has to be."

On Sunday, before we return to New York, I stand alone in my bedroom looking out at the view. The sun is bright but no longer warm. The sea is disorganized, the froth of whitecaps obscuring any possible sign of a whale. I don't want to receive the message I am being given—that I must not become too attached to my idyllic memories. This barely blemished weekend will never be repeated. Next year may also be wonderful, or it could be marked by loss, illness, or discord. The only certainty is that it will be different.

As we leave the Vineyard, the plane flies directly over our house. I look down and have the sensation that I am still there, standing in my bedroom, waiting for the me up in the airplane to return. The feeling is strong enough to generate an actual image of my alternate self. My first impression is that the woman waiting by the window is trapped; she is too scared to leave her sacred haven even as her sight flies out to the ocean's vastness. My sorrow for her vulnerability, though, soon turns to anger. Why does she get to stay while I must return to my messy and complicated life? Finally, I reach pride. This woman will not be taken from her sea.

Sad, angry, strong—all three of these women reside in me. All three were tested, nurtured, and ultimately made more powerful by mothering Nadia during her cancer. All three have made me the mother that I am.

In the spring of 2004 I will have to call upon this woman as Nadia approaches another surgery. Because of partial nerve damage resulting from the removal of her fibula three years earlier, she has developed a progressively worsening foot drop. She can no longer lower her left heel to the floor when she tries to stand flat-footed and is unable to rotate her ankle outward. Her gait and body alignment are becoming lopsided. An Achilles lengthening and tendon transfer are proposed.

The surgery is not performed at MSKCC. I am relieved; the prospect of seeing Nadia succumb yet again to anesthesia—to have her removed to a different plane of consciousness than the one I inhabit—is enough of a return to cancer for me. Instead, she is admitted to the Mount Sinai Medical Center, the place where she, Max, and Frannie were born; where Max spent time in intensive care and the emergency room because of asthma and anaphylactic episodes; where John and I have gone for our various minor medical procedures—all with perfect outcomes.

Once again, Nadia goes off to her twilight state with a face still damp from crying, the anesthesiologists thinking they could simply take her alone and aware to the surgical suite where they would insert the IV and begin sedation.

"There must be some way you can start out here in the pre-op area," I say. But it is Nadia's tears that convince the doctors to do this more than my words.

After surgery, John and I are called to the recovery

room. We are greeted by Nadia's screams. They are primal, full of rage, pain, and fear. Her arms are pinned by a nurse; she twists to try to get away. It is her mind, though, that is trapped somewhere in an alternate universe. But she recognizes me. "Is it over? Is it over? Please tell me. Am I dreaming? It feels like someone is slicing my foot."

"It's done, Nadia," I say. "Look at me. It's over."

Nadia just keeps shaking her head, not understanding. The agony in her screams is escalating.

"Can't you give her something?" I plead.

One, two, three shots of Demerol. After the last injection, Nadia smiles at the nurse and says, "Thank you." Then her whole body finally slumps in total collapse against my shoulder.

The same nurse says, "At age twelve, isn't she a little old for this?" I wish Nadia would wake up to take back her gratitude.

The next scene in the nightmare: Dr. Murphy arrives on rounds. He discovers the antibiotic Nadia is getting is a relative of Ceclor, which all her charts say she is allergic to. The resident says I told him she had had this drug before, and for more than a minute I doubt myself rather than believe he would lie.

The final scene of our drama goes through the night until morning. For her pain, Nadia is given Dilaudid, not morphine. It makes her nauseous. "Why don't you give her morphine?" I suggest. "She's had it before, and it works perfectly for her."

"No, we prefer Dilaudid here," I am told. "She will get a basal rate, but she can receive a boost every ten minutes by pressing her button."

Nadia's vital signs are suppressed. When she sleeps, she doesn't get enough air. Our small double room rings with alarm bells.

"Can you please give her some oxygen so she can sleep?" I ask, wondering why I have to keep asking for the most obvious things.

For two hours, Nadia sleeps. The alarms are silent. At 4:30 A.M., she wakes in pain and starts pressing the button on her pain medication pump as if groping for a just-out-of-reach lifeline. The pump malfunctions. I call the nurse.

"She was never receiving a basal rate," the nurse tells me as if I must have dreamt our previous conversation.

"How did you expect her to get any sleep then?" I ask, incredulous.

A shrug is my answer; the nurse is tired of me. She fiddles with the IV pump's lines, supposedly fixing the problem. But every push of the button produces the same rapid beeping, indicating a problem.

"She's still getting the medicine," the nurse assures me.

"I'm not, Mama, I'm not," Nadia insists. "Can't they just give me a push?" Nadia begs, referring to an injection of painkiller directly into her IV line.

Three more nurses join us. Each one fights for territorial control over the pump, which continues to bleat its malfunction with Nadia's every frantic push of the button.

"I want to be back at MSKCC," Nadia cries. Doesn't anybody understand how desperate she must be to want to go back to a cancer hospital?

I will not allow Nadia to be treated this way anymore. "Stop," I command. "Listen to me. This girl has been through hell, and never has she been in this much pain. You get her a new pump right now and give her the push she asked for."

The four nurses scurry away, a new pump appears, a push is given. Nadia vomits from the Dilaudid.

"Please, can't you just give her morphine?" By 7:00 A.M., thanks to the intervention of Dr. Murphy, Nadia gets her morphine and her sweet opium smile returns. A change of shift puts an end to our nightmare.

Throughout all this, Max is calling me. "Mommy, I miss you." The words are the same each time, but his voice grows increasingly hoarse.

He stops calling me at 1:00 A.M. but the phone rings again at 6:15. "I missed you so much last night, and I couldn't sleep. I was coughing so much."

As he takes a breath before the cry that I know is coming, I hear the wheeze. "Go get Daddy, Max." But he is already crying, and I can't hang up until the coughing fit ends.

Margie arrives to sit with Nadia. I go home to Max and whisk him to Dr. Murphy, who has just arrived at his office from the hospital.

Max is lucky. It is the croup, not asthma.

A week later, Frannie will break her foot: two girls on crutches, one boy still clutching his inhaler.

I remember my anxiety before Nadia's surgery. I had felt guilty. It was such a minor procedure compared to what she had been through. Indulging my emotions—fertilized in the soil of flashbacks, watered by old tears—felt so self-involved. But my sister understood. "Everything is its own event," she said, "and you need to take things on their own terms."

The terms are never what you think they will be. Nadia has been in remission for three years, the point at which the chance of recurrence falls dramatically. She is as beautiful as ever. Periodically, I come upon her looking in the mirror, lifting her chin up to see her scar or turning her face sideways to view the slight depression in her cheek. I admit that John was more honest than I was when he worried about how Nadia would look. So far, she has refused any consideration of surgery to fill out the left side of her face.

She has grown taller. I no longer have to lean down to look in her eyes—eyes that no longer beg me to stay by her side or weep when we part. Soon I will be looking up to read her face and will find eyes that censor what they allow me to see. The journal of Nadia's soul will no longer be open to view.

It is time for the exaggerated mother to go into remission, too.

Fireflies are abundant on Martha's Vineyard in the summer of 2004. Each night in early July I walk among them as if strolling among the stars. As I navigate the dark path, the fireflies part to form an enchanted aisle to guide me and a glittering canopy to protect me.

Is this an omen, I wonder? What do fireflies signify? Is it good or bad? I should call Nadia. Together, we can imagine we are surrounded by fairies. We can ponder life.

The aisle in front of me narrows. There is only room for one person to pass. This event is meant only for me, and I surrender to the beauty and the magic as if nothing came before and nothing will follow. For this moment, I am just me.

Epilogue

How Is Nadia?

February 2010. Nine years into Nadia's remission, I am sitting in the auditorium of the Nightingale-Bamford School waiting for her to dance. She has a solo, she told me, in the dance specially choreographed for graduating seniors. My hands are clutched around a ball of tissues. John, Frannie, and Max are faint shadows in the disappearing background of the audience as my eyes remain riveted on the stage. I have waited for this moment all year, for the opportunity to resurrect, for one last moment before Nadia leaves for college, that intensity of motherhood I experienced caring for her.

The seniors come on stage and begin their dance, a modern choreography to the voice of Tom Waits. Nadia is not among them. I remain waiting.

The stage empties, the music shifts, and Nadia enters.

She is tall now, almost 5 feet, 7 inches. Her hair is cut in a fashion-forward pixie. The tank top she is wearing emphasizes the leanness of her body. Through years of hugs and hand holding, my fingers have memorized the feel of the muscles that lie underneath.

As Nadia walks across the stage, I wait for my eyes to well with the many-generations-removed tears I had shed eight years earlier, when Nadia entered the gym a hero and marched her way toward the climbing rope. But I am too drawn into her movement, the way she transforms a simple walk into a mood.

For the next five minutes, while Nadia is on stage alone or with a partner, she is no longer my daughter. She is an artist. She is too good, her dance too compelling, for me to generate any tears.

Medicine saved Nadia's life. Dance, which replaced gymnastics as Nadia's passion in middle school, has returned her to aliveness. It has not been a direct route to this moment, and this is not to be a recitation of all that has taken place since I walked the path of the fireflies. But one particular memory holds enduring significance.

There is a bridge on Martha's Vineyard that spans an ocean inlet. It is a popular spot for jumping into the water below. Nadia was about eleven when she went with Frannie, Max, and friends for her first-ever jump. I wasn't there that day, but I was given a series of photographs documenting the event. In the first, all the kids are lined up holding onto the outside of the railing. In the second, everyone but Nadia is in midair. The third one shows the jumpers in the water, their faces turned up to the bridge where Nadia still braces herself. There is no fourth picture depicting Nadia's ultimate choice. I find this appropriate. Nadia will often be brought to the brink of who she used to be—the strutting fearless girl who wished she could fly. Sometimes she will leap; sometimes she won't be able to.

One of her biggest leaps was her decision to go to summer camp. She was thirteen and the only one among her friends who had never been away for the summer. She was intrigued by the opportunity to build new friendships or maybe to reinvent herself among people who knew nothing about her. She studied the packing list the camp sent; we went shopping for sheets and shorts and one-piece bathing suits. She packed her duffel and rechecked the list to ensure she had the water bottle and flashlight, the insect spray and sun protection. She gave every impression of being eager and excited until the night before we were to take her, when she broke down, afraid to leave me. The pattern repeated itself for the next two summers, her separation anxiety never lessening, although in the winter months she babbled happily about her friends, camp traditions, and the privileges they would get the next season. Nadia's third year was the most difficult. I could see no reason why, except that she was a year older and maybe growing up seemed that much closer. It was unclear whether she would make it through the season.

On my way from Martha's Vineyard to a surprise eightieth birthday party for my father in Boston, I got a call from the camp doctor on my cell phone. Nadia had gone to the infirmary after hurting her wrist playing volleyball. She had passed out, cracked her head on the floor, and had a grand mal seizure. She was on her way to the hospital. By the time John and I arrived, Nadia was stable. I know it's impossible to hold your breath for the three hours it took us to get there, but I don't remember a single inhale. Once again, what I was supposed to feel was dependent on what Nadia was feeling. The CAT scan she received at the hospital showed no sign of the subdural hematoma the doctors worried about or of the brain tumor John and I had feared the most.

We took her home. A neurological exam and an EEG turned up no abnormalities. I assumed she would remain on the Vineyard for the rest of the summer. She decided to return to camp, though, and suffered the predictable last-minute crisis. For ten minutes she cried, saying she didn't know if she wanted to go. For ten minutes I told her she could do whatever she wanted to do. It would be great if she gave it a try, but she'd have to decide in the next five minutes. I understood why Nadia was pushing herself. Despite having a legitimate excuse to come home, she felt disappointed in herself because she hadn't succeeded at camp. During a thirty-second period of calmness, she agreed to get in the car. Once we were on the road, she seemed more settled.

It appeared Nadia had made a full transition to camper, and I sent in the deposit for the next season without a worry. But when June arrived, she couldn't leap. She stayed on the Vineyard with me and worked as a waitress.

In retrospect, I can see that that summer began a course correction in our relationship. It was a summer without an agenda—no work on healing or growing up or separation to be done. We were alone a good part of the time. John, Frannie, and Max came in and out, depending on work or social schedules. Nadia and I had few decisions to make beyond what to eat, whether to turn right or left when we got to the beach, or what book we would read next. Nadia had been drawn into Nabokov's writing, and I told her that, when I was a teenager, *Lolita* was a book parents hid away in some secret location. I discovered my parents' copy in the basement alongside Henry Miller's *Tropic of Cancer* and Anaïs Nin's *Delta of Venus* as well as my mother's high school yearbook and my grandfather's prayer book. I read *Lolita* amid the sawdust of my father's woodshop and the cans of food stored away in case of an atomic bomb attack, and I jumped every time the boiler fired, thinking it was my mother or father coming downstairs.

For me, my summer with Nadia was unnatural in how natural it felt. I had not realized how much my mothering of her was still dictated by her cancer, as if the Nadia I had been raising was a copy of my real daughter. When she went to India in her junior year of high school with her world religions class, I saw the trip as a triumph over the post-traumatic stress of cancer. When she was unable, the subsequent summer, to complete an internship she didn't feel ready for, I attributed her reaction to the fear of being a grown-up that she had developed after treatment. When she agreed to receive a Courage Award at the Sarcoma Foundation of America's annual benefit and when, as head of community service at school, she collected used formal dress for MSKCC's annual prom, and when she wrote her college essay on how there is no answer to the question of why she got cancer, I interpreted these actions as attachment to disease, not involvement.

Now, a year after the dance concert, Nadia has left her school of thirteen years and is nearing completion of her first year at Brown University. The image of her on the bridge is as poignant as ever. Nadia did jump that day, and I saw that as a triumph over cancer, much the same way as I have been interpreting her battles with anxiety at college. I have viewed every victory and every retreat through the lens of illness, as if this is all that has shaped Nadia over the past ten years. I must reclaim my whole daughter.

"How's Nadia?" It's the question I get asked most frequently. "She's good" is my typical answer. It is shorthand.

It means Nadia is searching for her place in the world, just like every other nineteen-year-old is. What she carries with her is a history of cancer. It is useless to think about what she might have been without that history, as senseless as it is to attribute all of her emotions or actions to that past.

Useless and senseless and hard to avoid. But Nadia's move to college has made it easier. She is not in my view every day; her scars are not visible. Even after a phone call filled with tears, when all Nadia can say is that she wants to come home, I hang up the phone knowing I am as separate from her as I was when among the fireflies. Yes, I am heartbroken for her. But I haven't lost myself in her pain. I am recovering my life, just as Nadia is making her erratic leaps toward hers.

Acknowledgments

From my initial scrawling of every raw emotion through the completion of this book, Nancy Aronie's support has been as perpetual as the ocean. Leslie Sharpe showed me how to deepen and shape this work. Mark Donovan added the final polish and, more than that, was the ideal teacher for Nadia when she returned to school in the fourth grade. Joan Cusack Handler and her colleagues at CavanKerry Press drew words from me I didn't know I had.

Thank you to *The Healing Muse,* which published my essay, "The Limits of Swallows and Seals," adapted from this book.

Others who supported me as a writer or a mother include: Patty Sacks, Patty Newburger, Cathy Trentalancia, Dr. Maureen Strafford, Elizabeth Stern, Deborah Robertson, Margie Killeen, Elizabeth Doon, Pamela Brian, Claudia and Lew French, Lori and Craig Keefe, Richard Arlook, Rick Marotta, Kathryn Martin, Drs. Leonard and Gail Saltz, Dr. Michelle Friedman, Blanche Mansfield, Faith Cinquegrana Gong, and my colleagues at the Children's Museum of Manhattan.

To Nadia's lifesavers, we owe everything: Dr. Paul A. Meyers, Dr. Leonard H. Wexler, Dr. Dennis H. Kraus,

Peter G. Cordeiro, and Dr. Ramon J. C. Murphy. There are too many superlative adjectives to choose from to describe the nursing staff at Memorial Sloan-Kettering. To each one—but particularly to Rachel—thank you.

To call my husband's family in-laws does a disservice to what they mean to me. I particularly want to thank Maureen Coscino for giving me the support I needed to be able to care for Nadia. My father and stepmother, Seymour and Donna Goldberg, and my sister, Joan Roth, were unconditional in their love, as was my aunt, Esther Goldberg. Essie died before I learned of this book's publication, but she had enough pride in me to last forever.

Finally, to John, Frannie, Max, and, especially, Nadia—thank you for your generosity in allowing your lives to appear in these pages. I feel your love every moment.

OTHER BOOKS IN THE LAURELBOOKS SERIES

Life with Sam, Elizabeth Hutner

Body of Diminishing Motion, Joan Seliger Sidney

To the Marrow, Robert Seder

Surviving Has Made Me Crazy, Mark Nepo

Elegy for the Floater, Teresa Carson

We Mad Climb Shaky Ladders, Pamela Spiro Wagner

Letters from a Distant Shore, Marie Lawson Fiala

Little Boy Blue, Gray Jacobik